JANE BRADBURY   EDWARD MAEDER

AMERICAN STYLE AND SPIRIT

FASHIONS AND LIVES OF THE RODDIS FAMILY, 1850–1995

PHOTOGRAPHY BY GILLIAN BOSTOCK EWING
AND DOUG MINDELL

V&A Publishing

Contents

FOREWORDS   6

PREFACES   8

FAMILY TREE   12

INTRODUCTION

"Mute but Eloquent Testimony": Saving the Roddis Collection   14

CHAPTER ONE

Making the Best of a New Life:

Sara Denton Roddis Goes to Marshfield   22

CHAPTER TWO

From Cheese Boxes to Fine Flush Doors:

William H. Roddis, Gentleman Entrepreneur   42

CHAPTER THREE

Sewing and the Modern Woman: The Prindle Family   58

SAVING AUNT JENNIE'S ACCESSORIES AND DRESSES

CHAPTER FOUR

"Pure Princess Prindle" Weds Mr. Hamilton Roddis   84

CHAPTER FIVE

A Changing World: The Roddis Family in the Roaring Twenties   104

CHAPTER SIX

Pursuing Happiness in Hard Times:

The Roddis Family Faces the Depression   132

REDISCOVERED DESIGNER: GLADYS PARKER

CHAPTER SEVEN

Wartime Production, Wartime Restriction: The Home Front 160

CHAPTER EIGHT

Travel and Style: "Getting There is Half the Fun!" 186

REDISCOVERED DESIGNER: SAMUEL KASS

REDISCOVERED DESIGNER: DAVID E. GOTTLIEB, "GOTHÉ"

CHAPTER NINE

What Shall We Wear in Marshfield?

Hometown Social Functions and Daily Life 210

CHAPTER TEN

Let's Go Shopping! The Quest for Good Clothes 230

REDISCOVERED FASHION SALON: ROY H. BJORKMAN

REDISCOVERED FASHION SALON: RUTH MCCULLOCH

CHAPTER ELEVEN

End of an Era and Looking Back: Augusta and Dressing Up 262

AFTERWORD

American Style and Spirit 280

NOTES 283

ABBREVIATIONS 291

GLOSSARY 292

THE RODDIS COLLECTION Selected Catalog Entries 296

BIBLIOGRAPHY 309

PICTURE CREDITS 312

INDEX 313

ACKNOWLEDGEMENTS 320

Foreword Valerie Steele

It is a miracle that any clothes survive the ravages of time. If moths don't eat them, the fabric may split, fade, or otherwise disintegrate. In thriftier times, clothes were often remodeled into more up-to-date styles and then worn until they wore out. Fortunately some garments are saved and acquired by museums, but in many cases, the curators have no idea who wore them. If we *do* know their provenance, it is often because the clothes belonged to a famous and/or exceptionally fashionable person, such as the Countess Greffulhe, whose Worth gowns were donated by her descendants to the Palais Galliera, The Museum of Fashion in Paris. But it is a rare individual who saves the "old clothes" of an ordinary family for generations.

Those of us who work in museums with fashion collections know how extraordinary it is that a middle-class American family, living in a small town in Wisconsin, kept about 250 items of clothing and accessories, dating from the middle of the nineteenth century to the end of the twentieth century. We owe a great deal to Augusta Denton Roddis (1916–2011), who saved family clothing, along with thousands of letters, photos, and other ephemera.

In one of her letters, Augusta memorably described opening trunks in the attic and finding beautiful dresses that had belonged to her grandmother: "There were her clothes, bearing mute but eloquent testimony over the gap of the years to her very discriminating, fastidious, elegant, and feminine taste." She also wrote that she had "always felt that to destroy a letter is to destroy a part of a person." This mindset would inform her entire attitude toward the family heritage. After all, it is not unheard of for families to discover treasures in the attic.

However, until recently, it was also common practice to wear antique clothing—to fancy-dress parties, for example, or in amateur theatrical performances—which often irrevocably damaged the clothing. I myself recall wearing dresses that my mother and grandmother had saved, but, ultimately failed to protect. On one occasion, my grandmother's beautiful 1926 gown literally disintegrated as I wore it. The Roddis family also lost some garments this way, but, fortunately, Augusta was unusually protective of the clothing she had kept: "The way I feel about these older clothes is that it is nice to wear them but that it is also nice to save them ... they get increasingly interesting with each passing year."

The publication of this book—a true labor of love—will introduce a new audience to the Roddis Collection, providing insight into the role of fashion in the lives of ordinary men and women. It is often carelessly believed that only "frivolous" people are interested in fashion. Yet the Roddis family was composed of serious, educated individuals, who saw no conflict between civic activities, such as working for women's suffrage, and the pleasures of shopping, making, wearing, and saving clothes.

Valerie Steele, Director & Chief Curator of The Museum at F.I.T.

Foreword Patricia E. Mooradian

In 1929, Henry Ford created The Henry Ford in Dearborn, Michigan, as a place for hands-on learning. He believed in the power of learning from the past in order to create a better future, and he amassed an enormous collection of objects—artifacts—to tell great American stories of resourcefulness, ingenuity and innovation.

Today, The Henry Ford, an internationally recognized American history destination attracting more than 1.7 million visitors each year, is home to Henry Ford Museum, Greenfield Village, the Ford Rouge Factory Tour, the Giant Screen Experience, Henry Ford Academy and the Benson Ford Research Center. At its core, The Henry Ford has what has been called "the greatest collection documenting the American experience." This collection includes a rich array of more than 1 million 3D objects and 25 million 2D objects.

We are honored to include among our holdings the Roddis family's rare and timeless collection. These pieces—called "the best-documented collection of clothing from a single American upper-middle-class family, spanning generations"—reveal stories about a time and place, a family, and about self-expression against a backdrop of history. These remarkable and uniquely American stories, we are sure, will be an inspiration to all.

Patricia E. Mooradian, President and CEO, The Henry Ford

Foreword Jeanine Head Miller

Rarely does one family preserve so many articles of clothing—spanning so many decades and generations!

The story of the Roddis Collection's box-by-box attic discovery in the family home immediately caught my imagination. I pictured each garment as a springboard to stories of American life: Who wore each piece? And what can it tell us about the world it came from? So much clothing has lost its personal "story." But not these garments. Careful stewardship by the Roddis family has assured that generations of clothing have been preserved with family letters, photos, and stories that help bring these garments to life.

Clothing is so personal. Yet it provides not only a lens to the people who wore or made the garments—their individual style and aspirations—but also to the larger context of the American experience itself. These garments, stylish and discretely elegant, are indeed beautiful. Yet—as importantly—they are about people.

This collection, generously donated to our museum, is a perfect fit for The Henry Ford. Each garment—and the rich stories of American life that surround it—will be an endless source of inspiration for generations to come.

Jeanine Head Miller, Curator of Domestic Life, The Henry Ford

Preface
Treasures in the Attic

My aunt, Augusta Roddis, lived in her family home in Marshfield, Wisconsin, for over 90 years. Every year of my life, until she died in 2011, I would travel there to visit her. During my visit in the summer of 1972, she took me up to the third floor and unlocked the wooden veneered door to a large walk-in closet, known as the attic. The small room inside was filled to the brim with old suitcases, boxes, an enormous trunk, and many hanging garment bags. It was literally overflowing with clothing that I had never seen before, and mostly would not see again for another 40 years.

She took down a large brown box and carried it out into the playroom close by. With a sense of excitement, she laid it on the ping-pong table and gently lifted out an exquisite black silk velvet, princess-line presentation dress with a long, beaded train. I was absolutely stunned. Here was the fabulous "Aunt Jennie's dress" that I recognized from hours spent flicking through old photographs in our large family album. My aunt beckoned me to try it on.

As I carefully fastened the many hooks and buttons on this historic dress with its whalebone stays, I could feel myself being transformed from a 19-year-old girl into a veritable lady, standing with perfect posture, my head high, and, suddenly, a new self-awareness. In an instant, I sensed what my ancestress and namesake, Jane Prindle Gammon, known as Aunt Jennie, must have felt when she wore the dress for the first time, after purchasing it in Paris in about 1880. I found myself imagining the sound of carriages outside, and suddenly understood why her niece—my great aunt Edith Prindle—wanted to be photographed in the very same dress. At that exact moment, I grasped the transformational power of clothes.

Decades later, as I explored the clothes and hats in my aunt's attic one evening, I caught a glimpse of black velvet and white fur hanging on the back of a big wooden door. I was amazed to find an exquisite evening coat hanging behind it (see p.217). Full length, it was made of sumptuous black velvet and edged with white ermine fur. Was this what people wore in a small Midwestern town? That evening coat, and the wonderful hats and dresses I discovered that night alongside it, struck me as testament to the confident yet understated elegance of the Roddis women, and the high standards they maintained over several generations, without appearing vain or over-dressed within their immediate social circles. Seeing and

feeling those treasures increased my desire to reveal the clothes hidden away in the Roddis house to the outside world; I wanted to rediscover and share the stories behind them, and, in doing so, find out more about my own family, and the times in which they lived.

We can no longer risk trying on these historic dresses, as the fabrics have deteriorated over time and may be easily damaged. But I hope this book, and the accompanying museum exhibition at The Henry Ford, will convey some of the exhilaration felt by costume historian Edward Maeder and myself when we first began to unpack and catalog the clothing stored in the attic and the surrounding area of the top floor.

While researching the Roddis Collection for this book and the exhibition, we witnessed the clothes come to life as they were prepared and mounted on body forms in our studio. My niece, Gillian Bostock Ewing, photographed them all with painstaking care. Each and every outfit became a testimony not only to the taste of the Roddis family, but also to over a century of American fashion and social history.

Jane Bradbury (née Jane Prindle Lempereur)

Meeting Miss Roddis and Her Dresses

I recall the summer day in 1972 when I first visited Miss Augusta Roddis in Marshfield to see some of her treasured family dresses. Joan Severa, the Curator of Costume, Textiles, and Decorative Arts at the Wisconsin Historical Society in Madison, Wisconsin, had kindly driven me there for the meeting. At the time, I was working with Joan on an innovative project, supported by Miss Roddis, to create dress patterns to enable guides at historic houses and re-enactors to make accurate reproductions of nineteenth-century dress styles.

We pulled up to an imposing white, gambrel-roofed house in Marshfield, just 17 miles from the small village where I had grown up (fig. 4). As I entered the vestibule, I noticed many old oriental carpets, the tiny telephone room off to one side, and the richly paneled dining room ahead. Wearing a trim, floral cotton dress and cardigan, Miss Roddis greeted us rather formally. Draped on the Empire sofa in the living room were several dresses from the late nineteenth and early twentieth centuries that were of superb quality. It was clear, however, that several of them needed restoration. Our obvious pleasure in seeing her dresses seemed to dissolve Miss Roddis's reserve. Once the dresses had been safely set aside, our animated conversation continued over tea and homemade cakes and cookies.

The following year, in 1973, I was invited once more to visit the Roddis house, and it was then that Miss Roddis entrusted to me the task of restoring two of her grandmother's dresses while I was studying in England and Switzerland (see figs 13 and 16). From that time on, we corresponded, and she wrote to me several times to enquire about the progress of the restoration. After the two dresses were restored and returned to the Roddis house in 1975, we lost contact. However, in 2010, Miss Roddis's niece Jane Bradbury was able to find me online after reading her aunt's letters, which included my full name, and even my middle initial.

After Miss Roddis passed away, I was invited to the Roddis house once again, nearly 40 years after my first visit. On that cold February day in Marshfield, Jane and I met for the first time to photograph and make an initial list of the garments stored in Miss Roddis's attic. Once again I saw the dresses I had spent some 200 hours restoring—it was like meeting old friends. We were amazed by the range of other clothing that we drew from the closet and trunks in the attic. Even after two days of intensive effort, new items kept appearing. And so began the adventure that led to this publication, one that has occupied me for almost five years.

I am ever grateful that Miss Roddis supported the pattern project that I undertook for the Wisconsin Historical Society in the early 1970s: it was a vital boost to my early career. I am also thankful that she trusted me to undertake the conservation of two of her treasured dresses, a project that gave me the chance to explore and learn the latest textile conservation techniques. It is a rare privilege to find an unknown collection of clothing, and most fashion historians can only dream of also having access to letters and documents associated with a dress collection; for that, too, I am indebted to Miss Roddis for saving almost everything. One particular pleasure was reading the countless letters exchanged between the young Catherine Prindle (Miss Roddis's mother) and her sisters, written before her marriage. The animated descriptions of their sewing projects were completely absorbing; I felt as though I had picked up a telephone and was listening in on actual turn-of-the-twentieth-century conversations. It is through their own words in these letters that the clothes belonging to the Roddis women came "alive" for me. Further investigation and discoveries about the family history confirmed that the Roddis Collection is important: its survival is almost unique, and, as an archive for both fashion and social historians, it is endlessly intriguing.

Edward Maeder

Family Tree

Isabella Challacombe ══ **John Wesley**
(1827–1892)   **Hedenberg**
Mrs. John Wesley   (1820–1902)
Hedenberg (*c*.1847)

     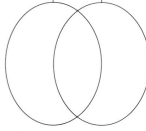

Elijah Gammon ══ **Jane Catherine Prindle**   **Mary Maria Prindle**   **Jason Richards** ══ **Isabella Arents**   **Cecilia Hedenberg**   **Cherrill**
(1819–1891)   (1833–1892)   (1835–1913)   **Prindle**   **Hedenberg**   (1860–1926)   **Hedenberg**
  Mrs. Elijah H. Gammon   Mrs. Don Carlos   (1844–1900)   (1850–1933)   Mrs. Henry   (1860–1935)
  (1856)   Newton (1853)   Mrs. Jason   Hedenberg   Mrs George G
    R. Prindle (1872)   Whitlock (*c*.1880)   Wells (1881)

Miriam Elizabeth   **Arents Legore**   **Richard Hedenberg**   **Edith Isabella**   **Lucy Adelaide**   **Catherine Sarah** ══
Prindle   **Prindle**   **Prindle**   **Prindle**   **Prindle**   **Prindle**
(1873–1959)   (1875–1962)   (1877–1957)   (1879–1945)   (1885–1974)   (1882–1964)
Mrs. Granville Waller   Mrs. John H. Holloway   Mrs. Hamilton Roddis
(1903)   (1912)   (1908)

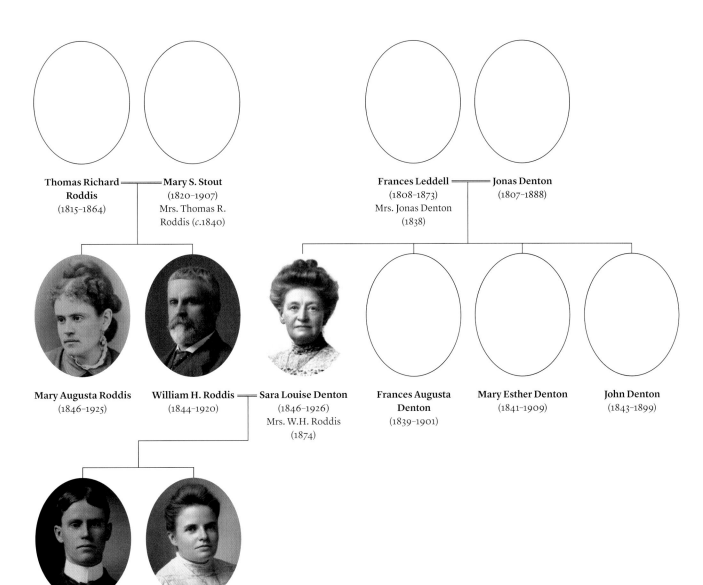

Thomas Richard Roddis
(1815–1864)

Mary S. Stout
(1820–1907)
Mrs. Thomas R. Roddis (c.1840)

Frances Leddell
(1808–1873)
Mrs. Jonas Denton (1838)

Jonas Denton
(1807–1888)

Mary Augusta Roddis
(1846–1925)

William H. Roddis
(1844–1920)

Sara Louise Denton
(1846–1926)
Mrs. W.H. Roddis (1874)

Frances Augusta Denton
(1839–1901)

Mary Esther Denton
(1841–1909)

John Denton
(1843–1899)

Hamilton Roddis
(1875–1960)

Frances Mary Roddis
(1877–1952)

Mary Isabella Roddis
(1909–2000)
Mrs. Gordon R. Connor (1929)

Sara Frances Roddis
(1909–1975)
Mrs. Henry S. Jones (1929)

Catherine Prindle Roddis
(1911–1986)
Mrs. Robert Beggs (1936)

Augusta Denton Roddis
(1916–2011)

William Henry Roddis II
(1917–2008)

Ellen Cecilia Roddis
(1923–1975)
Mrs. Glenn N. Lempereur (1945)

Introduction
"Mute but Eloquent Testimony":
Saving the Roddis Collection

Two generations of the Roddis family lived in the Dutch Colonial Revival house at 1108 East Fourth Street in Marshfield, a small town located at the very heart of Wisconsin, south of the swathe of dense forest that sweeps across that state and the other Great Lake states of Michigan and Minnesota (fig. 6). An earlier generation of the family had lived next door but their personal belongings had been transferred to this house in 1946. Thus, a rare collection of three generations of clothing from one extended family, dating mainly from 1850 to 1995, was found in the house built by Hamilton and Catherine Roddis in 1914.

Over the course of nearly a century, the structure and interior of their home hardly changed. The wallpaper was faded and marked, the oriental carpets worn and frayed, but the gracious old place remained essentially the same as it was when Augusta Denton Roddis was born there in 1916. One of six children, Augusta never married and lived in the family homestead for almost all of her life, until she died there in 2011, aged 94. It was here that Augusta chose to preserve her family history, following the tradition initiated by her mother, Catherine Prindle Roddis, and her aunt, Frances Roddis, of saving family clothing. The entire house became an archive, with nearly every corner crammed with letters, photos, documents, old newspaper articles, and ephemera—all evoking treasured memories. In the attic, the family collection of clothing, dating back more than 150 years, was carefully hung and boxed.

Augusta was frequently to be found in front of her 1950s typewriter (as seen in the still life opposite) on the third floor of the house. The old desks in the study were impractically small, so she sat at the ping-pong table in the playroom, writing long letters to her sisters, brother, and many nieces and nephews around the world. These letters were filled with thoughtful advice, news, and political commentary, yet it was her own personal stories that stand out the most. In her seventies, Augusta wrote a letter recounting her experience of opening trunks in the attic and finding a treasure trove of beautiful dresses that had belonged to her grandmother, richly adorned with lace, embroidery, and elaborate trimmings:

> *There were her clothes, bearing mute but eloquent testimony over the gap of years to her very discriminating, fastidious, elegant and*

FIG. 5
Clockwise from
top left: Augusta
Roddis's calling
card; her Smith
Corona typewriter,
1954, with letter
and envelope sent
to her niece Jane,
February 12, 1973.

feminine taste. I had always heard how she was the ceaseless striver
after excellence and perfection in all things, and it was fascinating to
realize that this extended to her clothes as well.

With her words "mute but eloquent testimony", Augusta described
perfectly the silent but powerful impact of those finely worked dresses;
she successfully communicates the notion that these garments reflected
her grandmother's love of beautiful clothes, as well as offering an insight
into her character. The same may be said for the ways in which the
Roddis Collection reveals the personal taste, as well as the individual
characteristics and family traits, of all its wearers.

Augusta Roddis certainly understood that clothes speak to us about
the past, and did her best to save whatever she could. Tucked away in
her house were nineteenth-century lace collars, widows' veils, crinoline

FIG. 6

Map of Wisconsin,
1892, with
the location
of Marshfield
highlighted. JBC.

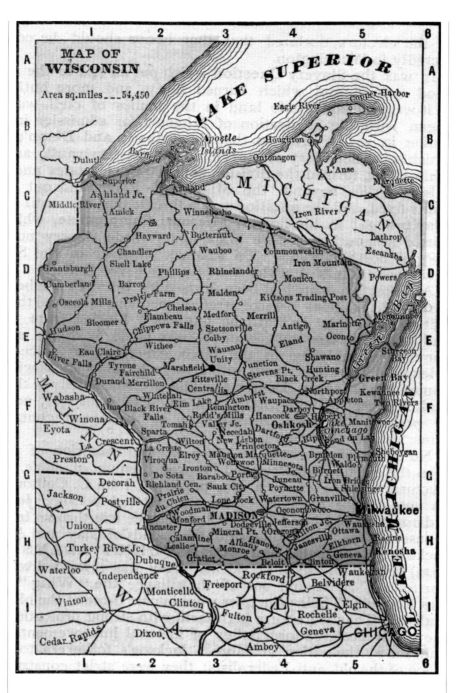

and bustle dresses, early twentieth-century lace blouses, 1920s beaded dresses, sleek 1930s gowns, sober wartime day dresses, exuberant floral hats to match 1950s ensembles, and quantities of suits and dresses from later decades, along with thousands of letters dating back to the late 1800s. Together, these clothes, objects, and written documents formed an extraordinary time capsule, enabling later generations to connect with the fashions and lives of the many and varied family members.

The Roddis Collection, as these clothes and ephemera have come to be known, consists of approximately 250 items of clothing and accessories, most of which were worn by women from both sides of the family—Prindle as well as Roddis relations. Unusually, the collection also contains men's clothes and accessories—including those belonging to William Henry Roddis and his son Hamilton Roddis. Christening gowns and some children's clothes also survive, along with nightwear and shoes—the latter two being categories that are rarely included in other large collections of clothing. The earliest garments represented in this collection are made by seamstresses or tailors, and there are several that were most likely made by Catherine Roddis herself. The remainder is ready-to-wear. The only dress that was definitely custom-made is the floral silk cocktail dress made for Ellen Roddis Lempereur in Paris in 1953.

Within the field of dress history, the survival of a collection of clothes from one family, as seen in the Roddis Collection, is rare. Others include the Palmer-Ward Family Collection at The Henry Ford and the Copp Family Collection at the Smithsonian National Museum of American History. These collections are notable precisely because these families were not famous. That the Roddis Collection is supplemented by a rich archive of letters and diaries written by the wearers of the clothes makes it even more remarkable.

More prominent in museum holdings are clothing made for the upper echelons of society: the wealthy and socially prominent. Notable among these are the collections of Elizabeth Parke Firestone (1897–1990), wife of the millionaire Harvey S. Firestone and considered one of America's best-dressed women in the 1950s, and Marjorie Merriweather Post (1887–1973), American socialite and founder of General Foods, Incorporated. In addition, the renowned First Ladies Collection at the Smithsonian in Washington, D.C., allows millions of visitors to see how the wives of former American presidents dressed. While collections based on the wardrobes of the American elite are artistically impressive, and can reveal fascinating information about how these women lived, they do little to enlighten us about the lives and interests of more typical American women.

The Roddis Collection reveals what a family of educated, civic-minded, upwardly mobile, middle-class Americans wore, and also where they shopped. It includes both evening and daytime wear, and even simple everyday wear. Thanks to a love of travel, and the expert dressmaking eye of many Roddis family members, their clothing not only shows what was worn in the Midwest, but also reflects the widespread influence of international fashion trends in North America.

The Roddis clothing was not so much collected as saved. A few of the surviving garments were in poor condition, but still they were retained. Objects stored in the attic would sometimes reflect a broader historical interest but they all served to keep alive the memory of those who had worn them, and were valued for the cherished memories they evoked for Augusta and her mother and aunt. Certain types of clothes were saved more than others: this may have been because they were associated with particular events, such as a wedding, an anniversary, or a special dance or trip. In a letter written in 1970, Augusta explained exactly why she preserved the garments:

What they are good for now mostly are ... for family keepsakes, the
historical record, for display as examples of the heights to which the
dressmakers' art rose during the latter part of the last century and the
early part of this one, and for limited wear under rarefied, controlled
conditions such as costume fashion shows, tableaux, and just possibly
a play in which one didn't have to be too active or sit down too much.

For Augusta, every object held a thread of continuity with the past. When asked by a younger family member if she could have any of the antique clothes in the attic, she responded: "The way I feel about these older clothes is that it is nice to wear them but that it is also nice to save them ... they get increasingly interesting with each passing year." Augusta once wrote that she had "always felt that to destroy a letter is to destroy a part of a person." This mindset may be the reason why she saved virtually all the correspondence of earlier generations as well as the letters she received, and may also account for her diligent preservation of her family's clothing.

The history of the Roddis family is a particularly "American" story. William Henry Roddis was the son of an immigrant from England who settled in the Midwest. Well educated, he earned a modest income in respectable white-collar jobs until middle age, when, with help from the windfall of his wife's inheritance, he invested in a failing wood veneer production company and transformed himself into a successful entrepreneur willing to push endlessly for new orders and explore forests in his snow shoes in search of hardwood trees. A devout Episcopalian, he treated his employees well and gained social recognition in his newly adopted community of Marshfield, Wisconsin, while also establishing an international reputation for his company. His son Hamilton joined his father to run the business, which capitalized on its reputation and played a role in contributing to victory in World War II. Hamilton was strict and hardworking, and led the family firm for 40 years after his father's death. He became the largest employer in Marshfield, and a wealthy man.

In 1908 Hamilton married Catherine Prindle. Also middle class, but of more modest means, the Prindles were Methodists who were noteworthy for their wide interests, their unusual promotion of a high level of education, and their acceptance of professional careers for female family members. They were also known for their excellent sewing skills. Common values and beliefs can be seen in both of these American families: religious faith, a Protestant work ethic, a firm belief in the importance of education, and the responsibility of every individual to make the best of their abilities.

Both sides of the family also took considerable care to dress tastefully. The clothes of all the Roddis and Prindle women reflect their elegance and respectability, and also the fashions of the day—almost always in moderation. These families were not big spenders. Thriftiness was in their blood; women on both sides of the family sometimes had a dress

remodeled to extend its life, and their selection of new clothes was achieved with careful deliberation. Although cautious as purchasers, they thoroughly enjoyed the thrill of a new suit or dress, as expressed in their many letters. Sewing was not always done out of necessity but often for the sheer pleasure of using their finely honed dressmaking skills.

These men and women all understood that clothes reflect the wearer's character and values. When dressing, whether consciously or unconsciously, the clothes we choose signal the interests, economic standing, background, sexuality, and other aspects of our identity. Like many of their contemporaries, the Roddis men and women believed that self-presentation should be taken seriously.

FIG. 7
Desk in Catherine Roddis's bedroom, stuffed with letters. Photo by Gillian Bostock Ewing, 2011.

In their own way, the Roddis family strove to improve their wardrobes just as they worked to better their lot in life. This desire for self-improvement extended to their wider family, their local communities, and even their country. Many of them were fiercely determined and exerted themselves to achieve their goals: this can be seen in Miriam Prindle's resolve to source the ideal suit, Ellen's training to be a civilian pilot during World War II, William H. Roddis's transformation of the veneer business, and Hamilton Roddis's success in keeping his family and the company afloat during the Great Depression.

The Roddis letters and associated archival documents reveal a side of early American entrepreneurial endeavor that is little discussed today. So while the Roddis Collection appeals to dress historians on one level, its significance also extends to other areas of social and economic history, thanks to the stories of each Roddis family member. Their lives overlapped with those of many other American families, and their clothes, letters, and ephemera help to complete a more general understanding of 145 years of American history.

There was little oral family history passed down, so the stories of the wearers and their clothes needed to be uncovered by other means. Through careful examination of the styles, labels, and standard of workmanship of the clothes in the Roddis Collection, initial clues and hints about the history of the clothing began to emerge. These were then pieced together with information gleaned from about 10,000 letters and other documents, along with some 2,000 photographs, family film footage, recordings, and the wide assortment of ephemera preserved in the Roddis house. Finally, newspaper articles were searched and family documents and period texts scoured for information that helped to place these articles of clothing into their historical context. Slowly, history was revealed.

The sophisticated clothes chosen by several generations of Roddis women, and preserved in the Collection, have exposed a number of American fashion designers and fashion salons whose very existence has been nearly lost within the history of American dress. In addition to an examination of the Roddis Collection, this book addresses this oversight.

Today, the history of dress is not confined to the study of high fashion or couture. Indeed, the study of dress history, argues historian Lou Taylor, is "more than a surface study of fleeting, pretty clothes." Instead, it is a "special combination of art, design, and social and economic history...." By researching and examining clothes, dress historians can "penetrate the major preoccupations of society and follow its changes and interests" (Taylor 1983 (2009), p.17). In order to achieve this, facts must be gathered about the source of various styles, the makers of the clothes, who wore them, and how typical such garments were in comparison to others from the same era. The Roddis Collection is an invaluable source for such studies.

In order to describe the wide variety of Roddis and Prindle family members and their clothes, and to set them into their historic context, the chapters are constructed around particular family members, or family experiences, set during a specific historical period. The sequence is essentially chronological, with particular attention given to common threads such as education, business development, sewing, leisure, travel, daily and social life, shopping habits, and prevailing attitudes about dress in America.

"The way I feel about these older clothes is that ... they get increasingly interesting with each passing year."

AUGUSTA RODDIS

This publication could not have been produced without the dedication and support of members of the extended Roddis family. Sara Bostock, Augusta Roddis's niece and executor, ensured that the daunting quantity of letters, china, books, linens, and clothes in the Roddis Collection was carefully sorted, documented, and shared among two-dozen relatives. The remaining unclaimed items were sold in an estate sale, held in the Roddis family house in July 2011. Of the thousands of letters found in the house, the majority was bequeathed to the Wisconsin Historical Society (WHS) and are currently held at the Archives Division in Stevens Point, Wisconsin. The Hamilton Roddis Foundation, the board of which consists of family members, funded the WHS's laborious task of archiving these letters and documents, known as the Roddis Family Papers, dating from 1884 to 2007. This archive offered an in-depth look into the lives of the Roddis family members, and will continue to prove useful for future historians. The Hamilton and Catherine Roddis house (as Augusta's house is now officially known) was placed on the U.S. National Register of Historic Places in July 2002; the house was sold in 2012, and a new family now fills it with life.

In a codicil to her will, Augusta left all but one of the early dresses from 1856 to 1926 to her niece Jane Bradbury, who had expressed interest in preserving the family garments. Jane obtained the remainder of the clothes dating up to 1995 from her aunt's estate. The long process of conservation and documentation of the Collection began in 2011, and both authors are indebted to the Hamilton Roddis Foundation for its generous support in this endeavor, which was essential in order to make it possible for the Collection to be shared with the public. In 2014, the majority of the clothes in the Collection were donated to The Henry Ford of Dearborn, Michigan— an institution that focuses on American material culture and innovation.

The determination of the Roddis women to save these clothes demonstrates their understanding of the vital role that clothing plays in the transmittance of historic and personal memory. Now, finally, these clothes, and the letters and diaries of this Midwestern American family, can divulge their previously concealed history.

MARSHFIELD, WIS.

CHAPTER ONE

Making the Best of a New Life
Sara Denton Roddis Goes to Marshfield

Augusta Denton Roddis described her grandmother, Sara Denton Roddis, as a "ceaseless striver after excellence and perfection in all things". How did a woman with such "discriminating, fastidious, elegant and feminine taste" end up living in the small town of Marshfield, Wisconsin, and how did she maintain her interests there?[1] What information is it possible to glean from Sara's surviving clothes, as well as documentary evidence and photos concerning her life, her character, and the times in which she lived?

Sara Louise Denton's mother, Frances Leddell, was from Mendham, New Jersey, where her family owned extensive property.[2] Her father Jonas Denton graduated from Williams College in Massachusetts in 1833, and from Princeton Theological Seminary in 1836. He became a schoolteacher until his ordination two years later. Sara was born in 1846, the youngest of four children. Although family genealogies indicate Mendham as the birthplace of all of the children, she may have been born in Canal Fulton, Ohio, where her father was a Presbyterian minister.[3] According to Princeton documents, Sara's family returned to Mendham in 1847; 12 years later Jonas Denton effectively abandoned his family in order to pursue missionary work in New York and Michigan.[4] Income from Sara's mother may have meant that his departure did not cause hardship for her family left at home, and that between this income and the respectability of her father's work in the church, she felt secure that her family retained status within the community.

FIG. 8, PAGE 22
Clockwise from top left: lace collar; hair comb; feather plume; photo of "Red Top", the Roddis house built in 1899; hat pin; photo taken from outside the Roddis house on East Fourth Street, Marshfield, Wisconsin; portrait of Sara; her dress, *c*.1895, with *c*.1910 alteration.

Training in Aesthetics

Sara grew up within a highly educated family environment, only six miles from Morristown, which had a rich history of events connected to the American Revolution and the creation of the new nation. Her interest in English history seems evident from the fact that she saved an illustrated panoramic history of the kings and queens of England. In 1868–9, she trained to be a schoolteacher at the Oswego Normal and Training School in upstate New York, founded in 1861, which became a fountainhead of teacher education in America.[5] The president of the school, education reformer Edward Sheldon,[6] was a convert to the methods of an object-based educational approach, which was innovative for the time.[7] The School's manifesto explained that teaching must involve: "… the cultivation of the aesthetic nature," developed through skills such as drawing, learning how to create perspective and shading, and also molding with clay. "In a well-arranged school curriculum," the manifesto continued, "boys and girls alike should receive careful culture in both of these directions. In practical execution of these ideas, some divergence is perhaps expedient as between the sexes … the girls with the shears, the thimble and needle."[8]

The Oswego Normal School's revolutionary change of approach to education involved a "practical" curriculum for the young ladies that involved an exercise to encourage refined taste in attire. The school required the making of a fashionable dress for a doll in the current style, colors, and fabrics of the day: "The girls are provided with dolls which they learn to dress in good taste, both as relates to form and arrangement, and the combination of colors…."[9] Sewing and needlework had been an important part of women's education for centuries, principally taught in the home, but here sewing and working with fabrics was part of a new hands-on approach to learning that was intellectually elevated above the merely practical. The school gained attention and its methods, known as the "Oswego Movement", were spread across the United States by its graduates, who opened other normal schools.

Marriage and the Trousseau

Sara attended this innovative institution during its exciting early years, graduating in 1869 at the age of 23 with certificates in Elementary and Advanced Education. School records indicate that she then taught for two years in Nyack, New York, probably at the Rockland Female Institute,[10] and then for a further two years in Milwaukee, Wisconsin. Sara was likely to have passed on the training she received at the Oswego Normal School, with its emphasis on aesthetics, to her students, and later to her own children.

According to a city directory, while teaching in Milwaukee, Sara lived in a boarding house.[11] This was normal at the time, when many middle-class families took in boarders, especially relations or relations of friends. A respectable young woman would not live alone. Still, in pursuing her career so far from home, Sara demonstrated a certain independence.

It was in Milwaukee that she met William Henry Roddis, a real estate man and an accountant from that city.[12] Letters from their courtship do not survive, with the exception of one written after they were engaged; William Henry, called Henry by his future wife, counted the days before their wedding and honeymoon in New York City, a city he had never visited: "I am so impatient to be with you that these few days seem to pass very slowly."[13]

Sara was a mature 28 when she married W.H. Roddis on 25 August 1874. Although not a classic beauty, she was famed for her beautiful and luxuriant golden red hair, and even though it was taken before the days of color photography, it is likely that the photo in the still life on p.22 was intended to show off her beautiful tresses.[14] As with all refined young ladies of this period, she was required by social convention to have a sizeable trousseau*, including several sets of chemises* (or shifts as they were sometimes called) and split drawers*, also known as pantalettes. Four of these sets of chemises and drawers survive, along with additional drawers (fig. 10).[15] Each of Sara's chemises was identified with the initials "S. L. D." (Sara Louise Denton) in permanent India ink, which was an alternative to "marking" with stitched, embroidered initials (fig. 9).[16]

A surviving sales receipt addressed to Sara's father, Rev. Jonas Denton, and dated April 1874 (four months before her marriage), is evidence that sewing was an important activity in the Denton family, and that these chemises were probably the work of her mother and two unmarried older sisters, if not partly Sara herself. Rev. Denton paid a long-standing bill to the dry goods merchant; the receipt itemizes two years of purchases, including 72 yards of three types of muslin* as well as calico, chintz, numerous threads, ribbons, and other sewing necessities. The majority of the purchases were made when the trousseau would have been the major concern of the Denton women.[17] No receipt exists for the Hamburg edging used as trim for these chemises,[18] but this popular form of cotton white-work embroidery was most likely purchased locally or even in New York City.[19] The one surviving

FIG. 9
Detail of Sara Louise Denton's initials written in ink on a trousseau chemise, 1874. THF 2014.24.13.1.

FIG. 10
Trousseau chemise
(THF 2014.24.13.1)
and drawers
(THF 2014.24.13.2)
belonging to Sara
Louise Denton,
1874. One of four
similar sets.

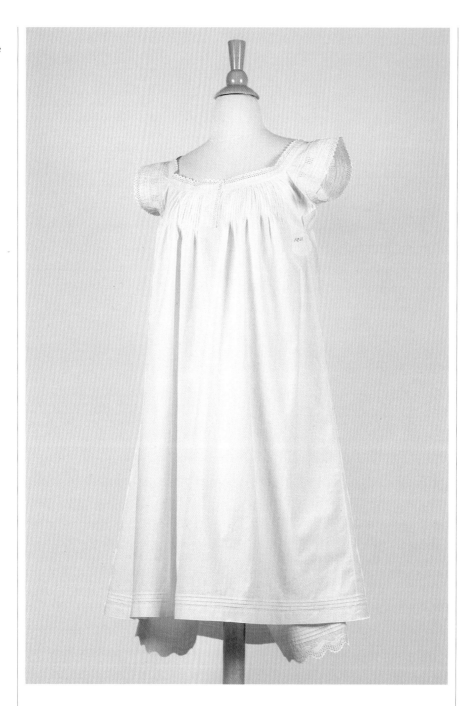

muslin nightdress from Sara's trousseau, which is full length with long sleeves, was undoubtedly also made at home (see p.301).

Starting a New Life

The couple settled in Milwaukee where two children, a son, Hamilton, and a daughter, Frances, were born.[20] They grew up and attended Milwaukee High School in the 1890s before a momentous change occurred in their lives: in 1894, 20 years after their marriage, Sara came into the sizeable inheritance of $14,000 (almost $400,000 in 2016) from her grandfather's estate after the sale of property in New Jersey. According to an existing legal document, at that time her husband had "very meager means," so this inheritance was significant for the family.[21] Augusta Roddis told the family tale that Sara's husband first considered using the funds to refurbish their house, but it was Sara who realized that this money offered him the opportunity to take charge of a company and be his own boss. This, she believed, was worth leaving a good job in Milwaukee for, and so she encouraged William Henry to move to a town "that offered little in the way of amenities in order to become the head of an enterprise."[22] Sara, therefore, was the hidden force behind her husband's new life and career. Using her money, he bought a majority share of the failing Hatteberg Veneer Company of Marshfield, took over its management (soon to own it outright), and developed a manufacturing company that would change the face of the community and build a national reputation in the United States (see Chapters 2 and 5).

The town of Marshfield, located 200 miles north-west of Milwaukee, had sprung up not because it had any advantageous natural features, such as a river, but because in 1872 it was deemed by the Wisconsin Central Railroad to be a good central location for a supply depot along their tracks. At that time, the federal government offered incentives to build railroads connecting population centers with the frontier, and this railway was one of many built to connect the wooded north of the Midwestern Lake states with towns and cities further south.[23]

Historian Helen L. Laird describes Marshfield's early days as a "wild, whiskey-soaked clearing in the wilderness with a log cabin inn, saloon, a log shack store and fewer than a dozen families." The settlement grew and then "survived almost total destruction by fire in 1887 to become a boom town."[24] The leading industrialist of the town, W.H. Upham, led the rebuilding effort after the fire and expanded his own industries there, sowing the seeds for the town's further growth.[25] It was most likely Upham who encouraged W.H. Roddis to move there and take a chance with the failing veneer company.

Marshfield was located in the heavily forested Wood County. By the time the Roddis family moved there, much of the timberland in the vicinity had been purchased by various lumbermen, who were busy harvesting the virgin pine trees. The cleared acreage sold cheaply as farmland and attracted families "searching for the American dream".[26] According to an historian writing in the 1920s, "the surrounding country, where the timber had been cut, was covered with stumps, presenting a rather desolate appearance."[27] Things had certainly improved by the time the Roddis family moved there in 1894, but even so Sara is reported to have exclaimed: "There are more stumps than people!"[28] Two decades had passed since the town was but a "ragtag whistle stop" clearing along the railway tracks, and it had grown to have some nearly 5,000 inhabitants and developed a new culture focused on civic pride and development.[29] In 1899, William and Sara built an imposing house, known in the town as "Red Top" (see fig. 8) due to its red painted clapboard sides, within walking distance of the new family firm, and set apart from the more

FIG.11
Postcard of
Central Avenue
in Marshfield,
Wisconsin,
postmarked 1908.
Telephone lines were
fitted on this street
in 1909, and brick
paving installed
1914–17. JBC.

fashionable part of town where other large residences were grouped. The photographs in the still life on p.22 show their new home and the wide dirt road outside it. Life in Marshfield for the Roddis family would have been different from urban Milwaukee, which was almost an eight-hour train journey away, and had a population of over 200,000.[30] The couple had taken a big risk; it fell to William to make this drastic move worthwhile. It would take much hard work for Sara and her children to adapt to a new life, and for the family to realize the dream of building a significant and prosperous company. Hamilton, aged 19, had graduated from high school and was attending the University of Wisconsin Law School in Madison, but his sister Frances, aged 16, would have had to cope with the profound change of a new school where she did not know anyone. It would be four years before she also left to attend the University of Wisconsin.

In a lecture that Augusta Roddis gave in the 1980s about the social history of Marshfield, she explained that in those early days of the town: "conditions were so primitive that it was necessary to carry a board around to get across the numerous mud puddles." Just as in other small towns across the country, Marshfield's unpaved streets were often thick with mud, causing a menace for footwear and the long skirts of the ladies, and hardly conducive to ease of mobility (fig. 11).[31] (Residents were pleased when boardwalks were constructed, and delighted when paving of the town's Central Avenue began in 1914.[32]) These conditions, continued Augusta:

> *... precluded very elaborate social affairs, but since human beings are naturally sociable creatures ... they are bound to find ways of getting together and the church social was the chief form of entertainment for a number of years.... But outside of church social activities, the pace of social life was not swift. When my grandparents moved to Marshfield in 1894, my Aunt Frances, who was a teenager, was afraid that she was going to stultify here.*[33]

Augusta recounted a story that suggests the Roddis family were under no illusions about their new home, even in 1899: "My father had gone out to Tacoma [Washington] right after his graduation from Law School and written back that Tacoma was a pretty rough town and my Aunt Frances wrote back to him and said, 'What do you mean rough? I can't imagine anything rougher than Marshfield!'"[34]

"I can't imagine anything rougher than Marshfield!"

FRANCES RODDIS

When the Roddis family first arrived in this small town, two-thirds of the population were German immigrants—many of them skilled woodworkers, farmers, and cheese-makers. Often the daughters of these new immigrants worked as live-in maids for families like that of William and Sara, who would have had one or two "girls" (most likely German or Scandinavian) living on the top floor of their house to help with cooking, cleaning, and laundry.[35] Although the town supported a German newspaper as late as 1926, these German settlers became increasingly integrated into the community.[36] By the 1890s, the population of Marshfield also included "Yankees", who had moved from New England, and others like Sara who also originated from the East Coast of the United States. A number of well-educated businessmen, doctors, and other professionals had settled in the town, and their wives, transplanted into this "rough garden", sought to cultivate their intellectual interests and those of their fellow residents.[37]

Homemade Culture and the "Can-do" Spirit

In 1894, a group of wives, including Sara Roddis, who was determined that *she* would not "stultify" in her new hometown,[38] founded the Ladies' Travel Class, the forerunner of the Marshfield Women's Club.[39] The travel of these industrious women was, for the most part, entirely cerebral. The close-knit group of about 30 educated women made careful preparation for furthering and presenting their knowledge at meetings by studying the literature and culture of different parts of the world, including the Scandinavian countries, and Spain and Portugal. To avoid the dangers of dilettantism, they unified their study through yearly topics. The women took turns giving short papers. Three existing annual programs for the Ladies' Travel Class survived in the Roddis house. They reveal that Sara gave talks on El Escorial in Madrid, and early Spanish literature, and that she served as president for one year. In 1905–6, the topic chosen by the class was the United States; the group discussed such topics as "Indian Policy" (the cover of that year's program featured the face of a Native American chief (fig. 12), and the history of Alaska and Hawaii, illustrated by glass slides.[40] They also enjoyed debating such subjects as whether

FIG. 12
Cover of the
program for the
Ladies' Travel Class,
1905–6, the year they
studied American
history, geography,
and culture. RFP.
Courtesy of the WHS
Archives Division.

UNITED STATES
1905-1906

Russian nihilism could be considered a political movement.[41] Augusta
observed that these women "were so earnest they did not take time to
take tea" and met in business-like surroundings, in the downtown offices
of their husbands.[42] Based on the findings of historian Karen Blair, the
format of this class was consistent with literary classes in "the dozens of
clubs that formed in almost every city, town, and village in the country."[43]

Sara was involved in other women's groups in the 1880s and early
1890s, notably the Ladies' Literary Society in Milwaukee. Her membership
in these clubs was consistent with Sara's desire to feed her mind. Augusta
used to tell family members that her grandmother subscribed to leading
newspapers from both New York and London: during her years living in
Milwaukee and later Marshfield, these newspapers would arrive in the
mail a month late, but Sara read them assiduously from cover to cover.[44]
In addition to the Ladies' Travel Class, while living in Marshfield Sara
also belonged to the Ladies' Shakespeare Club, membership of which
occasionally involved, in the name of culture, dressing up in costumes.
In March 1902, the *Marshfield Times* reported on "The Shakespeare Tea"
held at the "spacious" home of Mrs. W.D. Connor: the ladies dressed as
characters in the Shakespeare plays they had studied, with "Mrs. Connor
as the practical, high-minded Marina" (*Pericles*) and "Mrs. Roddis true to
character as Mistress Anne Page" (*The Merry Wives of Windsor*).[45]

These ladies' clubs often developed into organizations that established
libraries and made other civic improvements. Their members tended not
to challenge the concept that women belonged in the domestic sphere,
but they widened its scope to include "Municipal Housekeeping".[46]

In Marshfield, the Ladies' Travel Class devoted time and energy to establishing parks, playgrounds, and rubbish disposal.[47] In 1900, the club successfully campaigned to create a public library in Marshfield's new city hall.[48] Delighted with their success, the Ladies' Travel Class was inspired to devise a new slogan: "They can, who think they can."[49] The focus of the Travel Class evolved from the study of foreign culture to the promotion of intellectual and social improvements, and to the advancement of public welfare at home.[50]

By banding together, motivated women who belonged to these clubs sought to civilize their new hometowns while enjoying female companionship and mental stimulation. During the club meetings, the women gained confidence in public speaking, debating, and the animated discussion of ideas. Thus the clubs were regarded not only as a way of acquiring culture and helping their communities, but also, and even more importantly, as "agents of personal growth and transformation."[51]

Sara also aimed to encourage the education and confidence of her daughter Frances, who sometimes joined her mother in campaigns to create public parks and other amenities for the community.[52] Frances graduated from the University of Wisconsin, Madison, in 1902, following her brother Hamilton, who graduated from that university's School of Law in 1899.[53] Like her mother, Frances became a schoolteacher, working for two years (1903–5) in the town of Mondovi, Wisconsin, which was 80 miles from Marshfield. Her parents then allowed their daughter to take a break from teaching and live in Berlin for nine months, where she studied music and German, and traveled around Europe with a friend for eight weeks.[54] As described in Chapter 4, Frances returned in 1906 to work as a teacher of science and English in Elkhorn, Wisconsin. It was there that she befriended a fellow teacher, Catherine Prindle; Catherine met Frances's brother Hamilton, and a little over a year later, he became her husband.

Favorite Dresses

The Roddis family, like other similar leading families in Marshfield, was aware of its position in the community, and was socially as well as politically active. Sara's husband, whose business had flourished, and who served as mayor from 1908–9, took seriously his responsibility as one of the leading employers in the town and the holder of a controlling interest in the local First National Bank.[55] Appearance mattered. The family was obliged to dress in a manner that matched its leading position in the community. William and Sara shopped in Milwaukee and Chicago; he purchased suits and formal wear while she chose elegant apparel, consistent with her cultivated interests.[56] They also visited New York and are likely to have shopped there, too.[57]

Sara Roddis required a wardrobe of formal and informal day, evening, and leisure clothes. One of the dresses belonging to her, and much admired by her granddaughter Augusta, was made in the mid-1890s, when the

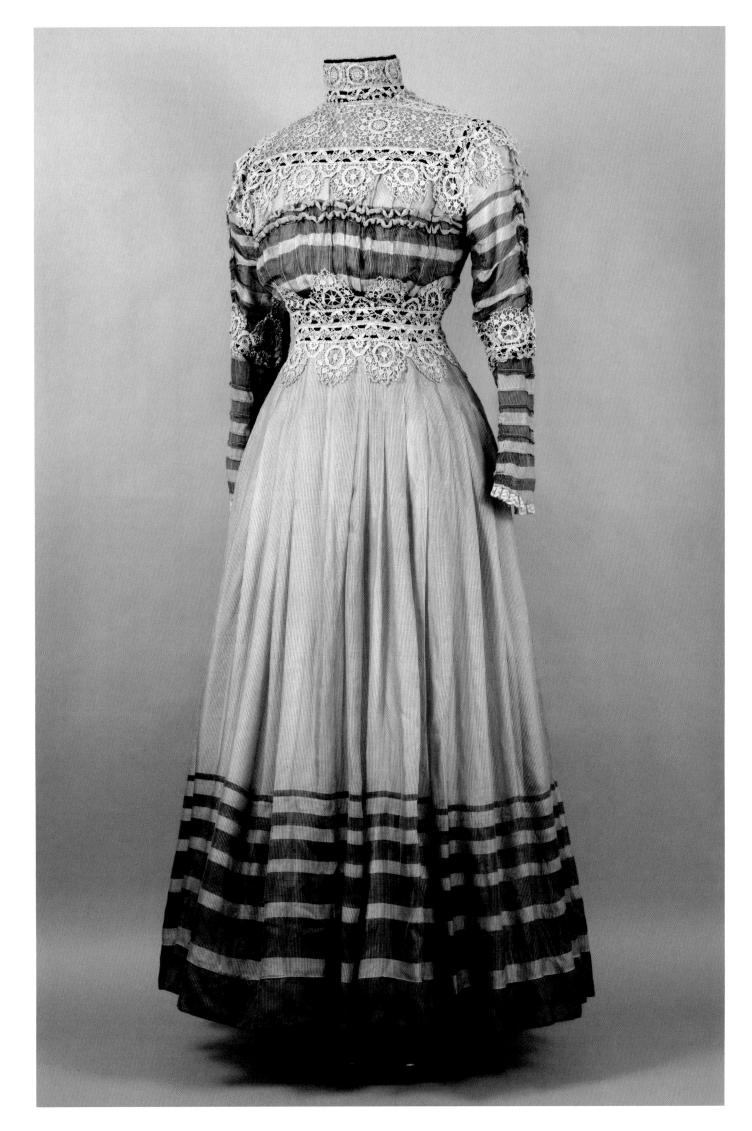

FIG. 14
Two portraits of
Sara Roddis wearing
the dress opposite,
*c.*1895 (left); *c.*1910
(right, with altered
sleeves). RFPA.

puffed leg-o'mutton sleeve* was fashionable (fig. 13). Two photo portraits exist of Sara Denton Roddis wearing this gray striped dress, with its broad collar of chemical lace* based on Renaissance prototypes (fig. 14). In the earlier photo (above left), the dress is seen in its original form, and Sara has a rather "Gibson Girl" hairdo,[58] while in the later photo (above right), the sleeves have been reduced and lengthened to match the long, fitted style that was more in vogue around 1910. Altering a much-loved dress was common in order to extend its life and avoid waste. Perhaps this dress was "updated" and then worn on the Roddis family European tour three years later in 1913, when Sara was aged 67.[59] An Italian needle lace dress collar insert, from about 1913, most likely purchased by Sara when the family was in Venice, also attests to her love of fine lace (see p.306).[60]

A letter written by Sara's daughter Frances suggests that in addition to her shopping trips to major cities, Sara depended heavily upon a local seamstress: "Mrs. Ashburn will probably not sew for us any longer. Mother and I are in a quandary about how we shall get our things made."[61] So it may have been Mrs. Ashburn who made new dresses for the Roddis women, as well as undertaking important alterations, such as removing, re-cutting, and lengthening the sleeves of the dress seen in the photographs above.

It is likely that Sara had a limited number of well-chosen dresses and wore them regularly; this was normal for upper-middle-class women.[62] In addition, there was a continuing call for dress reform, drawing upon common sense and science to stage a rebellion against both the current styles and the sheer wastefulness of having many outfits.[63] Prominent examples include the writings of Annie Jenness Miller, whose views were widely discussed at that time.[64] A friend of Sara's sister-in-law Mary

FIG. 13, OPPOSITE
Silk chiffon dress
with cotton lace,
*c.*1910. The yoke
is trimmed with
ecru chemical
lace inspired by
sixteenth-century
Italian *punto in aria*
prototypes.
THF 2014.24.25.

FIG. 15
Detail of the dress
opposite, with
gold metallic
chemical lace, silk
embroidered net and
silk, multicolored
floral motifs, c.1908.
RDC 3, Collection of
Sara Witter Connor.

Roddis wrote: "I believe in dress reform, not in extravagant costumes, but in wearing a dress until it is necessary to make it over as an economic measure, less time & thought spent upon what we put on our heads and bodies & more on what we put in them would conduce to better mental development & longer life."[65] Sara probably did not agree with the extremes of dress reform, but her wardrobe was moderate while remaining in style.

The most unusual of Sara Roddis's dresses to survive dates to c.1908, as determined by the silhouette and shape of the sleeves (figs 15 and 16).[66] This dress is made of deep blue silk gauze, through which a softly blurred underdress of pastel pink and gray floral-patterned French *chiné** silk taffeta is clearly perceptible.[67] The bodice is encrusted with gold

FIG. 16, OPPOSITE
Blue silk gauze
evening dress
with a *chiné* floral,
silk taffeta under-
dress, c.1908.
RDC 3, Collection of
Sara Witter Connor.

metallic chemical lace in a design that is based on Italian Renaissance prototypes. The layered, shimmering effect of this dress is reminiscent of the colors and iridescence seen in pieces of decorative glass by Louis Comfort Tiffany, the famous studio in New York that was influenced by the British Aesthetic Movement, and reveals the subtle influence of the later American Aesthetic Movement.[68]

A Most Important Party: A Family Wedding Reception

It is tempting to imagine Sara wearing this blue dress to the most important social event she had ever undertaken. Just as Augusta saw in Sara's dresses a desire for "excellence", so she recognized a similar spirit demonstrated by the lavish reception her grandmother organized for her son Hamilton and his new bride in 1908 after their marriage and honeymoon. (It was customary for a groom's family to give a reception or dinner for their newlywed son and his bride upon their return.[69]) The Roddis house was beautifully decorated for the occasion, according to a local newspaper, which described "the front lawn and exterior of the residence being lighted by strings of incandescent lights".[70] Another newspaper article described the event in greater detail:

> A very notable reception was given Thursday evening of last week at "Red Top," the beautiful home of Mr. and Mrs. W.H. Roddis. The grounds and house were brilliantly illuminated with electric lights, and on the broad piazza, the guests, numbering nearly two hundred, were served with frappe, and from behind a screen the orchestra furnished most delightful music. Cut flowers from the garden, artistically arranged, peeped out from among the green tendrils of the delicate asparagus, which was used in great profusion everywhere, and flowers of all kinds were used to further the elaborate decorations.... The fine menu, the splendid service and the pleasant time given each one will long be remembered as a social event of much merit.[71]

Augusta was incredulous that her grandmother could have attempted something so ambitious in 1908. With 200 guests, and no caterers available, Augusta surmised that she must have enlisted a hotel for help. In the heat of summer and before electric refrigeration, Sara daringly served frappé, "a semi-frozen dish", and Augusta assumed that she must have relied on the "great big ice closet" at her home. "Considering all the details of this," Augusta explained, "I was utterly amazed.... But ... my grandmother felt this was a once-in-a-lifetime situation—my father being the only son and newly married and my grandfather being mayor of Marshfield,[72] so she felt that this was the time to go all out."[73] Augusta drew further conclusions from this record of splendor in that small Midwestern town: "I think this is evidence of the great American spirit that the people made the best of things wherever they were ... they weren't going to be bound down by the fact that they were not living in a great metropolitan center; they were going to do things in the very best way...."[74]

Sara's meticulousness, and striving for excellence, extended beyond the realm of social entertaining, as her obituary in the *Marshfield Daily* makes clear. Her aesthetic eye was also focused upon her house and garden, and she worked unceasingly, with the assistance of gardeners, to create one of the most beautiful gardens in the vicinity. Her home on East Fourth Street was regarded as a fine example of the "show residences" of the city, "where her appreciation of nature, flowers, and trees, could be given full sway".[75]

"I think this is evidence of the great American spirit that the people made the best of things wherever they were...."

AUGUSTA RODDIS

This attention to detail is also evident in Sara's later dresses, especially her taupe dress from about 1914 (fig. 17). It consists of an attached tunic-like overskirt reaching just below the knee, worn over a long knife-pleated ankle-length skirt. Such long, smooth, columnar gowns of silk satin, with carefully placed silk embroidery and soutache* braid work as seen here, were typical of European fashion styles just before World War I. Sophisticated American ladies sought inspiration from France, in particular, in order to display their wealth and refinement, and consulted American fashion magazines, such as *Vogue* and the popular *Demorest's Monthly*, as well as French fashion publications, including *Gazette du Bon Ton*, *La Mode*, and *Belle Jardinière*, which were also sold in the United States. These featured dress styles just like this one.[76] This style was perhaps especially appealing to Sara because it suited the older woman, who had never quite escaped the comfortable shape of the ubiquitous mono-bosom* dating from the early years of the century (see Chapter 3).

Sara Mourns Her Husband

Around the time that Sara purchased this dress in 1914, there is evidence that she began to think about what would occur when her husband died. According to a legal document sent to the local county court, a large proportion of the shares he owned in the Roddis Lumber & Veneer Company "derived from" money she had inherited, and she had asked her husband to make an account to demonstrate the number of shares to which she should be entitled.[77] He delayed doing this until 1919, when, according to this document, Sara consulted an attorney and a settlement

was worked out: she would receive the bulk of his company shares upon his death, but requested that four-fifths of that total would be shared equally by their children Hamilton and Frances, with the remaining fifth given to her. A woman would not be expected to inherit as much as her brother, but Sara, it seems, was determined that her unmarried daughter Frances would be well taken care of, especially as she had run their household and looked after her parents for the past decade. The document also states that her husband had "promised to remunerate" his daughter for all that she had done for them. Sara did indeed become a shareholder and a member of the board.

After the death of her husband in 1920, Sara would have worn mourning black for the following 18 months, although it should be noted that black was a color Sara had chosen and worn earlier in her life. After a year and a half, wearing black (or mourning white) would have been optional. A photo portrait from around 1920 survives showing Sara, who was then in her seventies, as an elderly woman wearing a black silk crêpe dress with a tabard, or medieval-inspired panels (fig. 18). This dress dates from about the time of her husband's death, and it may be presumed from this photo that the dress was originally a mourning dress. Although restrained in design, this dress is elaborate in its decoration, richly embroidered on the front and less embellished on the back, and finished with flat silk tabs that end in glass-beaded tassels (fig. 19). Even the surface decoration of a black dress, either dull or shiny, was subject to the rules of mourning-wear etiquette, as laid down by fashion magazines of the late nineteenth century. These rules and regulations continued well into the twentieth century.[78] The one acceptable ornament, even in the first year of mourning, was made of black jet*, and when not available this was substituted with cut black glass, called "French jet", as used on this dress.[79]

The clothes in Sara Roddis's wardrobe all bear testimony to her education, her social background and her refined taste, as well as to her love of embellishment in the form of lace and embroidery. The success of an industrialist or businessman in the late nineteenth century was often reflected in his wife's wardrobe. This purpose in women's dress was famously articulated in 1899 by leading economist and sociologist Thorstein Veblen, who was born on the Wisconsin frontier. In his work *The Theory of the Leisure Class: An Economic Study in the Evolution of Institutions* (1899) and a related article in a widely read science magazine, he observed that "expenditure on dress is always in evidence and affords an indication of our pecuniary standing to all observers at the first glance."[80] There is little doubt that Sara would have wanted to reflect and enhance the prestige of her husband and their social position in the community, but she was far from the female clotheshorse Veblen described. It is apparent that she did not indulge in an excessive quantity of clothes nor other ostentatious forms of "conspicuous consumption". Sara may have been "ornamental", like the wealthy wives Veblen described, but she was certainly a well-educated

FIG. 17, OPPOSITE
Silk day dress, *c*.1914. The collar and lower sleeves are made of net with cotton machine lace insertions. Label: Marshall Field & Co., Chicago. THF 2014.24.28.

woman who was also active and useful to her family and community. As Augusta Roddis muses when writing about her grandmother in 1973, there was more to Sara than her handsome dresses:

I am glad that we have her clothes, which are so beautiful as mementos, but it would be wrong to judge her solely by them as they only represent one facet of her remarkable character. She had an enormous range of interests—was marvelously well read, both in the classics and current affairs, was an avid gardener and horticulturist, a dedicated homemaker, and was deeply religious and patriotic besides. Grandfather Roddis was of course pretty much in the same mold, and they really were a very happy couple who achieved so much more in their lives than most people do.[81]

FIG. 18
Sara, Mrs. W.H. Roddis, wearing the dress opposite. Portrait taken after the death of her husband in 1920, *c.*1921. RFPA.

FIG. 19, OPPOSITE
Silk crêpe mourning dress, *c.*1920. Black, the accepted color of mourning, is embellished here with black glass beads. THF 2014.24.57.

CHAPTER TWO

From Cheese Boxes to Fine Flush Doors
William H. Roddis, Gentleman Entrepreneur

William Henry Roddis's career developed late in life: he did not start work in the lumber business until he was 50 years old. Born in Troy, New York, in 1844, he moved with his family to Milwaukee at the age of four, where his British-born father ran a meatpacking business. William Henry (known as Henry to his close family and friends, and "W.H." to his descendants) went on to graduate from the Milwaukee Academy, completing his educational training to become an accountant, and also working as a businessman involved with real estate and loans (fig. 21).[1] He possessed an "absorbing interest in mathematics", attracting "attention with his unusual ability to add columns of figures in his head with great rapidity".[2] He also knew English history "backwards and forwards".[3] In 1894, after his wife inherited a sizeable sum of money (see p.26), W.H. invested $5,000 in the financially weak Hatteberg Veneer Company in Marshfield, Wisconsin. He was surprised when the directors insisted upon his "taking entire charge of the business" without assistance of the founder, who was apparently a poor businessman.[4] And so it all began: W.H. Roddis found himself presiding over an insolvent business in a strange territory, and operating in a branch of work with which he was entirely unfamiliar.[5] An understanding of veneer panels, cheese boxes, flour barrel headings, and butter tubs would now form the basis of his new profession.[6] Undaunted, over the next 26 years, W.H. Roddis successfully developed his company into a prosperous and internationally recognized business.

FIG. 20, PAGE 42

Clockwise from top left: leather satchel full of letters from the late 1800s; horn walking stick; decorative fob with the initials "WHR" in a gothic style; portrait of W.H. Roddis; the frame of a pair of his pince-nez reading glasses; photo of a Roddis Lumber & Veneer locomotive used for logging.

FIG. 21
William Henry Roddis as a young man, c.1865. RFPA.

By the 1850s, lumber was the second largest manufacturing industry in the United States, after flour and grist (ground grain).[7] The industry had begun in Maine, then moved into the state of New York, but by the mid-nineteenth century had shifted to the Midwest, where a great expanse of virgin forest stretched over much of Michigan, northern Wisconsin, and parts of Minnesota.[8] Lumber was big business in Wisconsin: between 1890 and 1910, timber and timber products exceeded all other manufactured products in the state.[9] W.H. Roddis would have been aware of lumber barons like Frederick Weyerhaeuser, who had built up a lumber empire worth an estimated $70 million by the 1880s.[10] But despite similar success stories, and a prevailing demand for timber, lumber was a notoriously boom or bust industry.[11] Lumber mill fires were frequent, and large tracts of forests could be set ablaze with fatal consequences.[12] In the previous year, America had experienced what is now known as the Panic of 1893, the serious economic depression that was still causing unemployment, making any new venture seem all the more perilous. After assessing the risks and potential gains, however, W.H. moved with his wife Sara and two children from the large city of Milwaukee to the small, developing town of Marshfield.

New Job, New Church, New Home

Within a week of his arrival, a local newspaper reported in March 1894 on Mr. Roddis's purchase of an interest in the Hatteberg Veneer Company, commenting that he was "a very pleasant gentleman" who had already made a favorable impression: "He has a true business air about him and appears to know what he wants and how to go about getting it."[13] The veneer plant prospered under his management (fig. 22). Hatteberg, an inventor and the founder, had developed a technologically advanced veneer cutter that, he boasted, "was the largest in the country, capable of handling a log that was 10 feet long and 4 feet in diameter".[14] Now an ambitious entrepreneur, W.H. was keen to maximize the company's potential: he eventually phased out the production of cheese boxes, and expanded the company's product line of hardwood veneers to include high-grade panels for folding beds, desks, pianos, and organs, all of which were items that could demand higher margins.[15] In possession of considerable business acumen and unflagging energy, W.H. was able to "recognize opportunities for innovations in the business", and turned the young company around.[16]

In November 1896, the *Marshfield Times* reported on the growing success of the business: "W.H. Roddis, the hustling veneer man, is making an extended trip over parts of Michigan and Illinois, and in these McKinley times, will come home with both arms full of orders."[17] His mother wrote

FIG. 22
The Roddis Lumber & Veneer Company in Marshfield, Wisconsin, *c.*1900. The mill was rebuilt in 1897, but the water barrels on the roof could not save the plant from another fire in 1907. RFPC.

to him expressing her delight to hear he was on "the road to wealth ... & honors".[18] But in April 1897, her "heart stood still" when she heard the news that her son's factory had burned down.[19] Fire leveled the building, and as one newspaper succinctly put it: "ONLY ASHES REMAIN".[20] Undeterred, W.H. built a more modern factory immediately. Helped by his son Hamilton, the lumber mill was up and running again in just two months.[21] The local newspaper commented approvingly in June 1897: "the business was in the hands of men in whose lexicon there was no such word as fail."[22] The other shareholders were relieved to sell out following the trauma of the fire, and so W.H. became the sole owner, renaming his enterprise "The Roddis Veneer Company".[23]

Just as his wife had set out to contribute to the cultural life of her new hometown (see p.29), so W.H. Roddis, a committed Episcopalian, filled what he felt was a gap in its religious landscape. Almost as soon as he arrived, W.H. spearheaded plans to build an Episcopal church in Marshfield, where he and his family could worship.[24] With the help of the local bishop and his own financial contributions, St. Alban's Episcopal Church was built in 1898, and W.H. served as senior warden there for the rest of his life. He then turned to his own needs: by 1899, the company had turned a profit of $30,000 (approximately $860,000 in 2016), and, according to his granddaughter Augusta, "William H. Roddis thought he had made his fortune."[25] He was now confident enough to spend $3,000 to build a fine house for his family.[26] Proximity to his work was paramount, so he chose a lot on East Fourth Street, outside the town's fashionable neighborhood and just half a mile away from his mill, allowing him to walk back and forth in snow or rain.

The Roddis belief in the importance of self-presentation, both in one's choice of clothing and home, is revealed in the quotation chosen by W.H. and his son for the front page of a Roddis Company sales booklet: "The house a man builds reveals his personality, through its doors, its halls, and its porticos runs the story of his life—Shakespeare."[27] W.H.'s own house featured up-to-date architectural details reflecting the influence of the Arts and Crafts Movement*, while dark wooden cross-beamed ceilings, wall paneling, and doors, all undoubtedly made by the Roddis Veneer Company, dominated the interior. Stenciled wallpapers and embossed friezes lent a decorative touch, and lighter white lace curtains were used instead of heavy, old-fashioned drapery. Period photographs reveal furnishings that were a blend of the fashionable Dutch Colonial Revival* and Arts and Crafts styles, and an interior characterized by a sense of restraint (fig. 23).[28] The relative simplicity and choice of furnishings would have given the impression that this was the home of a discerning gentleman and his wife.[29]

Once settled into his new home, W.H. turned his attention to the future of his business, especially since it was clear that local timber was becoming scarce. The lumber industry had been based on softwoods,

FIG. 23
The library of "Red Top", the home of W.H. Roddis and his family, built in 1899. Courtesy of Grace Roddis Hoffmann.

especially white pine, which was superb as a building material and could be successfully floated down rivers to the mills. For making veneers, however, W.H.'s company required hardwoods, which were not plentiful nearby and difficult to access since they would not float. In 1903, he turned to the northern woods of Wisconsin for new supplies. Walking in his snowshoes through the thickly wooded areas there, he observed abundant hardwoods, including oak, maple, birch, and elm.[30] Tracts of white pine that were inaccessible to rivers also remained. W.H. bought a 36-acre site at Park Falls from the Wisconsin Central railroad in order to build a new mill. He also acquired timberland in the vicinity and, through skillful negotiation, convinced the railroad company to build a 10-mile track from Park Falls to this new logging area; this spur of railway became known as "The Roddis Line".[31] W.H. organized moveable camps with new log cabins to be built in the woods to feed and house the loggers. When the job was done, the railway tracks and camps were dismantled and rebuilt in other parts of the forest. The use of railways within forested areas was not new, but it was an astute business decision; two lumber competitors in Marshfield had also developed railways that ran into their timberlands. Railroads were the main form of transportation of timber in the United States until the mid- to late 1930s.[32] With the new mill now handling lumber as well as veneer, and with the best logs being sent to Marshfield, the company name was changed to "The Roddis Lumber & Veneer Company".

A Gentleman's Wardrobe

In his book about the Roddis Line, Harvey Huston describes how W.H. Roddis "presented a rather imposing appearance, regularly wearing a hard derby* hat, frock coat*, and striped trousers, and carrying a gold-headed cane."[33] Dressed as a gentleman, W.H. would have blended into fashionable Chicago, New York, or even London, but it seems that he wore this urban dress even on his work trips into the forest. Yet the formal appearance of W.H.'s everyday attire was not so unusual in the small town of Marshfield: historian Helen L. Laird records that one of his competitors, fellow lumberman W.D. Connor, "revealed his standing as a 'millionaire' businessman and one of the county's leading citizens with his bowler* hat, immaculate wardrobe, soft-spoken voice and elegant manners."[34]

W.H. Roddis had not yet achieved "millionaire" status, but he certainly dressed like one: his surviving garments are of the highest quality and in the most current taste, a reflection of the society in which he moved. Men's clothing, particularly in the late nineteenth and early twentieth century, took advantage of the latest developments in American manufacturing technology. The innovation of the sewing machine, combined with the traditional European-based tailoring techniques used by the many skilled immigrant tailors, meant that American-made men's attire could be of fine quality. This is evident in the few remaining clothes belonging to W.H. Roddis. Due to the common tailor's practice of using labels with their name and location, as well as the name of the client and the delivery date, much information can be gleaned about W.H. Roddis's wardrobe. For this reason, we know exactly when most of the pieces owned by him were made, where they were constructed, and by whom.

An unusual number of W.H. Roddis's suits, waistcoats, shirts, collars, hats, and even shoes were saved in the attic of the Roddis house.[35] The more recent clothes of his son, Hamilton, were also preserved. Historically, it is women's clothes, rather than men's, that are more often preserved for posterity; consequently female fashion predominates in most museums and private collections. Their survival in this instance is testimony to the reverence with which the Roddis women—W.H.'s wife Sara, daughter Frances, and granddaughter Augusta—held their menfolk. This preservation also suggests that the family understood instinctively that clothes were important, not only as carriers of memory but also as objects and recorders of history in themselves. The cherished clothes belonging to W.H. Roddis were moved from his former home in 1946, and carefully packed away in the attic of his son's house next door, waiting to be rediscovered 91 years after his death.[36]

W.H. Roddis had his suits and shirts made-to-measure in the fine men's clothing stores in the growing cities of Milwaukee and Chicago. A surviving letter of 1902 from W.H. Roddis to his daughter Frances, then a student at the University of Wisconsin in Madison, reveals his sensitivity to the subject of men's fashion, as well as his sense of self-renewal. In this

FIG. 24, OPPOSITE
Cutaway coat ensemble, tailored by Wilkie & Sellery, dated March 24, 1920. As worn by W.H. Roddis, often with his derby hat, c.1920. THF 2014.24.147.

letter, he shares his surprise at the formality of men's attire in Marshfield at the turn of the century:

> While in Milwaukee I ordered A full dress suit* for swell Occasions & took two coats, one a dinner Coat & the other the regulation Swallow tail*—so you see your P o f [poor old father?] is trying to keep up appearances and actually hoping to renew his youth—Marshfield is becoming more dressy & the Married Peoples dances are Setting Quite a pace—Two Thirds of the men go full dress*, Whereas two Years ago hardly a swallow tail could be seen.[37]

Keeping up appearances was important to W.H. Roddis: in the earliest surviving photographic images of him (fig. 21), he appears perfectly attired in what has now become known as the three-piece suit, a costume that evolved in the late seventeenth century and, after many modifications, is still being worn today. The style of jacket he favored was called a cutaway*, known as a morning coat in Britain (fig. 24).[38] Subtle stripes in wool, sometimes including fine threads of lighter shades of gray, almost always running vertically, added to the visual impression of the wearer's height.[39] In this ensemble, the coat and waistcoat were of matching fabric, with slightly darker trousers. By the last quarter of the century, this fashion had become normal work attire for gentlemen (the cutaway jacket, originally created for horseback riding, allowed the wearer to sit at a desk with ease—crucial for the enterprising businessman). W.H. does not appear to have worn the more modern sack suit* that came into common use as work and leisure wear during the mid-1880s and, by 1900, outnumbered cutaway coat ensembles for daywear by two to one.[40] Regardless of the style, most men's clothing was made of wool, which was practical, versatile, and could be easily cleaned and maintained.

By 1900, records indicate that the majority of menswear was mass-produced, with sales of ready-to-wear clothing made in factories outstripping tailor-made clothing by two to one.[41] W.H. Roddis, however, always had his suits made-to-measure. Following the great success of the 1893 Chicago World's Fair (officially known as the Columbian Exposition), hundreds of tailors' shops sprang up in Chicago. W.H. Roddis was a client of a reputable tailoring firm whose changing partnerships are indicated by the labels sewn inside his waistcoats.

These include a cream silk version, dated 1913 by Carver & Wilkie & Carroll McMillen Inc., Chicago,[42] and another of gray and white striped, ribbed silk with the label "Wilkie & Sellery, Tailors, Chicago", dated 1915.[43] A later black, ribbed-silk waistcoat dated 1/27/[19]19 (figs 25 and 26)—a detail of which can be seen in the photograph in still life on p.42 and which may have been worn with one of the two surviving suits purchased by W.H. a year later, including the suit above—was also made by Wilkie & Sellery. It is likely that these waistcoats and suits were not bespoke (entirely

FIG. 25, LEFT
Evening waistcoat
made by Wilkie &
Sellery, for W.H.
Roddis, dated
January 27, 1919.
RDC 181, JBC.
Photo by Eli
Dagostino.

FIG. 26, BELOW LEFT
Detail of the
label inside the
waistcoat above.
Photo by Eli
Dagostino.

custom-made), but instead made-to-measure: the tailor's standard designs were adapted to fit W.H.'s measurements. This would have been less expensive and more convenient, with fewer fittings required than for a bespoke suit.

Travel to and from work required the wearing of some sort of hat, and in the case of W.H., he seems to have preferred a derby, reserving his top hat for more formal or evening occasions, as was the prevailing custom.[44] W.H.'s surviving derby from around 1920 was made expressly for Chicago's Marshall Field & Company by Woodrow, located on Piccadilly in London (figs 27 and 28). Early in the twentieth century, when the bowler became popular in America—where it was known as the derby—it was considered "the true daytime hat".[45] On the eve of World War I, these were worn almost everywhere, except for ceremonial occasions.

The "gold-headed cane" belonging to W.H. Roddis, as noted in the description of him above, provides a further glimpse into the world of elegant men's accessories at this time.[46] Examples of quality walking sticks survive throughout this period, suggesting they were a consistently fashionable accessory. Unlike canes, sticks do not have curved handles. Rarely functional, they were a symbol of affluence and power. The surviving multi-layered "stacked" walking stick belonging to W.H. Roddis is bronze-tipped and made from several types of horn, including stag and cow horn, indicating a high level of sophistication (fig. 29). Probably purchased in either London or Germany during the family tour of Europe in 1913, this stick reflects W.H.'s eye for the unusual, and also his means to travel and make purchases abroad.[47]

The gold fob belonging to W.H. Roddis, engraved with his initials in gothic letters, may be seen in the still life on p.42.[48] Although it looks very much like the personal stamps used on wax seals for authenticating documents and securing letters, a fashion that was revived in the Victorian

FIG. 27, FAR LEFT
Man's derby, or bowler hat, *c.*1920; pictured on a John Cavanagh hat box, *c.*1925–40. THF 2014.24.155; THF 2014.24.190.

FIG. 28, LEFT
Detail of the label inside the derby hat on the left, *c.*1920. THF 2014.24.155.

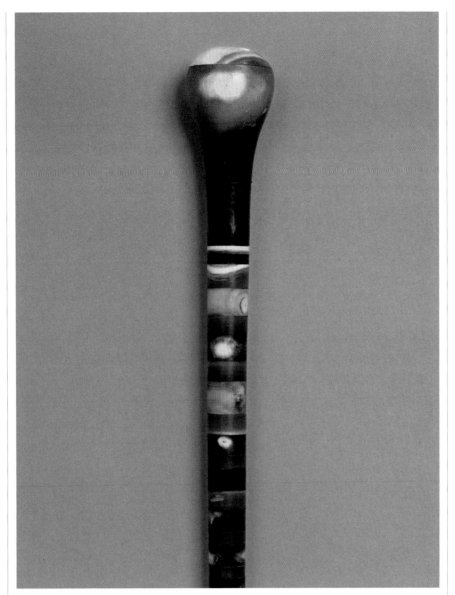

FIG. 29
Detail of a stacked
horn walking stick,
c.1913. This walking
stick belonged to
W.H. Roddis and was
possibly purchased
during his three-
month European
tour in 1913.
THE 2014 119 13
Photo by Eli
Dagostino.

period, the initials on this fob are not engraved in reverse and therefore it
was purely an accessory. W.H. would have attached this fob to his surviving
gold pocket watch, with the latter hidden in the watch pocket of his
waistcoat. Since jackets were often left open, this fob itself would have been
prominently displayed, making it the focal point of his masculine finery.

W.H. Roddis also took care to purchase fine quality shirts. One
surviving example was made by Phillips-Jones, which was established
in 1862 and became the largest shirt manufacturer in the United States
by 1910 (fig. 30).[49] The label reads: "The 'Fraternity' No Bulge Bosom",
along with a variation of the British royal coat of arms with "Britain" and
"P.J." within it and below "Made in U.S.A." (fig. 31). Advertisements for
this company included the phrase "They Fit Royally" alongside a crown,
clearly promoting an association with English men's shirts, however
unfounded. (Given W.H.'s pride in his English heritage, this link may
well have appealed.) The collars, however, were not necessarily made by

the same company and were usually interchangeable.[50] Detached collars had already appeared in the 1820s and rapidly gained popularity—they conveniently solved the problem of laundering a whole shirt when only the collar needed to be cleaned. Similarly, detachable cuffs were also available. By the end of the nineteenth century, collars averaged over four inches high (see the 1899 photo of Hamilton, and the example featured in the still life on p.160), and extreme examples could be as high as five inches.[51] The collar tips were turned over to resemble wings (the term wing collar* seems to have originated in America and was imported into England by 1906).[52] Heavily starched, these collars were attached to the collarless shirts at the front and back, often with gold or gold-plated studs, and were worn by all men of a certain social standing. Even workmen, such as cabinet-makers and other skilled craftsmen, adopted this symbol of the gentleman. Underneath these collars, W.H. would have worn either the knotted "four in hand" necktie still common today, or variations of what would have been referred to as a cravat*.

W.H. Roddis paid attention to every aspect of his self-presentation, including his footwear. A surviving pair of shoes from about 1910, suggest that his brand of choice was John H. Hanan & Son, Inc., a company founded in New York in 1882 (fig. 32). Hanan shoes were well-made and popular, and were also worn by W.H.'s son Hamilton during the first two decades of the twentieth century (Hanan also made women's shoes; see p.98).

Although W.H. Roddis followed some new fashions (he was among the first to buy an automobile in the early twentieth century, joining a small group of men in Marshfield who drove past their neighbors' carriages unnerving their horses), he stopped short at a smooth face. His sister felt that he should "cut off his moustache & shave his face clean & be in the fashion,"[53] but her conservative brother never took up this suggestion.[54]

FIG. 32
Men's shoes, by
Hanan & Son, *c.*1910.
THF 2014.24.160.

Hard-earned Success

W.H. Roddis was to retain his gentlemanly appearance, and his beard, through thick and thin. He and his company faced several serious setbacks before the marriage of his son Hamilton to Catherine Prindle in 1908. In January 1907, extreme weather conditions closed the Roddis railroad for several days and caused a shutdown of the Park Falls mill. A month later, fires once again broke out, devastating both Roddis plants in Marshfield and Park Falls within eight days of each other.[55] However, just as in 1897, W.H. and Hamilton rebuilt and reopened the mills quickly. Weak demand for forest products in 1908 brought more difficult times, but in March of that year Hamilton wrote: "Business is quite good. Hardwood lumber is firm and we are recovering from that sick feeling...."[56] Despite the fires and the periodic shutdowns of their mills when the market dropped, the company continued to expand and W.H.'s influence in the town grew. By the summer of 1908, W.H. Roddis, who was not a politician by nature, found himself mayor of Marshfield,[57] and the family had ample reason to give a lavish garden reception for Hamilton and his bride, Catherine Prindle (see p.95).

One of the reasons for the success of the Roddis Lumber & Veneer Company was the production of flush doors (flat slab doors) for which it had become famous in about 1912 (figs 33 and 34). Although they did not invent the flush door, W.H. and his son are credited as being the first to understand their potential and to manufacture them on a scale that led them to become the world's largest producer in the early 1900s.[58] Architects immediately recognized their advantages; Roddis flush doors did not shrink or swell, they retarded fire and sound, and had no joints to loosen or crack. These qualities made them highly suitable for large-scale commercial buildings—hotels, hospitals, schools, and apartment buildings. Photographs and testimonials from across America were featured in a Roddis promotional catalog from about 1913: the Immigrant Station at Ellis Island, the Bellevue Hospital in New York City, and the governor's mansion in Olympia, Washington, among many others.[59]

W.H. attributed a large part of his success to the quality of his employees, many of them fine woodworkers of German heritage. He sought ways to promote worker stability and loyalty, and to ensure they had access to safe, clean, and affordable housing. From 1910 to 1919, his religion-based, progressive approach led the Roddis Company to assume the role of guarantor to the various banks that lent money for the construction and purchase of workers' homes. This was typical of W.H. and resulted in the local newspaper noting his "kind and generous traits".[60]

In 1912, W.H. Roddis invited a friend and his wife to join him, along with his wife and daughter, on a three-month trip sailing to "Naples and from there to Rome, Venice, Switzerland, Dresden, Berlin, Paris and London."[61] The son of an English immigrant who had made the one-way journey to the New World less than a century earlier, W.H. had become a prosperous lumber industrialist with the time and money to travel back to the Old World. This trip, which he took with his family in 1913, was made in the tradition of the "Grand Tour"—a rite of passage throughout the eighteenth century for aristocratic British men and women who wished to immerse themselves in European art, culture, and history.[62] In the same letter, W.H. encouraged his friend that they need not stay in the most expensive hotels, reflecting his characteristic fiscal prudence.

The Roddises took this trip the year before World War I began, by which time the family firm was well established. The Roddis Lumber & Veneer Company had branches in New York, Minneapolis, Oklahoma City, Grand Rapids, Los Angeles, and Chicago. In a letter dated as early as 1898, W.H.'s mother had congratulated him for tapping into international markets in England and Germany.[63] By 1901 the company was also shipping to France, and during World War I shipments were made to both France and Italy.[64] By the late 1920s, the Roddis Company had become the largest employer in Marshfield.[65]

RODDIS LUMBER & VENEER COMPANY

RODDIS LUMBER & VENEER COMPANY

"R-642"
Striped Mahogany entrance door with
sidelights to match. Special design of
inlay.
Construction: RODDIS STERLING.

"R-702"-French Door.
Birch 10-light Door.
Special Colonial Curve Top Design
producing a very pleasing effect.
Construction: RODDIS STERLING.

Page 38

FIGS 33 AND 34

Illustrations from
the Roddis Lumber
& Veneer Company
catalog, entitled
*Roddis French and
Flush Doors, c.*1923.
THF 2014.115.1.
From the
Collections of
The Henry Ford.

When W.H. Roddis died in 1920, the value of his estate was about
$750,000 (the equivalent of over $9 million in 2016). As discussed in
Chapter 1, his children Hamilton and Frances inherited company shares
from his estate, making them comfortably well off, at least on paper.
However, the value of those privately held shares could have been
underestimated to avoid additional estate tax, so the true value of their
father's estate may have been much higher—by the time of his death,
W.H. Roddis may have actually been close to being a millionaire.[66] A
Roddis Lumber & Veneer Company catalog from the early 1920s attests
to the growth of the family firm under his stewardship: it boasts of 40,000
acres of "the finest northern hardwoods", traversed by 27 miles of Roddis-
owned railroad, as well as "the largest factory of its kind in the world".[67]
W.H. had come a long way from his modest circumstances at middle age.

Marshfield mourned the death of W.H. Roddis: the flag on the city hall
was lowered to half-mast, and the mayor asked all businesses to close for
the two hours of his funeral.[68] W.H. had been an alderman for many years,
mayor for one term, and had ensured that jobs and national recognition
were brought to the town. A letter of condolence describes W.H. as one
of the few "old pioneers" left in the area.[69] Fifty years later, Hamilton
described his father's key qualities: "An insatiable thirst for knowledge,
a sternness tempered with an understanding and love of humanity, and
an inexhaustible supply of energy, all of these were responsible for his
great enterprise."[70] By the end of his life, W. H. Roddis had distinguished
himself as an astute entrepreneur and industrialist, developing a failing
veneer business into a world-class company, spanning the United States
and even extending to Europe. In doing so, he transformed the fortunes
of his family and his descendants. His success is reflected in the quality of
his surviving garments. They clearly indicate a man of conservative and
refined taste who was comfortable with the formality of his attire.

CHAPTER THREE

Sewing and the Modern Woman
The Prindle Family

Sara and William Henry Roddis created a prosperous way of life in Marshfield, which was reflected in their activities in the town, as well as in what they chose to wear. Likewise, their children were making choices about their own lives to match the social and sartorial aspirations of their parents: Frances, who had a slightly hunched back, never married and looked after her parents until they died, when she was free to live during the winter in New Orleans, a city she loved; Hamilton was destined to marry Catherine Prindle, and thus link his family to hers. In doing so, the conservative and religious Roddis family intersected with the equally religious but more artistic Prindles.

Both families had daughters who, unusually for that time, were university educated and became teachers. The Prindle women differed, however, in their excellent sewing skills, their ability to draw well, and their exposure to progressive ideas about the role of women. By examining the similar characteristics of the parallel family of the Prindles, the social and cultural changes that affected many middle-class American families in the late nineteenth and early decades of the twentieth centuries become apparent. The complexities of the diverse, and sometimes conflicting, influences of domestic realities and intellectual ambitions of this era are particularly relevant in the context of the Prindle and Roddis women, and were strongly felt in both families. Catherine's upbringing offers an insight into the woman who would become the next matriarch of the

FIG. 35, PAGE 58
Clockwise from top left: Catherine's sample book (with fragment of beaded dress trimming, 1912); postcard from the Armour Institute, 1904; detail of Miriam Prindle's letter, with shirtwaist sketches, 1905; shirtwaist drawn-thread-work collar, c.1905; thimble; graduation photo of Catherine, 1906; set of needles; gingham embroidery sample by Catherine; portrait of the Prindle family women, 1902.

Roddis family. The fashion choices of the Prindle women also reflect some of the larger economic, political, and social forces that were prevalent at this time. Likewise, they hint at a family sensibility, as practical as it was creative, which was passed to Catherine, and then from her to her children.

> *"Arranged my hair in braids with green ties, and wore my white mohair & black basque. I looked well I knew ...."*

ISABELLA A.H. PRINDLE

Remarkably, the attic of the Roddis house also housed clothing, letters, and even artifacts from this Prindle side of the family—items that were evidently saved by Catherine, who shared this desire to preserve family history with her sister-in-law, Frances. Correspondence, diaries, and scrapbooks, as well as some garments, reveal a remarkable amount of information about Catherine's grandmother Isabella C. Hedenberg, her mother Isabella A.H. Prindle, and herself and her siblings. The surviving photos attest to the Prindle women's long tradition of being well dressed in the latest fashions, and their letters demonstrate that sewing and creating one's own clothes was an activity woven into the very fabric of this close-knit family. The sisters appreciated beauty in fashion, and lovingly saved two particularly fine dresses that belonged to their father's sister, Jane Prindle Gammon, known as "Aunt Jennie". These dresses extend the range of the Roddis Collection into the "crinoline" and "bustle" periods of the mid-1850s and the 1880s. The Prindles' interest in sewing and clothes was complemented by other artistic accomplishments, such as an active participation in the fields of drawing and music, while family scrapbooks clearly indicate an interest and a curiosity in philosophy, science, and especially new ideas about the role of women.

Personal Style and Artistic Endeavors

In 1870, at the age of 19, Isabella Arents Hedenberg was listed in the U.S. Census as a teacher living in Chicago with her parents, John Wesley and Isabella Challacombe Hedenberg—yet another teacher in this extended family.[1] A photo taken in late July 1871 reveals that Isabella is dressed in the height of fashion (fig. 36).[2] The use of black Chantilly lace over light colored silks, as seen on Isabella's dress, seems to have come into fashion in the United States at about the time when Mary Todd Lincoln, wife of President Lincoln, appeared in engravings wearing this style at White House functions in 1862.[3] This use of lace and its variations remained popular during the following decade. By the early 1870s, the wide

FIG. 36
Portrait of Isabella
Arents Hedenberg,
called "Belle" by her
mother. This *carte
de visite* is dated
July 28, 1871. RFPA.

crinoline* skirt had disappeared and was replaced by a bustle*. Isabella's dress hints at the beginnings of a bustle, although it is not visible in the photo of her seated. A new square neckline also appeared in the early 1870s and is evoked here with ribbon and lace, a style that suited the fashion-conscious Isabella.

Just seven months later, in 1872, Isabella married Jason Richards Prindle. Isabella's diaries describe her husband as loving, and able to "charm away all [her] troubles".[4] One entry in her diary details how she dressed as a young wife: "Arranged my hair in braids with green ties, and wore my white mohair & black basque*. I looked well I knew, and was glad for I love to appear beautiful in Jason's eyes and my only wish [is that]

I were ten times more so for his sake, and those who will be so dear to us in the future—our children."[5] Her diaries are also filled with reports of her sewing activities; of those projects she worked on alone but also with her mother, and how together they re-made old dresses, created new ones, and were busy "repairing garments".[6] There is scant evidence concerning the economic situation of this young middle-class couple living in the busy city of Chicago, but Isabella's diary reveals that financial worries burdened her; she wrote that when they had begun to live "alone" she felt she was willing to "undertake the work, washing and all" and knew Jason would "help" her, but the tyranny of housework (clearly without a maid to help her) and trying to live on "$10 per week" (around $200 in 2016) was difficult.[7] (The census of 1880 lists the couple as living with his parents on Jackson Street in Chicago, so perhaps they were unable to live independently for long.[8]) A few weeks later, Isabella admitted that Jason was much in need of a new suit, but seemed to put off spending on himself since his job, as a clerk, was not sufficiently remunerative.[9] Isabella was disturbed that he looked "shabby" but noted: "I dared not urge him to get another suit as much as my pride in his appearance inclined me. I wish we had a little more money, but I have so much I would not exchange for that, that the wish dies before it's uttered."[10] Isabella wrote this during the 1870s, a period when there is no information about the financial situation of Sara and W.H. Roddis with which to compare this statement. But the relative wealth of Sara's family probably protected her from this sort of experience. Despite financial hardship, Isabella was determined

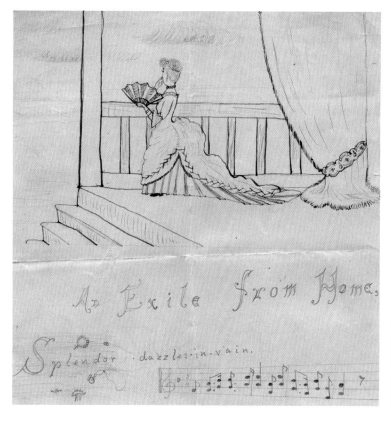

FIG. 37, FAR LEFT
Ink sketch by Miriam Prindle, entitled *An Exile from Home, Splendor dazzles in vain*, 1887. RFP. Courtesy of the WHS Archives Division.

FIG. 38, LEFT
Ink sketch by Miriam Prindle, pasted inside the scrapbook belonging to her mother, Isabella A.H. Prindle, *c.*1887. RFPC.

FIG. 39
Illustration by
Miriam Prindle for
her poem, *A Song
of Life*, with her
entwined initials
on the lower left,
undated but *c*.1905.
RFPC.

that she and her husband would remain well dressed, a desire that she passed down to her children along with the practical training and skills to make that happen. Thus, while the early photograph of Isabella on the previous page is reminiscent of images in the popular fashion magazines, such as *Godey's Lady's Book* or *Harper's Bazaar*, her ability to maintain a fashionable appearance clearly involved thrift and resourcefulness, as well as considerable skill with the needle.

Isabella and Jason Prindle had four daughters[11] and two sons, born between 1873 and 1885. The girls were all trained in sewing and, even as a child, the eldest daughter, Miriam, displayed great talent as an artist. An ink sketch entitled *An Exile from Home, Splendor dazzles in vain*, which she made and dedicated to her mother at the age of 14, in 1887, shows a fashionably dressed lady gazing out across a balustrade (fig. 37).[12] The prominent bustle and long train indicate that Miriam was aware of the current fashions, perhaps from reading about them in fashion journals of the time. The style of the dress in Miriam's illustration also suggests that she was familiar with the dramatic black silk velvet French "presentation" dress* purchased in Paris several years earlier by her father's sister, "Aunt Jennie" (Jane Prindle Gammon). One of Miriam's teenage ink sketches won a prize and was published in a local newspaper;[13] she also had an illustrated lullaby published while she was a student, and she continued to write poetry.[14] A further example of her drawings of women in fashionable dress may be seen opposite (fig. 38). The first daughter to attend college (having received a Church scholarship),[15] Miriam graduated from Northwestern University in 1896. She went on to use her artistic talent in the household business she subsequently set up, making notecards. She then continued her education at the Chicago Art Institute, studying decorative design. Her work must have been considered very good: one of her creations was included in a 1905 exhibition at that institution— a silk fan decorated with a delicately painted stencil of mermaids.[16] That fan does not survive, but an undated drawing to illustrate her poem, entitled

FIG. 40
A card written
by Isabella A.H.
Prindle to her
daughter Catherine,
explaining the
significance of her
nickname, "Pure
Princess Prindle",
September 24, 1887.
RFP. Courtesy of
the WHS Archives
Division.

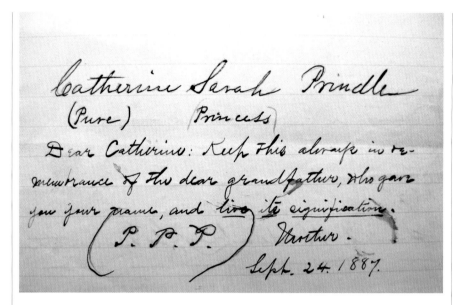

A Song of Life, offers a sense of Miriam's decorative and Art Nouveau*-influenced style (fig. 39).

The second oldest daughter, Edith, had excellent sewing skills. In 1899, aged 19, she enrolled as a student at Northwestern University but made it clear that she did not expect to graduate.[17] Stylish and skilled like her mother, Edith attended the Armour Institute in Chicago where a new "Domestic Arts" program for girls had been introduced.[18] Edith's accounts of the wonders of the new styles she witnessed while window-shopping on State Street in Chicago attest to her fascination with fashion. In 1902, she wrote: "I walked down State Street this noon, and my head is one giddy-go-round of white wool gowns, black lace waists and flowered trimmed chiffon parasols and every other frill and furbelow you can imagine, and some you can't."[19] (She continues to admit that shopping was out of the question that day since she only had "one dollar" to her name.) Perhaps it was admiration for the elegance of past decades that caused her to have a studio photograph made of herself wearing Aunt Jennie's black presentation dress (see figs 2 and 61).[20] Edith took a job teaching domestic science in 1904–5, after which time she returned to live with her mother Isabella in Kirksville, Missouri. She never married but remained a stalwart advisor to her sisters throughout her life on all matters relating to fashion.[21]

A note, written when the third daughter, Catherine Sarah, was aged five, was discovered among the family papers in the Roddis house and explains her nickname of "Pure Princess Prindle" (or simply "P.P.P."). As this card—as well as a further list of names and their meanings written by Isabella—reveals, the name Catherine was accepted to mean "Pure", and Sarah to mean "Princess". Catherine's name was given to her by her maternal grandfather,[22] and Isabella instructed her to "Keep this always in remembrance of the dear grandfather who gave you your name, and live its signification" (fig. 40).[23] Catherine was often said to have an angelic character, so it seems that she did indeed try to live up to her nickname. Isabella was certainly proud of her fifteen-year-old daughter's dedication to sewing: "[Catherine] finished the waist for Lucy, so that she could wear the red dress again. She is a darling—I wanted her to stop and not finish today, but she persisted and so it is done except the hooks and eyes to hitch the two pieces together. I helped some, but not much."[24] Lucy was Catherine's younger sister, who seems to have taken less interest in sewing and opted instead for a professional career in medicine. Catherine's brothers, Richard and Legore, were both accomplished musicians:[25] as young men, Richard sang in concerts, while Legore played the viola and then became a music instructor for the banjo, mandolin, and guitar.[26] Their educational level is not known, but if their sisters attended university, which was not typical at the turn of the century, it can be assumed that the two sons did as well.[27] It is clear that all six children had some level of university education, and they all pursued careers, whether in art, music, medicine, teaching, or business. They also took considerable care about their appearance, a trait emphasized and encouraged by their mother.

FIG. 41, BELOW
The Prindle family, Evanston, Illinois, 1897. The shirtwaists with puffed shoulder sleeves and simple, close-to-the-head hairstyles were the height of fashion in 1897. RFPA.

The entire family is portrayed together in a photo taken on the steps of their home in 1897 (fig. 41). The daughters' blouses all feature the highly fashionable inflated leg-o'mutton* sleeve (see p.66), which may also be seen in the photo of young Catherine below (fig. 42). This style of sleeve reached its most extreme form in 1895, before gradually decreasing in size and shifting location over the next several years; the fullness of the sleeve moved to the shoulder before disappearing altogether by the end of the decade. In this photo, the Prindle women are wearing blouses that reflect the latter stage of this development, and were at the cutting edge of the fashion for 1897.

As her surviving high school report cards attest, Catherine excelled in her studies, particularly in English history and languages.[28] But soon after

FIG. 42
Catherine Sarah Prindle wearing a jacket with inflated "leg-o'mutton" sleeves, Evanston, Illinois, c.1896. RFPA.

her graduation, in 1900, Catherine's family's aspirations and happiness were dealt a crushing blow with the death of their beloved father Jason. Photos of Isabella in full "widow's weeds"* date from this year: she wears a silk chiffon mourning veil that survived in the Roddis house (fig. 43). In a photo taken in 1902, about a year later, Isabella poses with her four daughters (fig. 44). Still mourning her husband, she wears a black dress, but it is now brightened by a white collar frill and lace jabot with a brooch. (It was customary then to add touches of white about one year or more after a husband's death.[29]) By this time, Isabella had moved with her family to her son Richard's farm, Elm Grove, in Bel Air, Virginia.[30] Despite financial troubles, this photo suggests that the Prindle daughters were still dressed in the very latest style, with the new sleeves that de-emphasize the shoulder. Details such as applied silk velvet ribbons, pleated and tucked bodices, a jeweled pin, and a strategically placed shoulder bow all indicate a consciously fashionable family. The girls' hairstyles, which were modest and showed only a hint of the more extreme, soon-to-take-over "Gibson Girl" style (see Chapter 1), confirms nonetheless that they were aware of, and continued to take an interest in, the developing trends of the day.

Education and Broadening of the Woman's Sphere

When her father died, "Pure Princess Prindle" had already begun her studies at the Armour Institute (see image in the still life on p.58), which she completed in 1901, along with her sister Edith. Catherine's workbook and notebook from the rigorous Domestic Arts course she took there have survived and contain many examples of her needlework skills, all of which were completed at the highest level. A surviving example of Catherine's mending technique is so finely executed that the repair is barely discernible. Her workbooks include examples of embroidery as well as technical dressmaking skills (fig. 45).[31] Catherine learned embroidery

FIG. 43, ABOVE LEFT
Portrait of Isabella A.H. Prindle in widow's weeds, taken after the death of her husband Jason, in October 1900. RFPA.

FIG. 44, ABOVE
Isabella A.H. Prindle (center) and her daughters, Miriam and Lucy (back row, left to right), and Catherine and Edith (front row), 1902. RFPA.

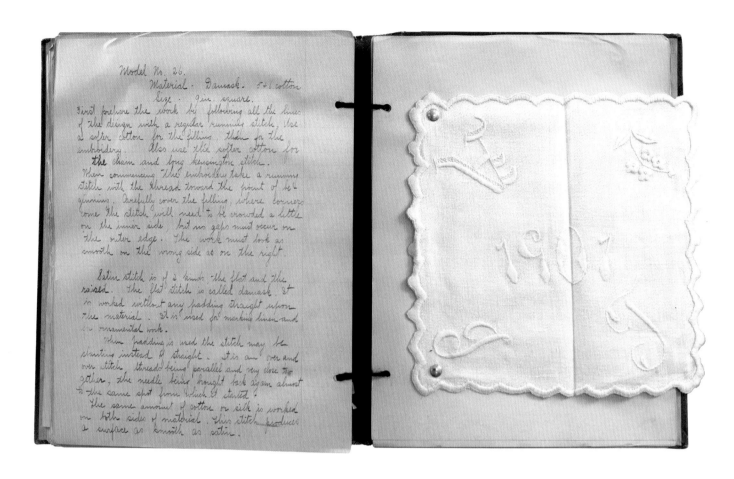

techniques such as satin stitch as well as the seaming of lace, darning, and smocking, all of which became the basis for her lifelong excellence as a needlewoman (see Chapters 5, 6 and 7). She would use many of these needle techniques in the clothes she later made for her growing family, as demonstrated by the smocking at the neckline of a child's shift that closely relates to a sample in her workbook. In 1901, Catherine was awarded an Elementary Teacher's Certificate by the Board of Education, City of Chicago.[32] Following the death of her father, money for tuition was particularly short, but fortunately her aunt, Mary Prindle Newton,[33] was able to underwrite her first year at college. Later, a Church scholarship[34] allowed her to complete the four years at Northwestern University, from which she graduated in 1906.[35]

During the mid- to late nineteenth century, men dominated the economic and political side of life and the women the domestic, but by the early twentieth century, this rigid view was increasingly questioned.[36] A more progressive viewpoint was held by the Prindle family members who were advanced in their thinking and valued personal growth for both sexes. The scrapbook belonging to Isabella's mother, Isabella Hedenberg,[37] with whom Isabella, Jason, and their children seem to have been very close, is filled with articles about the need for all women to broaden their horizons. It also underlined the importance of women's suffrage. This was a cause in which Mrs. Hedenberg was so involved as an active suffragist that the famous leader of that movement, Susan B. Anthony, described her in a personal letter of condolence to a family member as "noble" and "brave".[38] The girls' grandmother pasted newspaper clippings into her scrapbook between 1886 and 1892, and these examples are typical of the many quotes she believed worth preserving: "Woman's sphere is as varied as the form that water takes, which is always according to the vessel which holds it, or the channel in which it flows.... An uneducated woman, trained to dependence, with no resources in herself, must make a failure in any position in life."[39] Further articles about female novelists and leaders, science, religion, and philosophy testify to Isabella Hedenberg's wide interests. They also reveal her conviction that women should "broaden their sympathies", to use an expression from her clippings, and suggest that she may well have inspired the Prindle children. Their mother, Isabella Prindle, also kept a scrapbook from 1887 until about 1911; it is more heavily dominated by poetry, but clippings mentioning lectures such as the "Modern Woman" are also included. These collections of articles reflect the intellectual curiosity to which the Prindle daughters were exposed. It also helps explain the family's determination for the girls to obtain advanced education, which was rather the exception than the rule at the end of the nineteenth century.[40]

In wider society, the value of education for women was hotly debated. While so-called "evidence" was produced to prove that women studying at college suffered from poor health,[41] others argued that to educate a woman was to educate the next generation.[42] In 1890, only one college-age woman in 50 continued her education; by 1910 that had tripled, and increased yet further the following decade.[43] However, the "New Woman", independent and active in the outer world, was sometimes seen as a threat to the established social structure, and this antagonism often produced a backlash. One example that would have been frowned upon by the Prindles was the unexplained closure, in 1902, of the woman's division of Northwestern University's Medical School, a reversal of its co-educational policy, much to the dismay of women applicants.[44] "Educated" women were still very much in the minority. And yet all the Prindle girls attended university, and Lucy attended medical school, later becoming a doctor.

Sewing and Being Fashionable

Although they were encouraged to be educated and to engage in the wider world, Isabella's daughters were also planted firmly in the domestic world—by circumstance, it seems, but also by choice. In spite of the fact that the family did have some household help, they all participated in cooking and other tasks in the home, and dedicated a great deal of time to sewing and shopping for fabric, thread, and trims, as well as carefully selecting a very limited number of ready-made items of clothing. Whether it was store-bought fashion, clothes designed and stitched by family members (with or without the aid of local seamstresses), altered, re-made, or even dyed garments, clothing was a constant occupation and topic of discussion in

FIG. 46, ABOVE
An ink drawing of
a remade winter
jacket, from a letter
written by Miriam
Prindle to her
sister Catherine,
December 4, 1902.
RFP. Courtesy of
the WHS Archives
Division.

FIG. 47, ABOVE RIGHT
Travel brochure
for the Denver
Northwestern and
Pacific Railway,
featuring Art
Nouveau decoration,
and a lady fishing
while dressed in a
shirtwaist (often
associated with
the modern, active
woman), April 1907.
THF 2015.67.9. From
the Collections of
The Henry Ford.

the multitude of letters that sped back and forth between the Prindle women.[45] The verve with which they wrote about their sewing projects reveals their creative approach and the sheer pleasure they took in making and even remaking clothes. One of many examples is a letter from the ever-practical Miriam to Catherine, explaining in detail how, through well over two days of "dreadfully fussy, mussy" work, she turned an old plush cape into a chic winter jacket, ending confidently: "It will be very warm and cozy and look very sumptuous, and cost less than two dollars in cold cash".[46] Her sketch in the margins of the letter illustrates the stylish result of her new garment (fig. 46).

The correspondence between mother and daughters was often intended to be circulated, rather as emails are forwarded between readers today. Miriam was adept at observing and describing fashion, as well as those who were wearing it. In a letter to her mother, which she expressly requested be forwarded to her sister Catherine, she describes a couple she met at a library entertainment: although the wife had an "uppity, snippety foreign accent", Miriam immediately realized that her outfit was worthy of careful examination. The lady in question kept her cloak on, so Miriam was unable to "make any exhaustive study of its architecture, but the lace was superb." She described meticulously all of the other details of the woman's ensemble that she could see—another example of the way this family discussed and passed on fashion details.[47]

The World of the Shirtwaist

One of the most common articles of clothing for the Prindle girls, and all young women at the turn of the nineteenth century, was the "waist" or "shirtwaist"*. These linen or cotton daywear blouses could be either very plain, with a masculine-style detachable starched collar and cuffs (and worn with a bow tie as Catherine does in the photo seen in the still life on p.84, and fig. 75), or else highly feminine, with endless variations of pleats, tucks, insertions, drawn-thread work*, and trimmings of lace. Miriam's letters include descriptions of the latest waists she was designing and making, along with sketches of them that capture the very essence of the period and style with just a few strokes of the pen (see the still life on p.58).[48] This was a time when freedom of movement was important for young women, who were now working outside the home, riding bicycles, playing golf, and even fishing (fig. 47); these light, unlined blouses, which were easily washed and let the body breathe and move, became more popular than the stiff clothing that had long encased women's bodies.[49] However, the increased comfort afforded by these blouses was limited; corsets were still worn underneath them. Even so, such shirtwaists became the very symbol of the "New Woman", and, paired with a skirt or under a suit, quickly became a ubiquitous fashion statement of the era.

"The patterns are beautiful. If I wait till later all of the pretty ones will be taken."

FRANCES RODDIS

A letter written by Catherine's future friend and sister-in-law, Frances Roddis, reveals that women in her income bracket bought waists from specialist shops. In her case, the shop was in Milwaukee; there she was carefully measured by a man and charged $3.50 per piece. Frances reports that "in each style of goods they have only enough for one waist", and that she only needed two, since "the collars are separate and so the waists do not have to be washed so often" (just like men's shirts at that time). Frances asks her mother for permission to make the order: "The patterns are beautiful. If I wait till later all of the pretty ones will be taken ... [they] will be so much nicer than anything I can have made anywhere else."[50] This quest for the best possible waist is also the basis of an article in the June 1908 edition of the American magazine *Ladies' Home Journal*, which tells of a shop in Atlantic City, New Jersey, that specialized in shirtwaists from Paris and attracted wealthy customers from all over America. One such customer was a "... merchant's wife from the small town in the Middle West [who] always bought one shirtwaist at the most exorbitant price and took it home for her own little dressmaker to use as a model for the entire village."[51]

The shirtwaist was among the first products of the American women's ready-to-wear industry, and they became available to all.[52] These blouses were undoubtedly an American fashion craze: a women's magazine in

FIG. 48
Left to right: linen
blouse, 1905–10;
cotton pique and
eyelet blouse, c.1907;
embroidered linen
blouse, 1905–10.
These shirtwaists
have a "pouter
pigeon" front.
THF 2014.24.3;
THF 2014.24.5;
THF 2014.24.2.

1908 stated that "nothing has yet been found so economical, so useful, and withal so becoming to all classes of women as the shirtwaist".[53] No matter what income bracket a woman was in, she was sure to want several, and this new uniformity of look "blurred economic and social distinctions", reflecting a particularly American spirit.[54] About a half dozen of Catherine's waists survive, dating from 1900 to 1910 (fig. 48, and see p.301 for 2 more), along with a satin ribbon waist cincher, a minimally boned type of corset to wear under summer clothes (fig. 50). Catherine wears a similarly shaped belt in a surviving photograph (fig. 49).

As well as blouses, dresses too were often trimmed with ready-made embroideries—particularly those from the Philippines, a new protectorate of the United States with an international reputation for fine embroidery, particularly the floral style that was popular at this time. These embroideries were strategically placed on linen panels, which were then exported to America, purchased, and custom-made into dresses to suit the individual wearer. A Prindle example is a day dress of Catherine's, from around 1906 (fig. 51). Popular needlework magazines of the period included endless dress patterns that could be used at home, incorporating such panels. Some un-made, pre-embroidered panels were also found in

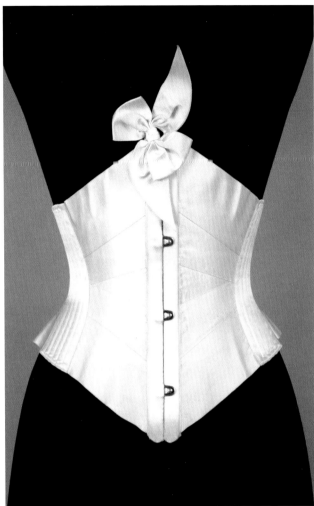

the Roddis house, suggesting that the Prindles may have assembled this dress themselves.[55]

Striving for the Best Possible Wardrobe

The interaction between the creative seamstress and the commercial world of the ready-mades collided in 1906, when Miriam determined to have the perfect suit. In an illustrated letter to her sister Edith, she wrote that she "planned a Directoire* suit (that style was always so becoming to me) of fine-twilled serge in an oak leaf brown, with revers* etc. of golden tan cloth like hickory leaves, and a little green velvet vest, like the green of the pine—an autumn symphony, you see...." Miriam added a sketch of this dream suit (fig. 53).[56]

Interestingly, this Directoire style of suit, and even the coloring, are similar to the brown velveteen suit apparently worn by her sister Catherine just before her marriage in 1908 (see figs 67 and 68). Miriam's long letter continued: "Mamma discouraged my idea of making my own suit, and as the 'National Suit Company' had no designs I liked, she told me to write to them and see if they could add some revers, deep cuffs & pocket flaps to a suit they had which would otherwise do...." This was achieved, but further

FIG. 51
Detail of a linen
day dress made
from Philippine
pre-embroidered
panels, *c.*1906.
THF 2014.24.29.

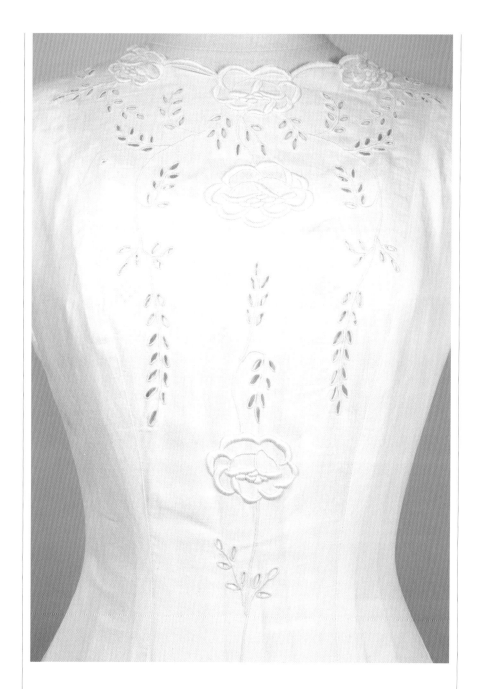

machinations followed in the quest for just the right colors and textures: "There is so much to do, and I have let my wardrobe get so run down, that I hardly know where to begin. It will be a great relief to have the suit question settled."[57] It would seem that the large choice of "tailor-mades"* (the *mot du jour* for ready-made suits at that time), produced by this leading manufacturer, could not satisfy the discriminating Miriam. She states that if the company wasn't able to fulfill her request, then she would have to make the outfit herself, although she would "grudge the time"—demonstrating her determination to have that ideal suit of her imagination.

Many of the letters about fashion and dressmaking that circulated between the Prindle women were illustrated: Miriam's drawings, in particular, often accompanied her descriptions of technical minutiae, such as the possible variations to be used in an arrangement of pleats.[58] Isabella

joined her daughters in the written dialogue about sewing projects, and photos suggest that she remained elegantly dressed throughout her life. No letter has been found that mentions the two-piece, black patterned silk ensemble found in the Roddis house, but based on style, size, and date, it is probable that this dress belonged to Isabella, and was possibly worn by her to Catherine's wedding in 1908, when it would not have been unusual for a mother-of-the-bride to wear black, particularly a widow (figs 54 and 55).[59] The skirt is lined with heavy silk taffeta of a rich shade of gray-green that must have caught the eye as she walked. At the neck there is a stylized black silk velvet collar in a curving Art Nouveau style, with a black lace dickey over white silk.

Domestic sewing and the alteration of clothing continued to be a typical and common feature of many middle-class women's lives at the turn of the twentieth century. The practical recycling of decorative fabric was testament to a woman's frugality, artistic skill, and ability to decorate her home without great expense. According to historian Harvey Green, "these activities and virtues were expected of all women, not just those with limited means".[60] Dressmaking in particular was considered an important part of the female sphere, and "was ambiguously linked with mental, moral, and physical health in the late nineteenth century".[61] It was the fashion, too. An article in a 1907 edition of the *Ladies' Home Journal* claimed that: "hand sewing is in great demand," arguing that women should be proficient in "decorative fancy stitches, hemstitching and especially lace inserting". The writer continued enthusiastically: "Hand-made clothes" are to "be more and more the style, and you can afford to wear them if you can do the work yourself".[62]

However, some women preferred to hide the fact that they were their own dressmakers, while dress reformers, continuing the arguments made by earlier leaders of the movement such as Antoinette Brown Blackwell and Abba Gould Woolson, would have criticized women like Miriam, who were content to spend hours indoors trying to produce fashionable clothes at the expense of "daily outdoor exercise".[63] As early as the 1850s, Elizabeth Cady Stanton, a social activist and early leader of the women's rights movement in the United States, much admired by the Prindle girls' grandmother, had been openly critical of women for being the "hopeless martyr to the inventions of some Parisian imp of fashion." In a letter to the Dress Reform Convention of 1857, she deplored women whose "tight waist and long, trailing skirts deprive her of all freedom of breath and motion."[64] Such criticisms continued into the 1900s. They could often be found in the same periodicals whose alluring fashion plates and readily available paper patterns encouraged women to follow French fashions.[65] At the turn of the century, women like the Prindles were pulled in different directions: they wanted to appear attractive and in vogue, spending precious hours deliberating before making purchases, and yet they also did much of their own sewing. At the same time, they were exposed to

new ideas of social change through their education and the media of the
day, including the concept that modern women could be independent
and strong, could push the limits, and perhaps break free altogether from
their traditionally prescribed domestic sphere. The Prindle daughters
loved having and creating attractive clothes, but this didn't conflict with
their desire to pursue higher education, or begin careers. In this way, they
earned their place as "modern women".

Saving Aunt Jennie's Accessories and Dresses

Catherine Prindle Roddis stored accessories and dresses that had belonged to her Aunt Jennie in the attic of the Roddis house. She also proudly displayed a painted portrait of this aunt in the living room there (fig. 56). Aunt Jennie was Jane Catherine Prindle (1833–92), the sister of Jason Prindle, Catherine's father. Jane, or Jennie, became Mrs. Norman Colton and later Mrs. Elijah Gammon. Having no surviving children, a few of her accessories and dresses were handed down to Catherine, whose first name was also Jane's middle name.[66]

In 1856, as a young widow, Jennie, a woman of "superior culture", married Elijah Gammon (1819–91), a poor farmer's son from Maine who had become a Methodist preacher and an ardent abolitionist. When he realized that his vocal cords were permanently damaged after a severe illness, he is reputed to have said: "If I can't preach for the Lord, I'll make money for the Lord."[67] After starting out in business with Jennie's brother-in-law, business acumen enabled him to make a fortune, and to influence the successful improvement of mechanical harvesters in western America.[68] From the early days of their marriage, Jennie "contributed her full share of the work, burden-sharing, and sacrifice to amass the fortune" that they would use for philanthropic purposes.[69] In 1883, they co-founded the first seminary for African-American men, located in Atlanta, Georgia, and over the years donated "his half million of treasure to perpetuate it."[70] According to one obituary, Jennie had shown resolution "even before her husband," to fund this seminary, and she maintained her interest in that institution, keeping up contact with its students after they had graduated.[71] When Gammon died, he made the seminary a legatee to one half the residuary portion of his estate. When Jennie died in 1892, a further $750,000 was thus donated to the Gammon Theological Seminary, bringing their total donation to over $1.2 million (over $31.5 million in 2016).[72]

FIG. 56, BELOW
Portrait of Jane Prindle Gammon, *c*.1867. Attributed to George P.A. Healy, a renowned portraitist of the time.[73] Jane is attired in a copper-colored, silk velvet dress with an Alençon needle lace* collar held in place by a brooch. RFPC.

FIGS 58 AND 59, PAGES 80 AND 81
Silk gauze dress with a floral multicolor printed pattern incorporating heart shapes, *c*.1856. Aunt Jennie may have saved this dress for sentimental reasons: it may be that she wore this at her wedding to Elijah Gammon in 1856. It may have been saved because it had other particular memories attached to it, or simply because it was beautiful. THF. 2014.24.54.

FIG. 57, OPPOSITE
Clockwise from left: double *gutta-percha** frame with portraits of Elijah and Jane Gammon, 1856[74]; paisley shawl, *c*.1860[75]; photo of the Gammon Theological Seminary, early 1900s[76]; whitework wedding cuffs, 1853; guide book from L'Exposition de 1878, Paris[77]; women's shoes, 1830–40; Edith Prindle modeling Jane Gammon's presentation dress, *c*.1918.

FIG. 60, OPPOSITE
Silk velvet, silk satin presentation dress by Mon. A. Angla ROBES, Paris, *c*.1880. Worn by Jane Prindle Gammon (label visible on p.296). THF 2014.24.34.

FIG. 61, LEFT
Portrait of Edith Prindle wearing Aunt Jennie's dress, *c*.1918. RFPA.

FIG. 62, BELOW LEFT
Detail of French wool jacquard shawl, *c*.1860. THF 2014.24.144.

FIG. 63, ABOVE
Pair of black silk shoes with elaborately tooled leather soles, 1830-40. These very rare shoes are difficult for shoe historians to date. They may have been saved because they had belonged to Jennie's mother, or because they were worn by Jennie herself as mourning wear when her first husband died in 1854. THF 2014.119.8.

With best Wishes

CHAPTER FOUR

"Pure Princess Prindle"
Weds Mr. Hamilton Roddis

At the turn of the twentieth century, teaching was considered the most appropriate career for a young, educated, single woman. After graduating from Northwestern University in 1906, Catherine Prindle (fig. 65), affectionately called "Pure Princess" by her mother (see p.64),[1] accepted an academic position teaching Latin and German in a high school in Elkhorn, Wisconsin, not far from Milwaukee.[2] Contemporary accounts describe the school as modern with excellent facilities and a teaching staff of the highest order. It was there that Catherine met Miss Frances Roddis, who was teaching history and English at the time, and they became close friends.

In April of 1907, Frances invited Catherine to visit her family in Marshfield, and it was during this visit that she came to know her friend's clever older brother, Hamilton. Catherine's teaching career was to prove short-lived and marriage followed.[3] Letters from this period reveal aspects of the couple's courtship, and the great effort involved in building a trousseau*, which was a point of pride for middle-class American women at that time. Catherine carried on the tradition of the hope chest, a box in which young women collected items for their marriage (an American evolution of the centuries-old European tradition of preparing a dowry chest), sometimes even before a possible spouse had appeared on the horizon.[4] Details about Catherine and Hamilton's wedding and honeymoon also tell us about the expectations women of a modest

income would have for these occasions. Likewise, records of Hamilton's planning for their new home reveal a great deal about fashions in interior decoration and house design.

We know from photographs and family testimony that Hamilton Roddis was handsome: his smooth red hair and fine features made up for his short stature (fig. 66). He liked to quote poems and passages from the classics, could discuss events in history in great detail, and felt he was best suited to being a lawyer. It was while he was studying law at the University of Wisconsin in 1897 that the Roddis mill burned down, an event that would change the course of his career (see Chapter 2). After an immediate visit home to console his parents, Hamilton continued with his studies until the end of term, and returned to Marshfield in June, by which time the new and improved plant was largely rebuilt. As his father evidently needed support, he did not return to law school but remained in Marshfield to help run the business while continuing his legal studies independently. Despite working 10-hour days, six days a week, he studied in the evenings and even on Sundays. In this way, he graduated with a law degree alongside his original class in 1899.[5] Hamilton headed west soon afterwards in order to establish his own law firm in the state of Washington. The economy there was flat, however, whereas Marshfield's was booming; a year later his father convinced him to return to Marshfield and begin a career in the plywood business.[6] Soon Hamilton became Secretary of the

FIG. 65, ABOVE LEFT
Catherine Sarah Prindle, often called "Pure Princess Prindle" by her family, c.1903. RFPA.

FIG. 66, ABOVE
Hamilton Roddis, c.1900. RFPA.

family business, and took on multiple roles as plant, sales, and advertising manager.[7] It was at this point that Catherine came into his life.

Hamilton fell instantly in love with his sister's friend. Within days of her first visit to Marshfield, they began an active correspondence. Hamilton addressed her formally at first, as "My dear Miss Prindle", but soon he was writing to "My dearest Catherine".[8] They wrote to each other every day, sometimes even twice a day. Just five months later, Hamilton informed his mother that he had proposed to Catherine and had been accepted, and that he was "very much in love".[9] Hamilton likened himself to the Count of Monte Cristo—the character in Alexander Dumas' novel of the same name, who had "discovered the great treasure".[10] He begged Catherine for speed: "... the sooner you marry me—the sooner you will cut off the flood of correspondence", and signed off one letter with "lots of love for your hands and cheeks and lips, dearest".[11]

Engagement and Wedding Preparation

Catherine's mother sensed the pending engagement even before it occurred. In her account book, Isabella made an entry on July 28, 1907, a year before the marriage, for "Wedding expenses ... $325.00". In the following month, on August 11, there is another entry for "a sewing machine ... $16.00",[12] possibly purchased with the making of Catherine's trousseau in mind, or possibly as an additional one for her household.

In September 1907, Catherine wrote to her sister Edith from Batavia, Illinois, where she was visiting relations: "Sunday Hamilton came out in time to go to church with us. He brought me the most beautiful diamond ring from Hyman Berg's."[13] Shortly afterwards, he wrote to her: "I feel that I am very undeserving of such a lovely—sweet and altogether beautiful girl...."[14] Catherine's protestations of love were rather more restrained; she cloaked her most open admission in German: "*ich liebe dich*".[15]

Catherine's career, if not her happiness, was cut short by an incident well before the wedding. While Hamilton was driving, the couple were involved in a car accident in which Catherine's knee was injured, forcing her to resign from her teaching job.[16] Hamilton was mortified, begging to be allowed to compensate for the salary she would have received. Catherine received treatment for her injuries every week, but she wrote to Hamilton that she was happy and did not have "much trouble in keeping cheerful for I know you love me and that counts for more than anything."[17]

Hamilton was indeed in love with Catherine. During their courtship and engagement, however, he was hard at work managing the business: "I have simply lived to work with a few hours for eating and sleeping and writing to you, dearest."[18] He even had a desk set up in his bedroom specifically to write to her. In addition to the hundreds of letters between Catherine and Hamilton, this pre-nuptial period was filled with correspondence between both families: Hamilton's parents wrote to Catherine praising her and welcoming her into their family, but his father requested that they wait until July of 1908 to be married;[19] Hamilton's sister, Frances, was delighted, if a little shocked by the speed of their engagement, cautioning that they must always have a chaperone;[20] Isabella wrote to her daughter that she was happy with her in her happiness; while Edith sent Catherine an "embroidered corset cover" to start off her trousseau.[21]

Catherine had settled on a small wedding, but there was still a great deal to think about in preparation for the all-important day. As she wrote to Hamilton: "It's lots of fun to buy things for my trousseau, but at the rate I've been going, it will not take long to reach the limit I've set." Later she reports that an aunt and friend are "simply bristling with suggestions. I ought to have this and I ought to have that, and I ought to do this and that, until if I acted on all this advice I'd be kept very busy."[22]

In a letter to her sister, Catherine continues with a description of the clothing she and her mother were making: "Last week I began a gingham* morning dress and if I have good luck I can finish it this week. Then the next thing is the flannel kimono.[23] Mamma has done more than half of the hemming on my lace petticoat flounce." Catherine signs off this letter by thanking her sister Edith for two more gifts destined for her trousseau— "a hand embroidered nightgown", and a fine lace yoke*: "The yoke is lovely and I appreciate it so much."[24] Clearly, the family was rallying around Catherine to support her.

"Then I have my suit, with sleeves & gloves to match & several new white waists."

CATHERINE SARAH PRINDLE

Catherine was always careful with her money, probably a combination of both her family's circumstances and her own character. Catherine writes to Edith: "I'm not going to have such an awful lot of new dresses. I have engaged a dressmaker for May 1 and when the things begin to take shape it will really be easier to tell about them, but I am going to have the green crinoline* & the white dress made by then."[25] She goes on to mention blouses called shirtwaists* or waists that were so ubiquitous at that time: "Then I have my suit, with sleeves & gloves to match & several new white waists".[26]

It is clear that Catherine Prindle's budget was limited. She fretted about whether to wear any of her new clothes before the wedding: "If I go to Chicago & it's warm I will not have a thing to wear but the brown suit, will it spoil the charm to take the newness off it, for I certainly can't afford to buy another suit & I want to look well when I go around with Hamilton in Chicago."[27] The suit Catherine is referring to may be the brown cotton velveteen suit made by Franklin Simon & Co. (fig. 67) that was found in

FIG. 67, OPPOSITE
Walking suit, from Franklin Simon & Co., c.1908. Made of cotton velveteen in the popular Directoire style, with a built-in faux waistcoat. THF 2014.24.95.

FIG. 68
Detail of the walking
suit on the previous
page, c.1908.
The formal and
rather military
look of this suit
is enhanced
by contrasting
decorative braid.
THF 2014.24.95.

the Roddis house. This style would have been considered a walking or traveling suit, and the false "waistcoat" front is typical of the Directoire* revival at the time (fig. 68).[28]

Catherine also confided her anxiety about the wedding party to Edith. She felt she ought to invite short and stocky Frances, Hamilton's sister and her friend, to be a bridesmaid, but she worried that she would tower over her, let alone over Hamilton who was himself slightly shorter than his bride. Catherine tried to assure herself that this did not really matter, especially at such a small wedding, but she admitted that it did matter to her "pride".[29] In the end, Catherine did ask Frances to be her bridesmaid, and her own sister Edith was maid of honor. It was not considered necessary to have new dresses for them. Catherine wrote to Edith: "Maybe you would rather have a white and pink dress, but you can see there is no cause for any special outlay ... tell me what you decided about hats. Do they all have to be alike? White with pink ribbon or roses would be very pretty."[30]

Catherine's trousseau would be the focus of her attention, and she approached its organization like a military campaign.[31] In April, three months before the wedding, she was still hard at work: "Yesterday I began on my under-wear in earnest, took stock of what I already had and planned what more I wanted. When that part is done I shall really feel as if progress had been made."[32] Calm as she was normally, one of her letters admits that there were moments when the wedding and the preparation of her trousseau got on her "nerves".[33] In a long missal to her sister Edith, she wrote: "As to the sewing I've done ... I have now marked with P a dozen napkins & washed & ironed them all ready for use. I have another dozen hemmed & have the monograms worked on 2. I want to mark my towels as well as napkins and tablecloths but it certainly is a tedious job."[34] There is evidence from late nineteenth-century catalogs that, along with feminine apparel, towels and household linens would have been part of a trousseau for American brides of modest means.[35]

The popularity of monogramming underwear and household linens experienced a revival among the middle classes in England and America, and women's magazines promoted the trend.[36] Rather than embroidering her own trousseau, Catherine's future mother-in-law Sara Roddis had in 1874 chosen inked identification on her chemises*, a less time-consuming method which had begun to be used in the late eighteenth century, and used her three initials (see p.25). Catherine only embroidered the letter "P" to signify her maiden name Prindle on her trousseau linens. A more intimate and traditional article, her wedding handkerchief, was embroidered with "C" for Catherine. After becoming Mrs. Roddis, Catherine embroidered "R" on household items; a few of the napkins she monogrammed survive, along with a wood and brass pattern block with the letter "R" that she used for setting out the design (figs 69 and 70).[37]

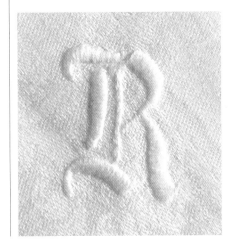 

Hamilton was also busy during the same period, planning their new home. By March 1908, he had already signed the lease to rent a house in Marshfield for $25 per month. It was a "good-sized house with a parlor", had "electric lights", "running hot and cold water", and was only a fifteen-minute walk to the factory. In June, Hamilton purchased a set of library furniture in the "Modern English Style" (known today as the Arts and Crafts* style), as featured in an article in a recent 1908 issue of *Vogue* magazine.[38] The set consisted of a wooden settee, two rockers and two chairs of fashionable fumed oak, one of which was referred to as a "Morris chair" on the receipt (fig. 71).[39]

Additional receipts demonstrate that Hamilton also purchased around two dozen more items of furniture for their home, including a set of bedroom furniture. Catherine tried to slow him down, writing in February 1908: "Speaking of splurge, you know, dear, I don't care for that to any great degree."[40] She pointed out to Hamilton that they would appreciate their possessions even more if they could "add to them gradually".[41] Catherine did, however, meet him in Chicago in order to select "accessories", possibly including the Brussels and Wilton carpets that Hamilton purchased from Marshall Field & Company, which was the leading department store in Chicago at the time.[42] Catherine had arranged to meet Hamilton there at least once in the wood-paneled, club-like waiting room on the third floor.[43]

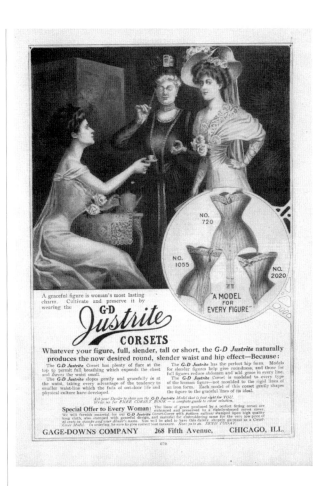

FIG. 72
Advertisement for
Justrite Corsets,
1908. EMC.

The Wedding: Dress, Ceremony and Honeymoon

Meanwhile, progress with her wedding gown preoccupied Catherine: "As for my dress I have about decided on white net. I have the silk lining but haven't the outside." She sought out ideas from her sister Edith, and commented: "I really don't want a train, though they seem to be creeping in again." Her letter continues about the design of her future dress: "Yesterday a corset woman came around and now I am the proud possessor of a habit bask [basque*] corset (cost $5) and it gives me a grand figure. I am even aspiring to a princess gown."[44] Perhaps bolstered by this new corset, Catherine's wedding dress was indeed shaped by seams from shoulder to hem without a separate seam at the waistline—known as a princess line* (figs 73 and 74).

No wedding portrait survives, but Catherine would proudly don her wedding dress again a half-century later to mark her fiftieth wedding anniversary to Hamilton Roddis in 1958 (see p.264).The wedding was to take place in the only Episcopal church in Kirksville, Missouri, where Catherine was currently living with her family. Although raised a Methodist, Catherine switched to be Episcopalian like Hamilton in order to maintain matrimonial harmony, an act much appreciated by her future husband.[45] Although she mentions a marriage feast in one of her letters, it seems there was not much time for socializing given the brevity of the wedding: "We practically decided the wedding is to be July 7th at six or

FIG. 73, OPPOSITE
Wedding dress worn
by Catherine Prindle
for her marriage to
Hamilton Roddis,
July 7, 1908. Fine
cotton net, princess-
style dress, with
three graduated,
horizontal bands
of silk satin ribbon
at the hem.
THF 2014.24.31.

FIG. 74
Detail of wedding
dress opposite, 1908.
The boned bodice is
shaped with vertical
tucks and includes a
false bertha of cotton
chemical lace around
the shoulders.
THF 2014.24.31.

six-thirty for we are to take the 8:08 train for St. Paul and go from there to Yellowstone.... Hamilton can hardly realize, I think, what a very small modest affair it will be, but I did my best to impress that fact upon him."[46]

The wedding was modest, but formal nonetheless, since it was to be an evening wedding. Catherine explained why Hamilton was to wear formal attire: "You see anything after 6 can be counted an evening affair, so Hamilton will wear a dress suit*."[47] She continues to discuss her own attire: "though [Hamilton] suggested my wearing a traveling suit, I think I might as well wear a white dress, for Mrs. Roddis is going to give a reception for us after we get to Marshfield, and I suppose my wedding dress will be the proper thing to wear for that."

Catherine did indeed wear her wedding dress at the early August reception in Marshfield (see Chapter 1). A newspaper article about the

FIG. 75
Catherine and
Hamilton Roddis
on their honeymoon
in Colorado Springs,
1908. RFPA.

gathering mentions her attire: "Mr. and Mrs. Roddis presented the
bride, Mrs. Hamilton Roddis, who was charmingly gowned in white, and
who most graciously acknowledged each introduction at once, by her
prepossessing manner, won the hearts of everyone."[48]

During their honeymoon, the couple posed for a photographer in
their city clothes (fig. 75). Catherine is wearing an oversized hat that was
in fashion at that time. The couple is also captured in a more relaxed
moment in a snapshot taken during their trip to Yellowstone National
Park in Wyoming (as seen in the photo in the still life on p.84). This was a
joint honeymoon taken with another couple, and, according to Augusta,
a female chaperone. No evidence has been found as to how unusual this
would have been at that time.

Building a Family and a Home

In 1909, the young couple became the proud parents of twin girls, named Sara Frances and Mary Isabella; in 1911, another daughter was born, christened Catherine Prindle (also known as "Pickle" and then "Pickie" due to her mispronunciation of her own middle name).[49] Hamilton felt the time had come to build a home to accommodate his growing family. He debated the social disadvantages of building on the lot next to his parents' house, but in the end that is what he chose to do. Working with Marshfield architect, Gus A. Krasin,[50] he designed a three-story Dutch Colonial Revival*-style house, and its construction began in 1914 (fig. 76).[51] The house showcased many of the Roddis Lumber & Veneer Company products, including inlaid flush doors and dining room paneling made from richly grained walnut veneer from Russia. As a younger man, Hamilton had been captivated by modern innovation and design. In 1897, he had written enthusiastically to his father about "the best bicycle he had ever heard about".[52] This interest was also manifest in his choice of cars and company airplane. So it was typical of Hamilton to insist on several modern conveniences in his house: a telephone booth off the vestibule, a disposal shoot for burnable paper running directly from the kitchen to the incinerator, and a cutting-edge machine to suck up dust. These made

FIG. 76
Catherine and her young daughter Pickie outside the Roddis home, a Dutch Colonial Revival-style house, designed by Gus A. Krasin, 1914. RFPA.

the new Roddis home a thoroughly modern property.[53] Furthermore, in the new house, access to fresh air was a priority since physicians, architects, and even politicians were exhorting its importance for good health: the living room had an attached screen porch, two bedrooms benefitted from copper roof porches, and attached to Hamilton's study was a screened sleeping porch, where he often slept all year round.[54]

In this new home, the family continued to grow. Augusta Denton Roddis was born in 1916.[55] One year later, Catherine and Hamilton finally had a son, too: William H. Roddis II.[56] Always organized and eager to do her best, Catherine ordered a set of booklets offering advice to parents.[57] An interest in psychology and its importance for the successful raising of children had developed in the United States over the past decade, and this set of over 40 booklets produced for American Motherhood of Cooperstown, New York, included such titles as *The Father as His Son's Counselor*, *Work as An Element In Character Building*, *Cheerfulness in the Home*, and *The Cigarette and Youth*.

A Changing World: Dance and Fashion Trends

As the Roddis house was being built in Marshfield, the world was changing dramatically: World War I began, and America declared its neutrality while firing up its industry to supply and feed Europe's war machine.[58] By 1910, over a million telephones had been sold in the United States, and telephone lines linked New York to San Francisco for the first time in 1914. Public life was evolving at a similarly fast pace: by the middle of the decade, dancing became all the rage across the United States, with dances like the tango spreading to small towns like Marshfield.[59] Even Catherine, who was not the kind of woman to fall for any craze, felt she needed to be able to dance well for Hamilton's sake as well as her "own pleasure". So in 1908 she took a few lessons, focusing on the waltz, until she was informed that she was so good that she needed no more instruction, only practice.[60]

For dancing and eveningwear, appropriate shoes were a necessity. The label on Catherine's pair of bronze beaded leather pumps with a "Louis"-style heel reveals they were purchased in the grand Chicago department store, Carson Pirie Scott & Co. (fig. 77).[61] They probably date from 1905–10, about the same time period as another pair of shoes believed to have belonged to Catherine—a pair of black silk *peau de soie* pumps. Made by Hanan & Son of New York and Chicago, a shoe manufacturer also favored by her father-in-law and husband (see fig. 32 and fig. 140), this pair of shoes has removable rectangular clips of faceted, steel-cut decoration, in imitation of marcasite; these clips appear to have been infrequently, if ever, used by conservative Catherine (fig. 78). The "Louis"-style heel was revived in the 1920s, so she may have continued to wear these pumps well into that decade (perhaps congratulating herself on saving shoes of a style that had come back into fashion).

Evidence that Catherine discussed fashion with her sister-in-law is found in a letter of 1912 from Frances to her mother: "Hamilton is going to send twenty-five dollars. Catherine, after hearing about my pongee*, said she wanted one too. But of course you will not get trimming like mine for her. There was a lot of trimming on my other pongee and it was always admired so much."[62] A surviving silk pongee Roddis dress of this period may be the one for which Sara, Catherine's mother-in-law, selected the trimming (fig. 79). This dress consists of wide linen bobbin lace insertions in a symmetrical pattern repeated on both the front and the back of the dress from the shoulder to above the hem. The benefit of lace inserts is that a colored silk underdress, worn under the pongee, enables the wearer to alter the appearance of the dress for different occasions, a practical feature that may well have appealed to Catherine since it was a way to efficiently extend one's wardrobe.

Another surviving garment thought to be of Catherine's is a short wool coat that was practical enough to wear during her pregnancies (fig. 80). This elegant outer-garment was made by Maklary Ladies Tailors: Hungarian tailors who settled in Milwaukee in about 1900.[63] Fine tailoring creates the flowing shape of this popular style, and subtle tailors' devices, such as embroidered arrowheads, are used to reinforce the edges of

FIG. 77, ABOVE LEFT
Bronze beaded leather pumps with a "Louis"-style heel from Carson Pirie Scott & Company, Chicago. Worn by Catherine Roddis, c.1905–10.
THF 2014.24.138.

FIG. 78, ABOVE
Silk *peau de soie* pumps with faceted, cut steel shoe clips, from Hanan & Son, New York, Chicago c.1905–10.
THF 2014.24.133.

FIG. 79
Detail of silk
pongee dress with
linen bobbin lace
insertion, 1912.
THF 2014.24.26.

pockets. Inside, there is an extravagant printed silk lining of modern design (fig. 81), strongly influenced by the Wiener Werkstätte*.[64] War in Europe led to military themes and khaki colors being used in women's fashion in the United States; this coat fits into this trend, while concealing an unexpected flamboyance inside.[65]

No clothes belonging to Hamilton from this period survive, with the exception of attachable collars (which could also be from the 1920s) and a fine pair of standard spats*, short for spatterdashes (see pp.160 and 305). (These date from anytime during the first two decades of the twentieth century, when they were popular, and so could also have belonged to his father.) Originally a functional item, spats were worn over the instep and ankle to protect shoes and socks from mud or rain. These are made from taupe English box cloth*, and feature four horn buttons on either side and leather straps with metal buckles. Spats became an element of fashionable dress when new city streets made of asphalt and concrete rendered them redundant. In Marshfield, for example, the paving of the main street, Central Avenue, began in 1914 and was completed by 1917, and the principal streets of the town were paved by 1923.[66]

The Impact of the "Great War"

The European war was encroaching. In 1915, a German U-boat sank the R M S *Lusitania*, killing 1,198 civilians, including 128 Americans, and two years later the United States declared war on Germany in April 1917.[67] At this time, a busy family life occupied Catherine, while Hamilton and his father rushed to fulfill orders for plywood for use by the military in France, Italy, and England. The local and federal governments encouraged everyone on the home front to help ensure the nation had enough food supplies for the war effort. Commercially canned foods were needed to ship to the troops; by growing their own vegetables and fruits and observing the institution of "Meatless Monday" and "Wheatless Wednesday", the American population was able to avoid government-imposed rationing. Catherine managed the large fruit and vegetable garden at the rear of the Roddis house, undoubtedly with the aid of a gardener, and she used glass

FIG. 80, BELOW LEFT
Wool coat or jacket with silk lining, by the ladies' tailors, Maklary of Milwaukee, c.1915. THF 2014.24.83.

FIG. 81, BELOW
Detail of the printed silk lining inside the jacket below left, c.1915. The design of the lining echoes designs by the Wiener Werkstätte, a cooperative of artists in Vienna from 1903 to 1932. THF 2014.24.83.

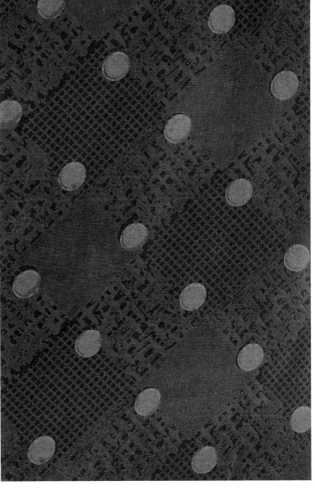

jars for preserving much of the produce, as well as turning her multitude of berries into delicious jam. Her management of the vegetable garden became a near obsession for the rest of her life. Aided by a housekeeper, Catherine also partly undertook, and usually oversaw, the household food preparation.

Hamilton established daily routines that he would continue for decades. He became accustomed to the ritual of walking home from the factory to join his children, who walked home from school, for the main meal of the day at noon. The dining table was always formally set, and Hamilton served from the head of the table (fig. 82). A hired girl passed around rolls, cleared the plates, and brought in the dessert. Hamilton's routine also involved retiring to his sleeping porch for a post-meal, twenty-minute nap, after which he would stride back to the office to work for the rest of the day. In his free time, he continued his tradition of making sure his children learned to read at an early age and were well supplied with the classics of literature. Keen on "mental improvement", he restricted the number of toys allowed into the household; instead, he encouraged physical activity for health benefits, such as lifting and throwing the heavy medicine ball that was to be found on the top floor for decades.[68] Hamilton indulged his children by playing ping-pong with them on the dining room table, but later he had a standard-size ping-pong table (fig. 83) made in

FIG. 82
The Roddis family dining room, set for a noonday meal. Photo by Gillian Bostock Ewing, 2011.

the factory and installed on the third floor (allowing Augusta to practice so much that she became the girls ping-pong champion at Northwestern University).[69]

Hamilton's employees soon began to leave the Roddis plant to enlist, and on June 5, 1917, the United States selective draft swung into action, depleting ranks still further. The sight of many blue stars hanging in the windows of houses to indicate homes of Marshfield servicemen was a constant reminder of the danger they faced in Europe. When these blue stars were replaced with gold ones, to signify a casualty, the gloom of war was hard to avoid. Out of the 450 men who enlisted from Marshfield, one in 10 died as a result of either military service abroad or the influenza epidemic that followed the conclusion of the war.[70]

The ensuing years after the marriage of Catherine and Hamilton in 1908 had been marked by disruption and change in America. For the couple themselves, however, it was a creative and productive time, both in their family life and their business. By the time of the Armistice on November 11, 1918, the difference between the "Old" and "New" worlds had widened. Europe had been set back by the war, whereas the United States had been given a boost and was now the world's leading economy and creditor.[71] More change was on its way, for the Roddis family, and for the country as a whole.

FIG. 83
The top floor of the Roddis house served as a ballroom for dance parties and also a playroom, especially for games of ping-pong. Augusta typed her many letters on this table. Photo by Gillian Bostock Ewing, 2011.

CHAPTER FIVE

A Changing World

The Roddis Family in the Roaring Twenties

The 1920s "roared" from New York to San Francisco, and from Paris to London and beyond, bringing a series of changes that would result in the modernization of society across the world. The devastating effects of World War I were still raw and recent memories for many, but with the rapid expansion of the press and of advertising, of Hollywood, automobile ownership, and household conveniences came economic growth and revolutionary social changes.

The 1920s was a decade when America was aware of its economic and military might as a world power. This confidence manifested itself through a shift in popular culture, with film, music, and fashion responding to a desire for frivolity. A new national identity had been discovered by younger generations of Americans who were optimistic about the future, and keen to shake off the social conventions of the past. International travel and a taste for exoticism blossomed; hemlines rose and fell; the "talkies" became the "movies"; and women could finally vote.

How the Roddis family chose to dress during this decade reflects the wide range of influences that impacted their personal choice of clothing, and also demonstrates a clear sense of the family's style and continued desire for quality. The upheavals of the period were felt in the Roddis home, and right across America, with national and global developments in fashion, news, and culture reaching even as far as small Midwestern communities, such as the ever-developing town of Marshfield, Wisconsin.

Central Ave. looking North from 3d St., Marshfield, Wis.

FIG. 84, PAGE 104

Clockwise from top left: Catherine Roddis's gold fan, *c.*1920s; her chiffon dress, *c.*1928; French beaded neckband, 1928; *peau de soie* pump with shoe buckle, 1905–10 (but in a style renewed in the 1920s); belt buckle of the chiffon dress.

FIG. 85

Postcard of Central Avenue, Marshfield, with electrical lighting at night, known by locals as "The Great White Way", *c.*1923. JBC.

Since 1894, when W.H. and Sara Roddis first arrived in Marshfield, the town's population had grown by more than two-thirds.[1] There was a wide variety of local industry, particularly in lumber products and the production and shipping of dairy products made in the surrounding agricultural area.[2] The town also supported many churches, newspapers, an opera house (a venue for theater, films, and music, as well as traveling opera productions), and an advanced medical clinic. There was even a department store, although it was not a place where the Roddis family seems to have shopped for clothing.[3] Telephones were becoming more common (1,404 existed in the town by 1922) radios were also becoming widely popular, and by 1923 most of the roads in town were now paved. There were so many more cars that seven traffic lights had to be installed (fig. 85).[4] Hamilton indulged in an innovative new car in 1921: a Franklin-Ritt sedan costing $4,090.[5] Despite these advancements, there were still more horses than cars in the state of Wisconsin, and many times more cows than people. Marshfield, like much of the United States, was caught in the sweeping change from "a culture not quite urban and yet not entirely rural ... and [it was] struggling to define itself."[6] There was growing prosperity in the town, as there was across the country, but, in both cases, any growth enjoyed was far from universal.[7] For the less prosperous portion of the population, the roar of the 1920s was but a faint whimper.

The prohibition of the sale of alcohol, begun in 1920 and continuing until 1933, had little impact on the Roddis family. W.H. Roddis was an adamant "dry", the term used for those who opposed drinking,[8] Hamilton and Catherine (a former Methodist) were largely teetotalers, while Hamilton's aunt, Mary Roddis, created a (possibly satirical) party favor in 1928 entitled

FIG. 86
Postcard of the
Pompeian swimming
pool on the S.S.
Leviathan, which
included wood
panels supplied by
the Roddis Lumber
& Veneer Company,
*c.*1923. JBC.

The GOOD that PROHIBITION Has Done The United States (visible in the still life on p.280).[9] Marshfield's saloons had become "soft drink parlors" but local arrests for public drunkenness were still common.[10]

In the same year, 1920, there was another major social breakthrough: after a long struggle, American women were granted the right to vote. This was the culmination of decades of activism for the enfranchisement of women that had begun as the Suffragist movement in the mid-nineteenth century. As noted in Chapter 3, Catherine's grandmother was a keen supporter of women's suffrage. Hamilton's Aunt Mary was also much interested in expanding women's rights, and she attended meetings with "bright brained women" at the Portia Club in New Orleans.[11] However, no surviving letters reflect the views of Sara, Frances, or Catherine on that topic.

The 1920 U.S. census lists William Henry, Sara, Frances and a live-in maid residing at their home, with Hamilton and Catherine and their five children and two maids, known as "the girls", living in the seven-bedroom house next door. The Roddis Lumber & Veneer Company, like many American industrial firms, had prospered during the war years, and, consequently, the Roddis family was now among the wealthiest members of the community. The Roddis Company was selling veneer products across the nation through distribution points that dotted the map from coast to coast. W.H. Roddis had built up a small fortune by the time he died in 1920, aged 76, leaving his son to run the family business (see Chapter 2).

As the new president, Hamilton successfully steered the company into prestigious new contracts, including the supply of wood panels for the S.S. *Leviathan*, the German flagship (originally called the *Vaterland*) requisitioned by the United States in 1917. This ship had transported over

100,000 American soldiers to and from the Western Front during World War I. During her 1922–3 reconstruction, she was entirely refurbished with American-made fittings and machinery, becoming "a German ship with an American soul".[12] Having become the finest, largest, and fastest ship in the world, the *Leviathan* became a Jazz Age icon and was seen in paintings and advertisements of the 1920s; it represented all there was to celebrate about a booming economy, exciting cultural extravagance in music, dance, and film, and the flamboyant "anything goes" attitude that emerged in America after the end of World War I. The Roddis Company supplied panels and doors for the lower levels of the ship, including the first class "Pompeian" swimming pool, where humid conditions made the anti-warp technology of Roddis doors highly practical (fig. 86).[13]

During the 1920s, architects increasingly used Roddis doors and panels: their consistent high quality ensured client satisfaction. Well-designed company brochures reflected an impressive range of Roddis French and flush doors, clearly directed at the most prestigious end of the market (figs 87 and 88). Business was booming.

Meanwhile Hamilton and Catherine's family was also thriving, with Ellen, their sixth and last child, arriving in 1923.[14] The family was dedicated to "God and country", as well as self and community improvement. Mary and Sara, the sororal twins, young Catherine (Pickie), and little Augusta too, were all growing up into fine young ladies. After meeting the daughters, a friend wrote to Catherine that they were "so full of such different characteristics that they are all intensely interesting individually."[15]

FIGS 87 AND 88
Illustrations from the Roddis Lumber & Veneer Company catalog, entitled *Roddis French and Flush Doors*, c.1923. THF 2014.115.1. From the Collections of The Henry Ford.

Film, Fashion, and Aspirations

For these vivacious young women and their parents, grandmother, and Aunt Frances living next door, awareness of the latest fashions and judicious choice of what to wear was the natural consequence of a family in possession of discerning taste. "Good clothes" mattered. Although books on etiquette had been printed for hundreds of years, in the mid-nineteenth century they became available to the broader population, and by the 1920s they had penetrated nearly every corner of American society, giving much needed advice on correct manners as well as proper dress. Perhaps the most famous was Emily Post's *Etiquette in Society, in Business, in Politics, and at Home* (1922). This publication advised the American public about correct form and the goal of gracious and courteous behavior. Post's book became a bestseller; indeed, a copy was always kept in a convenient location at the Roddis house.[16] Post emphasized the importance of fashionable clothes, which she argued were the principal markers of social respectability and an important part of the human landscape: "In the world of smart society ... clothes not only represent our ticket of admission, but our contribution to the effect of a party. What makes a brilliant party? Clothes. Good clothes. A frumpy party is nothing more or less than a collection of badly dressed persons."[17]

> *"What makes a brilliant party?*
> *Clothes. Good clothes."*
>
> EMILY POST
> *ETIQUETTE IN SOCIETY, IN BUSINESS,*
> *IN POLITICS, AND AT HOME (1922)*

The Roddis women accepted the importance of self-presentation, and appear to have mined ideas from newspaper fashion columns and women's magazines. This is evident from the large quantity of related ephemera found in their home, particularly *Vogue* magazines and carefully clipped newspaper articles about fashion from the 1930s and 1940s. With a growing family of daughters, it is probable that this was also the case in the previous decade. Across the country, these readily available magazines, newspapers, and mail order catalogs helped to emphasize the importance of fashionable dress, as they disseminated the latest styles. These periodicals created an important link between American women's awareness of fashion from coast to coast, and from large city to small town.

But perhaps the main reason for the increasing national uniformity of fashion styles was the impact of Hollywood—the most important cultural development of the decade. Silent films had begun to be made in the late nineteenth century but "talkies" followed in 1927.[18] "Going to the movies" became the national pastime: during the 1920s, the majority of

Americans, of every age and income bracket, went to the movies to see a film at least once a week, and many went even more often.[19] Films publicized new trends (elegant women smoking, for example) and new designs for furniture, interiors, and architecture; they also served to reinforce existing fashions.[20] Hollywood thus helped weave many of these aspirational choices into a popular shared aesthetic. Gracious living, with as many refinements as could be garnered, became highly desirable and its net spread across the United States, supported by related publications offering social advice, as detailed above.

Fashion Influences from Afar

In this era when feminine fashion was changing so radically, what were the Roddis women wearing in the Midwest? Surviving Roddis garments reveal that Catherine displayed an appreciation of the latest international trends. Archival family photographs (fig. 89) show her wearing a dress with a separate and slightly protruding overskirt that reaches just below her knees, a shape that was clearly influenced by the famous "lampshade" tunic designed in 1913 by French designer Paul Poiret (1879–1944). Judging from the age of her son Bill, who was born in the fall of 1917, these photos must have been from 1919 or early 1920. To see such innovative designs worn in a Midwestern town at this time speaks volumes about Catherine's personal sophistication and sense of style, as well as the continued wide-reaching influence of Parisian fashion.

    The day dress opposite that probably belonged to Frances, Hamilton's sister, is also linked to French design trends and was made from silk pongee* (fig. 91). Both Frances and Catherine had dresses made from

FIG. 92
Clockwise from
top left: Japanese
parasol, 1920s; silk
and paper Japanese
lampshade, 1920s;
North African
or Palestinian
embroidered bag,
*c.*1928; Catherine's
Palestinian dress,
1928; 1927 passport
of the Roddis couple;
kimono-style, silk
house dress, *c.*1919.
Photo by Doug
Mindell.

this fabric a decade before (see fig. 79). With its rows of bobbin lace and tucked inserts, this dress is stylistically related to the designs developed by the four sisters, the Callot Soeurs, who opened their Paris design house in 1894. The highly regarded Callot Soeurs were known for a series of dresses that set decorative elements—such as embroidered pieces and lace—onto starkly flat planes of fabric. Their fashion aesthetic, like that of other leading Parisian designers, was widely imitated in America until the firm closed in 1937.[21]

Other Roddis dresses are examples of influences from further afield than Paris, and demonstrate a fascination with the exotic. In 1928, Catherine and Hamilton joined the increasing number of Americans traveling abroad when they visited the Holy Land and Europe during a three-month trip (the joint passport they used for that trip is visible in the still life photo above).[22] While in Palestine, Catherine purchased a dress that was adapted from a Syrian *abaya* robe and probably the surviving embroidered bag as well, both also visible in the still life above.[23] Catherine also purchased Palestinian garments to be used for the annual Nativity plays at their church in Marshfield (fig. 93).[24]

Catherine's purchase of a Middle Eastern dress to wear back home in the United States reflects an interest in foreign fabrics and styles that had begun at the end of the previous century, and which had reached what could be called a "craze" by the early 1920s. Syrian fabrics like that of Catherine's dress, for example, were used by Paris-based designers who appreciated the remarkably similar Art Deco* aesthetic evident in these local, traditional textiles.[25] When the tomb of King Tutankhamen was discovered in 1922, the event caused an international sensation, and hieroglyph-like patterns appeared on many dresses and accessories as well as furniture and even buildings soon afterwards. In addition, oriental aesthetics inspired Poiret, among others, during the previous decade, and kimono-like dresses and coats became widely popular and persisted into the 1920s. Oriental-inspired dress patterns, such as the one for a dressing gown visible overleaf, also became available.

This pattern is very similar to the at-home dress probably sewn by Catherine Roddis to wear around the house in the early 1920s (fig. 96).[26] Made from red silk with round oriental medallions and kimono-style sleeves with black tassels, this garment is a pullover dress rather than a wrap-around kimono but is nevertheless strongly influenced by Japanese

FIG. 93, BELOW
Assorted Palestinian robes and headdresses purchased by Catherine Roddis in Jerusalem in 1928 to be used for the annual Nativity plays at her local church in Marshfield, RFPC. Photo by Eli Dagostino.

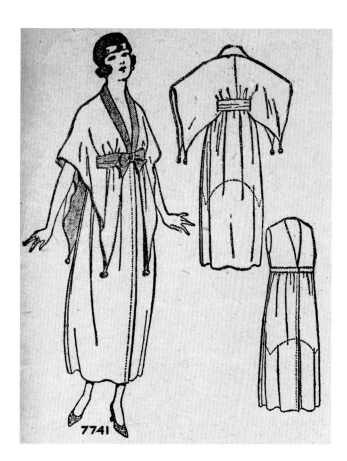

FIG. 94, ABOVE
Ladies' Empire
dressing gown or
negligée, *Pictorial
Review* 7741, 1918.
Courtesy of the
Commercial Pattern
Archive, University
of Rhode Island.

FIG. 95, ABOVE RIGHT
Japanese paper
parasol, 1920–30.
THF 2014.24.145.

costume. A Japanese parasol from the 1920s found in the Roddis house also attests to a fascination for, and acceptance of, these exotic fashions and accessories, and may have been used for theatrical productions or dressing-up parties (fig. 95, see p.269).

Dressing the Children

Surviving examples of clothing worn by Roddis children suggest that Catherine took pride in dressing them well. At that time, and certainly within the Roddis household, children were expected to be obedient, well behaved, and respectful of their elders. Always practical, as well as up-to-date, the style of their clothes reflects a certain formality. Augusta's little girl's dress (fig. 97), dating from around 1922, has straight, simple lines and many of the elements that were popular in the early years of the twentieth century: fine embroidery, lace inserts, a slightly dropped waist, and a tabular panel on the front that is held in place with decorative bands. These bands circle the waist and attach at the center of the back, accentuated with two silk bows. A blue and white girl's dress with a white sash, once again set below the waist, which was also found in the Roddis attic, dates from about 1926 (fig. 98). Its coloring resembles that of the boy's "buster suit" that belonged to young Bill, which is very similar to the one he is wearing while perched on his mother's lap in the photograph on p.110 (fig. 90).[27] This boy's suit was probably handmade and includes embroidery that strongly resembles examples of the same padded satin stitch embroidery

FIG. 96, OPPOSITE
Silk kimono-style
dress, possibly
homemade by
Catherine, *c.*1919.
THF 2014.24.44.

FIG. 97, ABOVE
Girl's linen dress
with cotton lace trim,
c.1922. This dress
was most likely worn
by Augusta Roddis.
THF 2014.24.164.

FIG. 98, ABOVE RIGHT
Boy's linen buster
suit, *c*.1920; and girl's
linen dress, *c*.1923.
Both are attributed
to Catherine Roddis.
The buster suit
belonged to her son,
William H. Roddis II,
also called Bill.
THF 2014.24.171 and
THF 2014.24.165.

found in Catherine's workbook from the Armour Institute (see p.68). It is likely that she made this outfit using a similar pattern of a later date.[28] This boy's suit was saved lovingly in a box inscribed with Bill's name, and is a testament to his mother's fine needle skills, as well as her personal pride in dressing her children attractively.

Photographs taken in about 1926 show young Ellen Roddis, aged two, Augusta, aged ten, and Bill, aged eight (fig. 99). Bill is wearing a dark tie, while Ellen has a black bow pinned on her white dress, and Augusta is wearing a straight, typically 1920s-style white dress with a black ribbon trim; these touches of black signify mourning, probably for their grandmother or their great aunt Cecilia, the sister of Isabella A.H. Prindle, both of whom died that year.[29] This mourning tradition for children dates back to late eighteenth-century Europe, when children under six years old were first allowed to wear white with black accents rather than all black.[30] Yet this custom was evidently still practiced in the American Midwest as late as 1926.

Attic Exploration and Playing Dress-Up

It was just before her parents left for the Near East, in 1928, when Augusta first ventured into the attic and discovered the trunks stored there. In one of her early diaries, written at the age of 12, she described how she dressed

FIG. 99
Ellen, Augusta, and
Bill, *c.*1926, the year
their grandmother
Sara Denton Roddis,
and great aunt
Cecilia Hedenberg
Whitlock died. The
bow on Ellen's dress,
the black trim on
Augusta's dress, and
the black necktie
on Bill all signify
mourning. RFPC.

herself and her little sister Ellen in some of the old clothes her mother had saved and paraded down the street in front of their home in Marshfield: "Took Ellen out for a walk. I got dressed up in mother's old-fashioned dress and put 1 of Sara's dresses on Ellen. The effect was quite amusing."[31]

Perhaps it is no coincidence that just two months earlier, an issue of *Child Life* magazine, to which the Roddis family subscribed for Augusta and her younger brother and sister, included a two-part story of a family that was likely to have had treasures hidden in their attic (fig. 100). As the children in the story search, they find trunks of clothes, which they examine and eagerly try on (fig. 101).[32] There is no proof that Augusta had read this story, but she was an avid reader who adored the *Child Life* magazines (she saved all the issues and later gave a subscription as a gift), and it was just the sort of fantasy she loved. It may well have inspired her to try her own exploration in the mysterious walk-in closet upstairs: the "attic". In a letter written in the 1970s to her niece, she recounts the fun she had there:

> *When I was a little girl, my best friend and I used to spend hours in the attic, delving into your grandmother's trunk and swishing around in some of her old evening dresses. We entertained ourselves endlessly this way, and when I think back on it, I marvel your*

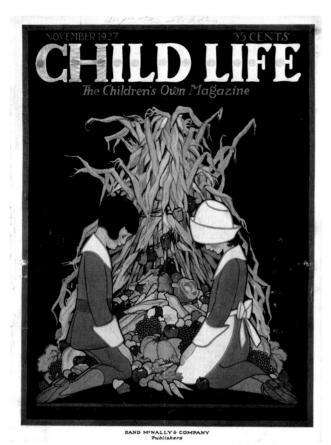

FIG. 100, ABOVE
Cover of *Child Life*
magazine, November
1927. Augusta
and her younger
siblings all read
these magazines to
which the family
subscribed.
THF 2015.10.83.
From the Collections
of The Henry Ford.

FIG. 101, TOP RIGHT
A story in the
Child Life magazine
above entitled
"The Secret of
Belden Place",
which featured
children discovering
historic clothes
in an old trunk.
THF 2015.10.83.
From the Collections
of The Henry Ford.

grandmother let us do it, but actually we were sufficiently impressed
with the dresses to be quite careful even at that tender age.[33]

Only a single image of Augusta playing "dress-up" has survived from
this period (visible in the still life on p.262). "Swishing around" in these
feminine dresses allowed Augusta and her best friend Ellen Sexton, also
in that photograph, to experience the transformational effect of donning
a special dress. Whether for dress-up or real-life occasions, Augusta never
lost her enjoyment of very feminine clothes.

The Flapper Style Takes Hold

By the age of 12, Augusta would have been aware of her three older sisters'
love of fashion and all the latest things to do and say. Mary, Sara, and Pickie
were sent to boarding school, where their parents believed they could
obtain an education that was superior to that provided by the local high
school. (Augusta recalled how as a young teenager she would soak up the
latest slang words from Pickie when she was home for school breaks.[34]) The
elder girls went to Grafton Hall, a private school in Fond du Lac, Wisconsin,
whereas in 1930 Augusta was enrolled at Saint Mary's School, New York,
for one year only (due to the impact of the Wall Street Crash on the family
finances). Augusta's older sisters enjoyed varying degrees of academic
success, but their father expected all of them to learn sound money

management: surviving correspondence from this period reveals how the three older girls were required to send meticulous balance sheets home to their father, Hamilton. These draconian measures demanded an account of how every penny of their allowance was spent, right down to the purchase of pencils, and any unaccounted-for sums had to be returned.[35] The 1920s was a period when the rampant consumerism continued its upward spiral, but restraint was still characteristically paramount in the Roddis family.

Despite their conservative upbringing, the twins, Mary and Sara, were not able to restrain themselves from adopting one of the newest fashions for women: smoking. In these changing times, it was no longer considered improper for girls to smoke. Many women, in a conscious effort to appear chic, would follow the example set by magazines such as *Vogue*, which often featured images of beautifully dressed women holding a long cigarette holder.[36] Like millions of Americans, the twins would have gone to the movies and seen actresses such as Clara Bow posing elegantly with a cigarette holder in one hand.[37] Mary and Sara were exposed to nightlife in the urban areas where they went to college, including New Orleans, Boston, and Madison, Wisconsin, and would have observed, and undoubtedly embraced, not only the fashions but also other behaviors of women in those cities.[38]

Another revolution took place in attitudes towards make-up, the wearing of which had previously been considered improper. The subsequent use of powder, rouge, and lipstick soared. Between 1914 and 1925, it is claimed that sales of cosmetics in the United States rose from $17 million to $141 million; there is credible evidence that by 1929, the annual spending on cosmetics and beauty services climbed further to $700 million.[39] In 1928, *Vogue* featured an article recommending that "the use of lip-stick, if not too vivid in tone", was suitable for débutantes, "but the healthy young girl of today should have sufficient color in her cheeks to forgo the use of rouge."[40] Photographs and film footage of the Roddis women at this time suggest that they followed this advice.

As teenagers, Mary and Sara certainly did wear dresses now referred to as being in the flapper* style. Members of the family remember several such dresses belonging to Mary, either sleeveless or with little cap sleeves, and in the latest fashion, with details such as tiny mirrors sewn onto the fabric.[41] These dresses were usually constructed using light fabrics that fell from the shoulders and were often gathered low on the hips, drawing attention away from the bust and the waist, and creating a slim, boyish, or *garçonne* look.[42]

In the 1920s, the word "flapper" was used to describe the new young women who would wear the latest fashions and make-up, know the latest dances, smoke, drink alcohol illegally, drive, and generally live a fast life. But the more conservative Roddis twins, protected within their strict family circle, could not be called true flappers. The term, which originates from sixteenth-century British slang, went on to become an appropriate way in which to describe the bird-like flapping of a woman's arms as she danced to jazz music.[43] The rising popularity of jazz brought about new, more vigorous and animated types of dancing, such as the Charleston, which in turn had a direct effect on fashion.[44] To be suitable for free body movement, the highly structured fashion styles of the early twentieth century, which weighed women down with heavy petticoats and corsets, had begun to be abandoned (see fig. 47). This development, reflecting women's desire to move more easily and accompanied by more progressive thinking, was now taken much further.[45] Corsets were largely replaced with new bandeau brassieres that flattened and smoothed the figure into the fashionable boyish silhouette. Not only were the new styles more comfortable and practical, they were designed with a keen awareness of how they would appear in motion.

> *"All the girls are getting permanents now—and not in the ruinous old way that Aunt Frances had either—so far they have all turned out beautifully."*
>
> SARA FRANCES RODDIS

The use of free-floating fringes and strands of beads became popular, partly because they emphasized the wearers' movements as they danced to jazz, a radical new form of music inspired by the syncopated rhythms of African-American music.[46] No typical flapper dresses are in the Roddis Collection, but two long-sleeved beaded dresses do survive. One of these is described below. The other beaded evening dress, on the opposite page, was damaged beyond repair by the weight of the decoration, and may have belonged to Catherine (fig. 102). Of particular note are the diamond-shaped beaded medallions, strategically placed on each hip, from which strings of iridescent turquoise and pink beads are suspended in strands of graduated color. More than two feet long, these strings would have been set in motion as the wearer walked or danced.

Vigorous movement wrought havoc on hair mounted on top of the head with pins, which is one reason why the short, easier-to-care-for hairstyles gained popularity. The fashionable new bobs featured sleekly smooth or curled styles. Fashion magazines in the 1920s were full of advertisements for permanents to create short, softly curled coiffures; the Roddis girls favored the short bob and young Sara sought out a wavy hairstyle, referred to by *Vogue* as the desirable *floué* coiffure.[47] She wrote home to her mother from school in 1924, when she was only 15, begging permission to have a permanent wave: "All the girls are getting permanents now—and not in the ruinous old way that Aunt Frances had either—so far they have all turned out beautifully."[48]

These short hairstyles also worked well with the new head-hugging *cloche** hats of the period, which were sensibly unobtrusive, especially when worn to tea dances or movie theaters, and more secure in open cars.[49]

FIG. 102, OPPOSITE
Elaborately beaded dress of silk crêpe de chine, mid-1920s. Two foot long strands of beads are suspended at the hips. RDC 124, JBC.

FIG. 103

Cotton net boudoir
cap with silk ribbon
flowers, *c.*1920.
THF 2014.24.127.

No *cloche* hats survived in the Roddis house, but there was a cotton net boudoir cap with silk ribbon flowers from *c.*1920. This cap shares a similar bell-shaped form and the pulled-forward quality that would characterize many *cloche* hats of the decade, when exposed foreheads were to be avoided (fig. 103). The ever-creative Miriam, Catherine's sister, wrote to her sister Edith in 1927 to describe how she had "brightened up" a little black felt hat "by running rows of silver ribbon through slits in the felt, in graduated effect, with flat bows in the front."[50] Miriam included a sketch of her "very pretty" creation (fig. 104). In a Roddis family film from 1929, most of the friends and family wear *cloche* hats with the exception of the ever-fashion-conscious Mary, who appears in a charming broad-brimmed picture hat, a style favored for occasions such as garden parties.[51]

Hemlines went through radical changes during the 1920s; they began and ended the decade nearly sweeping the floor. With the new right to vote and more progressive views about women emerging, a kind of freedom had materialized in fashion. Along with growing confidence

and optimism, skirts became shorter while necklines plunged, backs were bared, and sleeveless styles appeared. Generally, by 1925, skirts had risen to a position of about 14 to 16 inches from the floor, and were creeping up further. For the first time in Western fashion history, knees actually peeked out around 1926 and continued to be visible for about two years. It was in 1926 that Catherine's Aunt Cecilia wrote to her about a visit to New Orleans, where she helped alter clothes of Catherine's daughter Sara. Cecilia wrote that "two of her tub silks" (silk dresses that could be laundered in a tub at home) "had shrunken above her knees so she didn't like to wear them at school, so I dropped the hems three inches, just the length she wished."[52] Hemlines began to descend once more in about 1928.

French Imports and Novelties

France enjoyed great prestige as the ultimate source of fashion, and Catherine appears to have been drawn to the purchase of some clothes actually made in France, not just inspired by French designs. A remarkable survival from this period is a beaded silk dress by Adair of Paris, *c.*1923 (fig. 107). This luxurious gown was hidden away for decades in an old suitcase with a jammed lock. The suitcase was sold during the estate sale at the Roddis house in July 2011; when it was taken home by the buyer and pried open, out spilled this gown, along with another beaded dress that was described above (see p.120)—both were duly returned to the Roddis house by the honest purchaser.

The Adair dress, which most likely belonged to Catherine, is made of brown silk lace with gold and silver metallic silk thread in floral and geometric patterns, and enhanced with hand-stitched beading. It bears the label, "Adair D & O, 'The House of France', Paris, London, New York, Montreal, Made in France", a French fashion house that made beaded dresses for export (fig. 106).[53] The shimmer of this dress is further enhanced by two shades of blue and green glass beads, along with clear beads with silver-coated centers, (most probably produced in Czechoslovakia during this period). The silver foil-wrapped silk threads incorporated into the lace highlight eclectic motifs ranging from seventeenth-century floral set pieces to geometric stars and squares in arrangements reminiscent of Islamic art forms (fig. 105). The low-slung decorative belt, heavily beaded with turquoise-beaded half spheres, has an almost medieval quality to it— yet more touches of the exotic. This gown reflects the sumptuousness of high fashion on both sides of the Atlantic during this period, and hints at Catherine's venture into sourcing French-made clothing.[54]

Beadwork was often found on accessories as well as clothes in the 1920s: one small but typical example of the popular use of loom-woven beadwork is the narrow neck piece (which can be seen at the center of the still life photo on p.104; see also p.307) that Catherine sent to her mother, Isabella Prindle, from Paris in 1928. Isabella wrote to thank her daughter for this "latest Paris", which she proudly wore on Mother's Day.[55]

FIG. 105, RIGHT
Detail of the dress
opposite, *c.*1923.
THF 2014.24.24.

FIG. 106, BELOW
Label from the dress
opposite, *c.*1923.
THF 2014.24.24.

FIG. 107, OPPOSITE
Beaded silk lace
dress by Adair of
Paris, *c.*1923. This
dress includes a silver
lamé underdress
and a beaded
decorative false belt.
THF 2014.24.24.

The highly sophisticated dress opposite, found in the attic and undoubtedly worn by Catherine, appears also to have been purchased during this trip to Paris; an existing receipt from Adèle & Cie, dated April 13, 1928, lists one "mousseline" dress with multi-color roses.[56] This description would fit this printed silk chiffon dress with black and white stripes and floral bands, which is undoubtedly of French manufacture (fig. 108). The hem is created by stitching rectangles of the silk chiffon with horizontal stripes onto the edge of large scallops, creating graceful drapes and ending in a "handkerchief hem" that would sway as the wearer walked. The belt buckle is formed of red, blue, green, and clear stones, an aesthetic found in seventeenth-century Mogul jewelry. The length, waistline, and construction suggest the fashions of the next decade.

Two Weddings as the Decade Ends

The final year of the decade brought yet more change for the Roddis family. In April 1929, Sara was the first daughter to be married, betrothed to Henry Stewart Jones of Marshfield. In the portrait taken on her wedding day (fig. 109), she wears a fashionably short dress with satin pumps and two long strings of pearls—a classic bridal style of the late 1920s. As far more leg was exposed than in previous decades, shoes became a focal point in a woman's outfit, as this photo demonstrates. In 1928, *Vogue* had insisted on the importance of shoes, which it called "the criterion of the true gentlewoman".[57]

> *"It looks as though the rest of us will have to wait until a good long time—perhaps until we get married—before the paternal purse is fit to buy any more clothes."*
>
> CATHERINE PRINDLE RODDIS

That same year, Sara's twin, Mary, was courted by Gordon Robert Connor, the charming and jovial son of W.D. Connor, also a Marshfield resident. His Connor Lumber and Land Company had long been a Roddis family rival in this local industry, as well as in the realms of local social and political influence. A perfect gentleman at home, W.D. Connor was sometimes accused of using ruthless tactics in business and politics, and while he and Hamilton Roddis remained civil in public, everyone in the town knew these two families were actually enemies.[58] The Montague and Capulet courtship of Mary and Gordon caused great consternation in the Roddis family, and Hamilton tried his best to keep them apart. Mary's mother did not entirely agree with the ban—she was much more sensitive to the situation and permitted the infatuated pair to meet. The couple

FIG. 108, OPPOSITE
Printed chiffon evening dress, worn by Catherine Roddis, *c.*1928. THF 2014.24.48.

were sometimes allowed to drive off in Gordon's yellow convertible as long as they had some sort of chaperone, if only Mary's little sister, Ellen, and Gordon's nephew, Melvin Laird (aged five and six respectively).[59] Melvin, who later became a long-standing member of the U.S. Congress and the national Secretary of Defense, recalls those days: "Ellen and I served as chaperones for Gordon and her older sister Mary on occasion as passengers in the rumble seat in Gordon's yellow roadster... [Mrs. Roddis] thought they needed chaperones even though we were very much their juniors.... Gordon always got a pass if we rode with them."[60]

As the relationship became serious, there was increased opposition at home, but despite it all, Mary and Gordon were married in July 1929. Despite her father's initial dismay over the match, Mary was allowed to shop in the leading Midwestern cities for lots of new clothes for her trousseau*. She wrote to Augusta: "I have bought a few dresses and am going to Chicago, Milwaukee, and Madison next week to buy more."[61] (Indeed, Mary had such refined taste that her Aunt Frances once commented that she had expected her to end up "living in New York or Paris" rather than remain in Wisconsin.[62]) A few months later, her sister Pickie reported on the results of these shopping trips: "Mary got oodles of new duds in Chicago, Milwaukee, and points south. It looks as though the rest of us will have to wait until a good long time—perhaps until we get married—before the paternal purse is fit to buy any more clothes."[63] After Mary's spree—perhaps allowed since her extended honeymoon to Europe would be paid for by the groom's father, W.D. Connor[64]—the paternal purse did indeed freeze up due to Roddis resistance to big spending, and the developing economic climate.

A grand garden wedding was planned. Every detail of the event was captured for posterity on a rare, surviving film.[65] The styles of the dresses at Mary's wedding were straight out of fashion journals from Paris and reflected the recent shift towards more feminine and gracefully curved lines. This was a departure from the mainly vertical silhouettes of the 1920s.

Before Catherine was married in 1908, she mentioned to her sister Edith that there was no reason for her bridesmaids to invest much money on their dresses, and that she did not even mind if their dresses did not match (see p.90). For her own daughters' weddings, however, there was far more formality and considerable expenditure. The layered skirts of the bridesmaid dresses at Mary's wedding, visible in the photograph below (fig. 110), are similar to that of the pale peach gown of the same period, found crushed in a trunk (fig. 111).[66] Machine-embroidered with colorful flowers, the dress has two flared and shaped flounces set below the near hip-length waist seam and is made from cloth woven from the fibers of pineapple plant leaves, also known as piña. Piña fiber had been in use for

FIG. 110
Two bridesmaids at the wedding of Mary Roddis and Gordon Connor, held in the garden between the two Roddis houses, July 20, 1929. RFPA.

FIG. 111

Embroidered piña
fiber and silk tea
gown, *c.*1929. This
dress probably
belonged to
Catherine Prindle
Roddis, known
as "Pickie". The
style resembles the
bridesmaid dresses
in the photo on the
previous page.
THF 2014.24.33.

centuries in the Philippines, but it became available in Europe and America during the nineteenth century, and reappeared once again in the 1920s.[67] Its use in this dress demonstrates the Roddis family's continued fascination with imported, or unusual, materials. The use of these special fabrics exemplified the lengths to which the young women of the 1920s would go in their quest for uniqueness and novelty. With its perfect *jeune fille* style, this dress may well have belonged to Pickie, then aged 17.

Mary's silk wedding dress was also very stylish, and had the uneven hemline typical of the late 1920s: its front edge extended to a few inches below the knee and tapered into a train at the back (fig. 112). Ellen and Melvin

Laird were given the task of managing her long veil, with limited success, as the film footage of an encounter with a rose bush reveals.[68] Unlike Catherine and Hamilton's wedding, Mary and Gordon's was a lavish affair with 300 guests, and it proved to be the most notable family social event for the next decade. They left for their honeymoon, ignorant of the impending economic disaster that would take place only three months later (fig. 113). There was little indication of the straitened circumstances they would face, along with their family, and their town and nation, with the dawn of the 1930s.

The level of sophistication seen in the Roddis dresses from the 1920s, not only worn in their small town in the American Midwest, but also while traveling or at college, is in itself a tribute to their taste and their knowledge of fashion. It also reflects this complex decade at its most prosperous: a time when new urban fashions in dress and new urban ways of living spread across the United States.[69] Just over ten years had passed since the end of World War I. America had made great strides towards modernization and had developed great confidence, bordering on a conviction of its superiority, but remained a country of great social and economic contrasts. Few were prepared for the cataclysmic event that would mark the closure of this decade: the Great Stock Market Crash of October 1929—an episode that would supplant a sense of invincibility with the feeling of fragility. This would have a profound impact on the lives of the Roddis family, and on their fellow Americans.

FIG. 112, BELOW LEFT
Mary Roddis, with her father Hamilton Roddis, at her wedding to Gordon Connor, with Melvin Laird and her sister Ellen Roddis as attendants, July 20, 1929. RFPA.

FIG. 113. BELOW
Mary and Gordon Connor on board a ship heading to Europe for a three-month honeymoon, July 1929. RFPA.

Junior
Promenade

Eight-thirty o'clock
April 15th, 1932
PURDY GYMNASIUM

Prom Chr.—Patrick J. Finucane
Prom Queen — Augusta Roddis

CHAPTER SIX

Pursuing Happiness in Hard Times
The Roddis Family Faces the Depression

In March 1929, as President Hoover moved into the White House, he observed that Americans had more bathtubs, oil furnaces, silk stockings and bank accounts than any other nation in the world.[1] Little did he know— the honeymoon was almost over, and only six months later, America's boom years would succumb to a shock so profound that it would take most of the following decade to recover.

On Black Tuesday, October 29, 1929, the New York Stock Market experienced a major collapse that plunged the country, and ultimately the entire Western world, into a period known as the "Great Depression". In Roddis family circles, newly married Mary and Gordon Connor had returned from a glamorous honeymoon abroad only to face financially difficult times, along with virtually all their fellow Americans.

By the end of 1929, the family had undergone significant changes. The eldest daughters had both married and started new lives. The remaining three daughters and son would witness economic upheaval by observing it in the town and firsthand from their father's efforts to keep his business and family afloat. The Roddis household was certainly not immune to the hard times that ensued, but it probably suffered less than others. Unlike many who had to worry about such basic concerns as rent or mortgage payments, the Roddis family owned their house on East Fourth Street. The other major expense, food, was also less of a concern since Catherine had always maintained a substantial vegetable garden, as well as a number

FIG. 114, PAGE 132

Clockwise from
top left: Augusta
Roddis's Prom dress;
re-created rose
corsage; high school
photo of Augusta;
Prom dance book
with attached pencil.

of fruit trees and shrubs. She ensured that sufficient home canning and preserving was done to allow them to store vegetables and berries to last the entire year; this was a tradition that Catherine had begun by World War I. During the lean years of the early 1930s, Augusta recalled that they ate a lot of venison, which came from Roddis timber forests.[2] In spite of the hard times, her mother was still able to retain one live-in maid for $5 per week, plus room and board, which was "the common rate then", according to Augusta.[3]

Yet the family business was in such a "precarious state" that Hamilton reinvested all profits back into the company, and cut his annual salary as president of the Roddis Company from $15,000 to $7,200 in 1932, where it remained for several years.[4] As mentioned previously, in 1921 he purchased a new car for $4,090, a sum more than 50 per cent of what was now his yearly income. While this new salary must have felt meager indeed, it was large compared to that of his employees.[5] In accordance with the lumber industry code, as instituted by the National Recovery Administration, Hamilton agreed to pay a newly set minimum wage to his workers: those working in his mills were to get 30 cents per hour for a 40-hour work week, and those doing the more seasonal work in logging camps were to receive 27 cents per hour for a 48-hour week. This meant that all his workers must have been earning between 12 and 13 dollars a week.[6] However, a former employee once told Augusta that he survived one year during the Depression on only $300 annual pay.[7]

Hamilton was lucky not to be a bank stockholder, thus avoiding double indemnity (whereby shareholders were required to pay back the banks the value of their stocks in order for the banks to cover withdrawals from depositors). However, double indemnity led to "straitened circumstances" for Gordon (Augusta's sister Mary Roddis's husband) and his extended family. The once highly successful lumber industrialist W.D. Connor was forced to declare bankruptcy, along with many others in the area as a result of this banking policy.[8]

Despite the bleak economic climate, the Roddis family's concern for education was still a priority, so less than a year after the Wall Street Crash, in the autumn of 1930, Augusta was sent off to Saint Mary's School in upstate New York. The buildings and approach there resembled those found in traditional English schools, and the curriculum was similarly Anglophile. Augusta relished the discipline of memorizing all the kings and queens of England, she loved the careful study of classics such as Dickens' *A Tale of Two Cities* (1859), and she excelled in all her classes.[9] Augusta was also required to wear a school uniform, which she found most unbecoming. In an early letter home she told her mother that she was surprised to witness her classmates looking so "smooth" when dressed in normal clothes to go into the city. Luckily for future generations, Augusta followed in the Roddis family tradition and was an avid writer of letters. In October, she penned an anxious letter to her mother: "Is the depression so bad that the factory is about to be shut down or what? It looks as though I won't be able to buy my winter wardrobe in New York. Whatever prompted selling the cows, anyhow? I thought cows paid for themselves so beautifully."[10]

"Is the depression so bad that the factory is about to be shut down or what? It looks as though I won't be able to buy my winter wardrobe in New York."

AUGUSTA RODDIS

Augusta was right when she sensed the impending gloom. By 1931, the Depression had severely affected Marshfield, and the family business as well. She later recalled: "… in a sense the fate of the whole town depended on the success or failure of the Roddis Co. It was as though the sword of Damocles was hanging over us for several years."[11] With less building work going on due to the Depression, the demand for doors, lumber, and plywood decreased dramatically. To make things worse for the Roddis Company, a large bank had called in a company loan. Smaller, local banks, however, were considerate to Hamilton, partly because they knew he was the largest, most reliable employer in Marshfield, and that if he failed, then the families of his 500 employees would be destitute.[12] Hamilton's son, Bill, was only 14 years old but he had a farmer's driving license and was entrusted with the important task of driving many miles around Wisconsin to deliver payments to a variety of banks every Friday afternoon—further proof that his father's company was surviving on the edge.[13] The town of Marshfield itself was forced "to fall back onto its own inventiveness" at a time when limited assistance from federal programs or even state resources were available.[14] Local farmers also had to be resourceful; some could only pay for medical services with produce, as was the case with the father of Augusta's best friend, Ellen Sexton, who was a Marshfield doctor. Local groceries were forced to extend credit to their customers, while realizing that they would only partially be repaid.[15]

The Roddis Company was able to weather "the Slump" because the family business specialized in high-quality custom work, and as Augusta later recalled, "even in a depression … some people and organization[s] … want the very best and can afford to pay for it."[16] A photo of a veneer wall panel made by the Roddis firm depicting an elegantly dressed woman, along with other images of commissions from around 1934 (including a court house in Texas where oil buoyed the state economy), demonstrate the sort of high-end business that the company was still able to attract (fig. 115). These prestigious commissions were the key to the family firm's survival, and by default resulted in the continued employment of a large proportion of Marshfield families.

In addition, the Roddis Company had developed a national distribution system, so it was not completely dependent on only one limited area. In fact, about 90 per cent of the business was now out of town. Hamilton's keen business acumen certainly played an important role in his ability to keep the company from bankruptcy. Between 1930 and 1934, he opened three new logging camps on company land in northern Wisconsin to maintain a constant supply of hardwoods.[17] Hamilton was also sensitive to new markets; he recognized that many Americans were now spending much of their leisure time at home playing cards, so he cleverly concocted the idea of producing a line of card tables with beautifully inlaid and matched veneer tops. This Depression item was a great success, and helped bring in some much-needed revenue.[18]

Hamilton's skillful management paid off, and he was able to keep his company afloat, although money continued to be a concern. Boarding school for Augusta and her brother Bill was now out of the question, so they lived at home and attended public high school in Marshfield. Despite the superior academic experience she had enjoyed at Saint Mary's, Augusta viewed the return home with some relief. In another letter, she wrote that while living away from home she felt "completely isolated from the rest of humanity and civilization."[19] Much to her surprise, back in Marshfield she soon became a success, both academically and socially. She was naturally bright, and thanks to the rigorous intellectual environment she had experienced at boarding school, Augusta was able to skip a class, and by the time she graduated in 1933 she was the class Valedictorian.

A Party and a Dress for the Junior Prom Queen

There was a tradition for the young Roddis daughters to hold parties in their home, making use of the large wooden-floored room on the third floor. (This room had been referred to as a "ballroom" by a local paper in 1915, while also noting that "the little Misses Roddis" had quickly converted it to their "playroom".[20]) In the 1920s, for instance, the elder twins, Mary and Sara, enjoyed dance parties there, as well as a specially organized treasure hunt noted in the *Marshfield Times*.[21] In 1932, when Augusta was 16, she invited friends to a party by formal invitation, and it is probable that her party was also held on the top floor. Except for the non-alcoholic punch most likely served, this would not have caused any great outlay to organize. Although there is no example of this invitation, two letters of acceptance have survived in the family papers archive, one from a young man and the other from a young woman. Both are written formally—"Miss Virginia Vedder accepts with pleasure the kind invitation of Miss Augusta Roddis for Saturday, May the twenty-eighth at eight thirty o'clock"—and the tone of the party probably matched the formality of these replies.[22] An illustrated dance card found in the Roddis house (visible in the still life on p.210), may have been from this party, since one of the boys' names corresponds to a respondent.[23]

Soon after this party, young Augusta had the honor of being voted to take the prestigious title of Junior Prom Queen in 1932.[24] The Prom theme was "A Storybook Ball" and it presented the perfect opportunity to acquire a chic new dress (fig. 116). During those financially strapped times, this new purchase represented a thrilling distraction: "The evening dress I wore as Prom Queen of the Junior Prom cost $19.95, and I was very happy with it, and if there was anything better in the world, I didn't know it. The skirt of that evening dress was cut on the bias as many dresses in the thirties were, and it had a cowl neckline, and I felt very up-to-date in it."[25]

Augusta's Prom dress was indeed fashionably cut on the bias, a technique championed by Madeleine Vionnet (1876–1975) in Paris in the 1920s. Bias cut, meaning cutting diagonally across the grain of a fabric, resulted in a natural drape of sinuous folds that clung to the wearer's body, especially at the bust and hips. A dress constructed in this way could be stepped into or slipped over the head, eliminating the need for obtrusive fastenings at the back or front; the closure of this dress is tucked under the

left arm and further disguised by the two yellow and tangerine waist ties. Inspired by ancient Greek sculpture, Vionnet's designs and consummate technique introduced fluid gowns with Grecian cowl necks and crisscross ties, similar to those featured on this dress.[26] Vionnet often used oyster-colored fabric, an allusion to marble sculpture. Both the design and overall color of Augusta's gown suggest this Prom dress may well have been based on a Vionnet toile* (fabric pattern) from Paris.[27] Alternatively, the dress may have derived from a paper pattern: between 1925 and 1929, McCall's pattern styles included many designs based on the work of major Parisian couturiers, from Coco Chanel (1883-1971) to Vionnet, thereby aiding the growing democratization of fashion that would continue throughout the 1930s and 1940s.[28] In addition, Vionnet established an American Madeleine Vionnet company in 1924 to sell ready-to-wear clothing, and this firm lasted until 1932, so it is possible that one of these off-the-rack models may have been the basis for Augusta's dress.[29]

This dress is made from a newly popular material—rayon* crêpe. In the 1920s, rayon was regarded as a poor substitute for silk, but the grim reality of the Depression shifted opinion. It was featured prominently by department stores and manufacturers, and fashion magazines actively promoted this new fabric. Clothes made of less expensive artificial fabrics kept costs down; one historian claims that most dresses sold in U.S. department stores in the late 1930s cost less than $12.95—so Augusta's Prom dress must have seemed expensive by comparison, although still far removed from the price of Parisian couture (also available in some of these high-end stores).[30]

FIG. 116, OPPOSITE
Cream rayon evening dress with yellow and tangerine drapes, 1932. THF 2014.24.72. "The evening dress I wore as Prom Queen of the Junior Prom cost $19.95, and I was very happy with it, and if there was anything better in the world, I didn't know it."

FIG. 117
Detail of a photo of Augusta as Junior Prom Queen, wearing the dress opposite, Marshfield, Wisconsin, April 15, 1932. RFPA.

A photograph of the Prom Court with the other students (fig. 117) appeared in the Marshfield High School yearbook, *The Tiger*. A small dance book with the original attached pencil—to list one's dancing partners—has also survived, and both can be seen in the still life photo on p.132.[31] The population in Marshfield at that time was about 9,000, and there were 97 students in Augusta's junior class. Many of these students, as well as teachers, inscribed her yearbook with dozens of comments, praising her academic accomplishments and her witty personality. Yet it was the memory of the sheer joy of wearing a beautiful new dress that evening that would dominate her recollections of those two surprisingly happy years in high school; and so this dress, representing pleasant thoughts from the past, was carefully stowed away.

Both mother and daughter shared a taste for dresses with a feminine line, and would have surely delighted in the new styles of the 1930s, which discarded the once considered chic but shapeless shifts of the previous decade. In April 1932, *Vogue* pronounced: "Spring styles say 'CURVES'!"[32] Augusta's Prom dress, with its vibrant sashes encircling her tiny waist, would have accented her youthful figure.

A Quiet Anniversary and Festive Christmas Parties

In 1933, Catherine and Hamilton celebrated their twenty-fifth wedding anniversary quietly, at home, with close family only. Catherine chose to wear the ready-made, copper-colored, floor-length evening dress opposite for the occasion, made with cotton and silk lace, and with godets* in the hem to create the flare. The scoop neck is edged with a pleated ruffle and there is a large matching silk velvet rose at the center of the bosom. A long-sleeved jacket also forms part of the ensemble (fig. 118).

Lace had always been an important element in the wardrobes of the Roddis family women. Augusta admired the fine lace in the remodeled dress worn by her grandmother Sara Denton Roddis in her portraits of 1895 and 1910 (see fig. 14). Perhaps this is one reason why, decades later, during a fashion show of period garments from Marshfield families, Augusta explained why she remembered her mother's dress so vividly: "... it was the middle of the Thirties and things were so flat that nobody even thought of a party; we just had a little family meal at home, but my mother thought it was such an important occasion that she came down to dinner in [this] evening dress."[33] Times were hard. By 1933, the Great Depression had reached its nadir, with 15 million Americans unemployed.[34] Few people were buying new clothes, and Augusta recalled that her mother's wedding anniversary gown was not a new one.

By 1936, it appears that the financial gloom over the town was easing slightly. Some friends of Augusta instigated a light-hearted "formal" (dance party) on Christmas night of 1936. It was clearly such a success that a second one occurred the following year. These two parties were held in a rented space nearby, possibly in the guildhall of their church. A letter lists

FIG. 118, OPPOSITE
Cotton lace evening dress, worn by Catherine Roddis for her twenty-fifth wedding anniversary on July 8, 1933, purchased *c*.1932. THF 2014.24.81.

out all the expenses to be shared between the friends, including hiring an
"orchestra", renting a "hall", and purchasing "punch", assorted balloons,
horns, noise-makers, and confetti. The total cost was $45, or $6.50 for
each of the girls, which was not a negligible amount during the Depression
years. In complete contrast to the formality of Augusta's invitations
(based upon the replies mentioned above), the party programs devised
by these young women were wittily informal in every way. One of the
fellow party organizers wrote to "Ellen" (probably Ellen Sexton, Augusta's
best friend), suggesting that a program printed on fabric would be "quite
darling—and if we had something different it wouldn't be—just another
formal."[35] The cover pages were duly made from rustic burlap, and printed
with ironic titles such as "Our Formal Brawl" and "Our Second Formal
Brawl" (as seen in the still life on p.210). Inside, the words and names on

the dance cards were written in a mix of lower case and capital letters, sometimes with the characters facing backwards,[36] and often intentionally misspelled, in order to totally avoid "PHormalNeSS".[37] Names on the lists of dances inside these two programs reveal that these were mixed-age affairs; even the names of Augusta's elder sister, Mary, and her husband "Gordi" appear on the dance list from 1936, and it seems that her sister Catherine (Pickie) Beggs attended in 1937. However impudent the party programs, Augusta and her friends and family would have worn their best "formals" (the American term for full-length dresses) to these Christmas night parties, which were also called "formals".

During the late 1930s, the top floor of the Roddis house continued to be the scene of parties and amusements, as it had over the decades. The "ballroom" there still holds memories for Melvin R. Laird (see p.128). He recalls that Ellen, "Augusta's lovely sister", who was his first love in grade school and a wonderful friend later in life, and he "used to play together on the third floor, [and] learned to dance there."[38]

> *"My mother thought it was such an important occasion that she came down to dinner in [this] evening dress."*
>
> AUGUSTA RODDIS

Northwestern University Years

There was some question as to whether the family would be able to afford the tuition to send Augusta to college, but she herself had confidence that her father was "Super-Man" and could achieve anything he set his mind to.[39] Despite the odds, Hamilton did pull the family and the business through the Depression; he "had to scrape the bottom of the barrel" to send Augusta off to college, where she majored in English literature.[40] But Augusta recognized that achieving financial security for his family and his workers was "the most profound test of his life."[41]

When she began her studies at Northwestern University—the alma mater of both her mother (Class of 1906) and her Aunt Miriam (Class of 1896)—she brought with her a dress that had belonged to her older sister Pickie (fig. 123). Dating from about 1932, the dress was an elegant and much loved "hand-me-down" in an era when passing clothes onto siblings was considered a necessity, and even rather patriotic. This well-worn dress made of cream silk taffeta, with a plunging bare back, accentuated with a large butterfly-shaped bow of magenta silk milliner's velvet, and elaborately embellished with beads and paillettes*, was worn by Augusta to dance parties in the late 1930s. The sleek, modern aesthetic of the early 1930s was accompanied by a more extravagant style; by 1932, dresses

FIG. 120, ABOVE
Formal portrait
of Augusta by
Kay Carrington,
1937. RFPA.
THF 2015.10.63.

FIG. 121, TOP RIGHT
Norma Shearer as
Juliet in *Romeo and
Juliet*, on the cover
of *Motion Picture*,
October 1936.
Courtesy of the
Academy of Motion
Picture Arts and
Sciences, Margaret
Herrick Library.

FIG. 122, RIGHT
Publicity photo
of Norma Shearer
as Juliet in *Romeo
and Juliet*, 1936.
EMC.

appeared with details such as tiered ruffled skirts, much like this one. For a young, unmarried woman, these would have been considered more appropriate as eveningwear than a clinging dress.[42] A small loop hidden beneath one of the skirt tiers on the right side of the dress allowed Augusta to lift the skirt while dancing; this sort of loop had been known as a "dress elevator" from as early as the 1870s when dresses began to have longer trains.

Augusta adored the dress, and she is seen wearing it four years later in what could be termed an "art photo portrait"—taken in the Pi Beta Phi House at Northwestern, in 1937 (fig. 120). Augusta won the door prize at a "Gala Fashion Show; Bridge Benefit", on April 2, 1937, the prize for which was a formal photo portrait taken by Kay (Katherine) Carrington,[43] a famous Broadway actress and also a photographer.[44] The resultant portrait was prominently displayed on the wall of the main staircase in the family home on East Fourth Street for many years. The photo is strikingly similar to images of the (then) popular film *Romeo and Juliet* (1936) with Norma Shearer and Leslie Howard. Images of Shearer in her Juliet cap* appeared on covers of popular movie magazines (figs 121 and 122) and in publicity photos across America; the Juliet cap was a hit with audiences, spawning a craze for this pseudo-historical fashion.[45] (Augusta later lamented losing the one she wore in this photo portrait.) It is likely that Kay Carrington, having been a well-known Broadway actress since the 1930s, would have been familiar with, and inspired by, those images of Norma Shearer.

In a second portrait by Carrington (fig. 124), Augusta poses wearing a contemporary mohair sweater with a patterned silk neck scarf and a charming bracelet of wooden bells that looks like an early piece by American jewelry designer Miriam Haskell (1899–1981).[46] This photograph was never displayed at the Roddis home because Augusta's mother and father preferred the romantic innocence of the Juliet portrait to the more modern and glamorous image of their daughter. They considered the latter to be "too Hollywood", especially the neck scarf and bracelet— modish accessories worn by the fashion-conscious young Augusta.

In the spring of 1934, and still in the midst of the Great Depression, Augusta indulged in the purchase of a dress that became a favorite during her college years (fig. 125).[47] It was the work of a young designer who had only just burst onto the New York fashion scene: Gladys Parker. Hitherto known only for her witty and humorous fashion-oriented comic strips, Parker was a budding American fashion designer who epitomized the creative spirit of a generation stifled by economic depression but desperate to improve their lot. A powerhouse of creativity, but today almost forgotten, Parker used clever, catchy names for her first collection of dresses, such as "Stuffed Shirt", "Sugar", and "Damn Yankee". She designed primarily for the Junior Miss size, also called "subdeb" at that time, and was known for her "impudent, original, and practical" creations.[48]

FIG. 124
Formal portrait
of Augusta, by
Kay Carrington,
Pi Beta Phi House,
Northwestern
University,
1937. RFPA.
THF 2015.10.62.

The dress purchased by Miss Roddis was dubbed "Cocktail", a very early example of the use of that term in connection with a dress (see p.212 for further discussion of cocktail dresses). It was described in a newspaper article as "a smart interpretation of the striped theme for dancing. Made of crunchy taffeta, it gains youth and smartness through the upstanding frill across the shoulder line and the tiny little train."[49] A similar dress was shown at one of Parker's fashion shows in Florida in 1935.[50] Based on the sketches in her popular comic strip, "Flapper Fanny", Gladys used a narrow but bold black and white even stripe in crisp silk taffeta. The raised waistline of Augusta's dress emphasizes the elegance of the floor-length gown, which is enhanced with a knee-length train topped with a vertical pleated flounce. The horizontal stripes in the bodice accentuate the popular wide shoulders of the era, which are capped off with deeply pleated puff sleeves.

FIG. 125, OPPOSITE
"Cocktail", a silk
taffeta evening
dress designed
by the newly
prominent designer,
Gladys Parker,
1934. Label: "An
original design
copyrighted 1934
by Gladys Parker,
REG. US.PAT.OFF."
THF 2014.24.36

Even prior to the showing of Gladys Parker's first collection in New York in 1933,[51] extensive interviews with the newly discovered designer appeared in newspapers throughout the country; the Wisconsin newspaper, the *La Crosse Tribune*, featured her at the beginning of February 1934.[52] A month later, the "Cocktail" dress, costing the considerable sum of $35, appeared in the *New York Times* in a large advertisement for Best & Co. (fig. 126). It is likely to have graced the windows of that renowned New York department store during the month of March 1934.[53] Augusta may have purchased her Gladys Parker dress in New York in the spring of that year, but this designer's dresses were soon sold in leading department stores across the country.[54] This slim, chic, cocktail* and dancing dress was the epitome of youthful grace, and Augusta wore it for a first date, as she rather flippantly explained to her sister Ellen in a letter dated 1936: "Navy Ball is tonight and am going to wear my black and white formal. My date is a boy whom I have never gone to a dance with before so I figured I might just as well trot out one of my older numbers—hence the black and white dress."[55]

"A Century of Progress": A Perfectly Modern Dress

While Augusta was attending Northwestern University in Evanston, outside Chicago, in 1933–4, the Chicago World's Fair (entitled "A Century of Progress 1833–1933") was taking place. Despite the Depression, the fair attracted almost 40 million visitors to Chicago, and Augusta must have relished the excitement that would have accompanied such an influx of newcomers into the city.[56] A copy of the *Official World's Fair Weekly, Week ending June 3, 1933* was found in the Roddis home, so there is little doubt that she attended this remarkable exhibition. In complete contrast to the

Easter egg stripe
taffeta frock for
sub-debs 35.00

Gladys Parker
striped taffeta
sub-deb frock
35.00

Point desprit
net dress 29.75

PICTURESQUE FROCKS FOR SPRING PARTIES

FIG. 126
Advertisement
for Best & Co.,
New York Times,
March 10, 1934.
New York Times
Archive.

"White City" of the Columbian Exposition in Chicago only 40 years earlier, "A Century of Progress"'s temporary buildings made dramatic use of modern approaches to technology and style, while their bright colors reminded visitors of descriptions of the Emerald City in the popular children's book *The Wonderful Wizard of Oz*.[57]

The fair became a symbol of pride in America's success during the last century, and served as an uplifting beacon of hope. Although planning began before the Depression, "A Century of Progress" was an antidote to the hardships of the day. Such was its success that it was reopened in 1934. The following excerpt from a souvenir program for the fair captures the impression it aimed to achieve: "As he enters the grounds and moves down the fluttering Esplanade of the Flags ... [the visitor] finds himself lifted up in spirit. This is the impression which the Exposition would have endure beyond any other.... Look into the tomorrow! With our help the new day can be made so much more rich than the old!"[58]

At the historic Marshfield fashion show of 1988, Augusta stated that she wore a modern and fun dress as a student at Northwestern University, although it is not clear if she actually wore it to classes there.[59] The hemline is only about nine inches off the ground, reflecting the significant drop from the knee-high day dresses popular in the mid-1920s. It is a deep salmon, twill-woven dress of rayon with a prominent single fly-away lapel over the left shoulder, edged with shirred beaver. The lapel is held in place with a large domed silver button, which is complimented by the silver mesh belt, featuring a prominent industrial-inspired buckle (fig. 130).

It would have been fitting for Augusta to visit the World's Fair wearing this. The rich shade, the dramatically jutting asymmetrical front panel edged with fur, the ultra-modern metal mesh belt and silver button, and the sleek silhouette of this dress are typical elements of 1930s fashion. Moreover, they share the aesthetic of the temporary architecture at the fair, with its vivid, clean, abstract shapes. The brightly colored Travel and Transport Building, for example, used expansion bridge technology to support a dome and create the rhythmic, angled "sky hooks" of its roofline (fig. 127). It seems that the aesthetic of Art Deco*, and its younger cousin Art Moderne*, had been imbued into virtually all art forms of that period, from architecture to fashion. Augusta's dress also resonates with popular science-fiction characters of the era, as featured in the ten-minute Buck Rogers film that premiered at this World's Fair in Chicago.[60] The faces of Buck Rogers, and his successor, Flash Gordon, were familiar comic strip

characters in the 1930s, and their costumes had a strong, "futuristic" look, which became a key influence upon fashion designers of the period.

In the family newspaper clippings archive from the Roddis house is an advertisement from the *Chicago Sunday Tribune* (fig. 129),[61] which includes a design for a coat by the French couturier Jean Patou (1880–1936).[62] The illustrated coat bears a remarkable resemblance to Augusta's salmon dress with its fur-edged flyaway collar. As the dress has no label and the interior construction indicates that it was most likely homemade, it was probably made by Catherine, or else a local seamstress. The newspaper image, cut out and carefully saved, suggests it may have been the inspiration for this dress; at the very least it shows that Catherine and Augusta were intrigued by the Paris designs it depicted.

Sewing for Style

Catherine had grown up in a family in which dressmaking was a natural part of domestic life, and she continued that tradition by making clothes for her own children, sometimes with the aid of McCall's or Butterick patterns. While Augusta was in her second year of college at Northwestern University, Catherine wrote to her suggesting that she look at some numbers from the current "March and April" *McCall's Magazine* pattern section, and offered to make some for her when she came home: "I have been looking for patterns for your dresses and like the McCall's best

of anything I could find. I marked some I thought you might like in the pattern books I sent you ... it says in so many words: Chiffon will be worn this spring. The no's for chiffon McCall's 8270, 8251, 8125, 8207, 1723, 8254, 8456, 8286, 8252, 8293" (fig. 132).[63]

No such chiffon dress made by Catherine survives, but it is possible that she made for Augusta the blue satin-back rayon crêpe evening dress with circular rhinestone buckles opposite (fig. 133). It is very similar to a pattern from an edition of *McCall's Magazine* from January 1936 (fig. 131).[64] Simple but elegant, this dress has two wide panels extending from the waist and crossing over the chest, held together at the back by a smaller version of the two-piece buckle used to close the wide sash at the front, and then falling as two long flowing back panels to the knees.

This glamorous dress was undoubtedly influenced by the gowns worn in the popular Hollywood films of the day, as well as the Parisian designs featured in American newspapers and movie magazines. Such films were eagerly viewed by 85 million Americans each week, many of whom were unemployed and distressed;[65] escape into the fantasy celluloid world was an inexpensive way to experience the glamor of beautiful women and the clothes they wore.

Movies stimulated a consumer demand for the fashions seen on the screen. Shops began to sell ready-made screen-style dresses, while magazines sold paper patterns created by the film designers themselves.[66] In 1932, Condé Nast, producer of *Vogue* patterns, introduced a new, cheaper line of Hollywood patterns, with envelopes that featured a picture of a Hollywood star. This range cost 15 cents rather than the full $2.00 for a regular *Vogue*

FIG. 131, RIGHT
Dress patterns from *McCall's Magazine* (similar to the evening dress opposite, which was possibly made by Catherine Roddis), January 1936. EMC.

FIG. 132, FAR RIGHT
"For Fair May Days" dress pattern 8251 from the March and April issue of *McCall's Magazine*, April 1935. Courtesy of the Commercial Pattern Archive, University of Rhode Island.

NIGHT FLIERS

FIG. 133, OPPOSITE
Satin-back rayon crêpe evening dress with circular rhinestone buckles, c.1938 (possibly made by Catherine for Augusta). THF 2014.24.80.

pattern. They were a big success and gave women the opportunity to dress in clothes that imitated those of their favorite stars.[67]

A diary entry written by Augusta a few years later reveals that she loved wearing this blue evening gown, as well as her sister's dress with the velvet bow at the back. She enjoyed her previous visit to New Orleans in 1939 so much that she returned to stay with her Aunt Frances in 1941, with the intention of wearing both dresses to Mardi Gras balls.[68] However, her aunt would not allow her to wear them, perhaps because they revealed too much flesh for that conservative Southern society, instead insisting on another gown, much to Augusta's dismay: "It practically breaks my heart to have to wear that thing when I would feel so ravishing in silk in Pickie's old white taffeta or my blue satin-back crêpe—I guess I shall have to rely on my devastating personality—Hi-ho!"[69] Even though the blue dress may have been made at home by her skilled and practical mother, Augusta clearly was proud to be seen wearing it.

Both this homemade blue evening gown and the salmon day dress, along with her letter about the patterns, bear testimony to Catherine's determination to dress her eldest daughters in the most sophisticated fashions, despite the restrictions on family income.[70] Dresses made in the Roddis home were key to remaining up-to-date; they were clearly inspired by the latest styles from Paris and Hollywood, and often used better quality fabrics than may have been found in many ready-made clothes, even in the best urban stores. It is appropriate that this is precisely the message expressed in a 1931 booklet found in the Roddis house entitled *Modern Dressmaking: The Guide to French Chic and Smartness of Dress*, visible in the still life on p.266, in which the following edict advises: "The secret, then, of having all the lovely clothes you want is to make them yourself—to sew for style."[71] This message is much like the article featured in the *Ladies' Home Journal* of 1907, as mentioned in Chapter 3 (see p.75), which also encouraged women to sew if they wanted to have the best possible clothes.

This type of book and article, advising on dress style and sewing, is part of a tradition found in hundreds of American books published by women involved in home economics and art departments across the country. Historian of American law, culture, and dress, Linda Przybyszewski, refers to them as "Dress Doctors". She has noted the pervasiveness of their works, among them *Art in Every Day Life* (1925), which became the "bible" of home economics classes.[72] Written by Harriet and Vetta Goldstein, who were called "the Emily Posts of domestic art and decoration" by *TIME* magazine in 1941, new editions of this book were published every decade until the last appeared in 1954. Similar books were also published in multiple editions.[73] The philosophy of all the writers was high-minded— "harmony", "order", and "discipline" were watchwords of this movement, along with color theory, considerations of line, rhythm, and proportion; personal "vanity" was hardly ever involved, and probably discouraged. As one Dress Doctor argued in 1931, "the consciousness of being well dressed strengthens self confidence, gives poise and courage to do greater things, [and] provides a keener wit, tact and resourcefulness."[74] The principles of aesthetics taught by these Dress Doctors were a natural extension of the approach that Augusta's grandmother Sara Roddis had been taught at the Oswego Normal and Training School in the years following the American Civil War, with the help of dolls (see p.24). Catherine was influenced by this approach when she was growing up, and the notion that being well-dressed helped women be useful members of society pervaded American women's culture until well into the twentieth century.

Family films from the 1930s include glimpses of Augusta, always beautifully turned out, revealing the high standard she maintained on a daily basis, with the help of her mother. The few clothes Catherine and Augusta did make or buy during these Depression years were very well chosen, and subtly reflect the latest styles of international couturiers and Hollywood costume designers alike. As stylish women in their small Midwestern town, mother and daughter had fashion antennae that were globally attuned. However, being seen to be "in fashion" was not in itself the primary goal. Catherine would certainly have agreed with the idea that being well-dressed was helpful for a woman's personal achievement. She also recognized that clothes of distinction acted as signposts, signaling to the outside world the value she and her daughters placed on good quality, exquisite taste, and an openness to change and innovation, both socially and in the cultural arena too. Catherine refused to allow the financial difficulties of the Depression to prevent her from dressing her children in the best manner that her intelligence, sewing skills, and taste could provide. The quantity of Augusta's clothes was nonetheless limited, though each special dress she wore was an object of delight to her in those hard times. Like the cutting-edge architecture of "A Century of Progress", the female clothes of the Roddis family were small triumphs set against the background of several long, anxious years, for the nation and the family.

Resting in the Shadow of Approaching War
When the military build-up began in Europe in the late 1930s, American industry was kick-started into action, allowing the country to haul itself out of the deepest and longest downturn in the history of the Western industrialized world to date. The Roddis family had survived the lean years with determination, hope, and ingenuity—always anxious to do the very best they could for their own family, but with a sense of responsibility for others in their hometown too. Business at the Roddis Lumber & Veneer Company greatly improved, and by 1938 the family's financial situation had brightened.[75] This provided them with time to relax and recuperate, and for Hamilton to view the latest plywood production equipment made in Germany. In 1938, Hamilton, Catherine, and Augusta made an extended trip to Europe, driving around England and the continent in the Plymouth car they had shipped over for this purpose.

REDISCOVERED DESIGNER
GLADYS PARKER

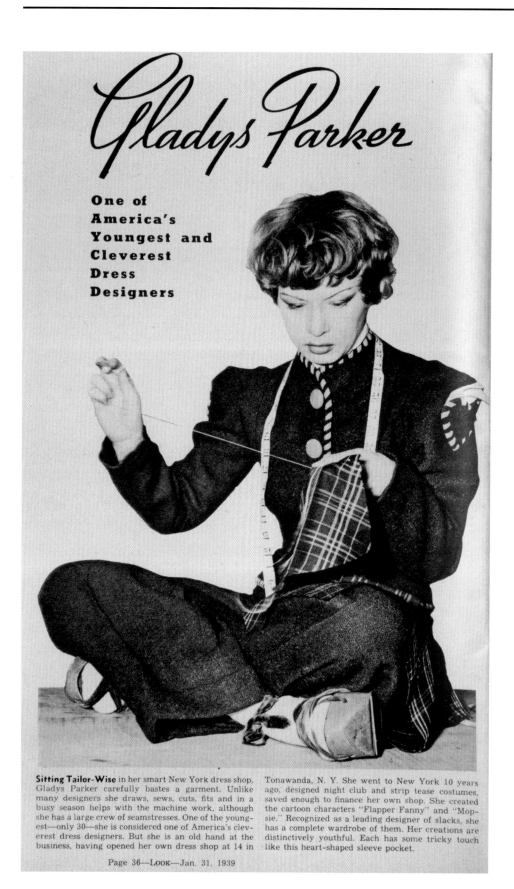

Gladys Parker

One of America's Youngest and Cleverest Dress Designers

Sitting Tailor-Wise in her smart New York dress shop, Gladys Parker carefully bastes a garment. Unlike many designers she draws, sews, cuts, fits and in a busy season helps with the machine work, although she has a large crew of seamstresses. One of the youngest—only 30—she is considered one of America's cleverest dress designers. But she is an old hand at the business, having opened her own dress shop at 14 in Tonawanda, N. Y. She went to New York 10 years ago, designed night club and strip tease costumes, saved enough to finance her own shop. She created the cartoon characters "Flapper Fanny" and "Mopsie." Recognized as a leading designer of slacks, she has a complete wardrobe of them. Her creations are distinctively youthful. Each has some tricky touch like this heart-shaped sleeve pocket.

Page 36—LOOK—Jan. 31, 1939

FIG. 134
Gladys Parker, *LOOK Magazine*, January 31, 1939, p.36. EMC.

FIG. 135, OPPOSITE ABOVE
Gladys Parker dress label, 1934 (copyrighted design). Parker's label features her self-portrait as a petite go-getter with tousled red hair. The same personal features were later used for "Mopsy", her cartoon character. THF 2014.24.36.

FIGS 136 AND 137, OPPOSITE BELOW
"Flapper Fanny", Sunday comic strips by Gladys Parker, *The Tulsa Tribune*, 1935. EMC.

BORN: 1909, Tonawanda, New York.

DIED: 1966, San Mateo, California.

EARLY CAREER: Moved to New York City in 1927 after winning a costume design prize, and studied briefly at the Art Students League and the Traphagen School of Fashion. In 1929 became a staff cartoonist and created her own comic strip called "Gay and her Gang". Took over the well-known cartoon "Flapper Fanny" in 1930. Showed her first dress collection in a rented suite at the Barbizon-Plaza Hotel in New York, September 5, 1933.

PEAK OF CAREER: In 1934 became associated with a New York manufacturer; together they opened a showroom on 7th Avenue. That year started copywriting her dress designs, sewing her own prototypes, and modeling her designs made for the Junior Miss size. They were soon carried in 150 American department stores, sold exclusively to one in each city. Launched a nationwide campaign in 1937 promoting the new rayon called "Vovita" with advertisements featuring four motion picture stars. Mentioned in *Vogue* in 1940.[76] During 1942, had her own fashion section in *SPOT Magazine*, featuring inventive designs for stars including Barbara Stanwyck and Veronica Lake.[77]

CLAIM TO FAME: Her fame as a highly regarded, young American fashion designer only lasted for slightly more than a decade. Best known for her originality as a cartoon artist: especially "Flapper Fanny" (1930–6) and the later "Mopsy", which began in 1941 and morphed into comic books (1947–65). These established her reputation as an icon of American popular culture. Both comic books and newspaper comics of "Mopsy" included a paper doll to cut out and dress in the latest fashions.

ALSO NOTABLE FOR: Attended the Beaux Arts Ball in New York in 1931 wearing her signature long "dance pajamas" in white velvet with the Empire

State Building appliqued in black velvet up one side, causing American newspapers to trumpet: "Flapper Fanny Turns Stylist".[78]

BIBLIOGRAPHY: In 1935, aged just 25 years old, she was selected for the book *American Fashion Designers*, by a panel of prestigious fashion writers.[79]

"Make me as brave as Washington, noble as Lincoln, smart as Roosevelt, with eyelashes like Marlene Dietrich — especially, please God— the eyelashes!"[80]

FLAPPER FANNY

Even with hindsight you can't see your own back.

FLAPPER FANNY

The choice of a party dress often depends on the party going along.

RODDIS
FLUSH & FRENCH
DOORS

B90SC3   Roddis Lumber and Veneer Co., Saw and Planing Mill, Park Fall

RODDIS LUMBER & VENEER CO.
Marshfield   Wiscon

ENEER CO.
SIN.

UNITED STATES LINE S. S. "LEVIATHAN"
LENGTH 950 Ft.   HEIGHT 184 Ft.   TONNAGE 59,956.

CHAPTER SEVEN

Wartime Production, Wartime Restriction
The Home Front

The Great Depression had been the most difficult period in the life of Hamilton Roddis and his family. Financial insecurity had affected every aspect of their lives, including their wardrobes; new purchases were limited, and Catherine returned to making clothes for Augusta, and possibly for her other daughters who were still at home. The next decade brought a new set of challenges. World War II would have a major impact on their lives, and government restrictions would even alter the design of their clothes. Thanks to Hamilton and his son Bill, however, the family firm made a significant contribution to Allied victory, and the war years would bring greater prosperity to the company and the Roddis family.

Hamilton maintained his father's entrepreneurial yet sound and successful approach to the family business.[1] He continued to feel a strong link to his energetic father. As previously noted, both father and son demonstrated a keen interest in the latest house design and trends in interior decoration, as well as the newest forms of transport. Just as William Henry Roddis was referred to as "W.H. Roddis" by the local press and business associates, so Hamilton became known as "H.R." outside the family. The paternal link even extended to Hamilton's shopping habits; all but one of his surviving suits were made by leading tailors in Chicago or New York, and both men wore the same brand of shoes.[2] Hamilton, like his father, appears to have kept pace with what was considered the appropriate attire of a gentleman, but whereas W.H.'s clothing was rooted

in the traditional nineteenth-century British style, Hamilton's wardrobe had a distinctly modern American look.

A Very American Suit

Once the financial difficulties of the Depression had somewhat subsided, Hamilton and Catherine went on vacation to Key West, Florida, in 1937. A photograph taken of H.R. in a relaxed moment (fig. 139) shows him wearing Oxford two-toned spectator shoes* just like his surviving pair by Hanan & Son, c.1930–5 (fig. 140).[3] The suit he is wearing appears to be either the same or similar to another in the Roddis Collection: a ready-to-wear two-piece suit by Lorraine Haspel of New Orleans, purchased from Marshall Field & Company, Chicago (fig. 141). Around 1909, Haspel launched a new lightweight fabric to the American market called seersucker*. Contemporary advertisements emphasized that Haspel suits were washable and "guaranteed not to fade, shrink or discolor";[4] Co-owner Joseph Haspel himself is said to have demonstrated this fact by swimming across the Mississippi River while wearing one.[5] Before the days of air conditioning, these cotton suits were popular summertime wear for affluent Americans, at garden parties and country clubs, as well as on Ivy League college campuses, Wall Street, and even the floor of the U.S. Senate. By the time Gregory Peck wore a Haspel suit for his role as the crusading 1930s attorney Atticus Finch in the 1963 film *To Kill a Mockingbird*, wearing seersucker had become a quintessential American style.

Hamilton's suit, dating from 1934–7, is made from a lightweight, unlined corded cotton—a more conservative version of its seersucker cousin. Intended as leisure wear, it would have been a refreshing change to wear this, rather than a traditional woolen suit, during the humid, hot Wisconsin summers, and also during the many family vacations in Florida, Bermuda, and Jamaica. This two-piece suit is in a half Norfolk* style, with a flat inset belt and large inverted vertical center pleat at the center back. In America this was known as a "fancy back" jacket; Clark Gable wore one in the 1934 film *It Happened One Night*, adding to the popular appeal of this style.[6] Less than a decade later, during wartime, Norfolk-style jackets would be banned due to the extra fabric required to create the back, which was sometimes gathered into the waistband.[7]

FIG. 140, BELOW LEFT
Men's spectator shoes, Hanan & Son, 1930–5. THF 2014.24.159.

FIG. 141, BELOW
Detail of striped suit with a Norfolk-style jacket by Lorraine Haspel, *c.*1937. THF 2014.24.148.

Hamilton's cotton Haspel suit was too informal to wear to an important business luncheon one hot summer's day in 1931, but even a traditional dark suit would have been in stark contrast to the attire of his German guest, Baron von Maltitz, who was representing Siempelkamp—a German manufacturer of plywood production equipment and glues. Hamilton's son, Bill, was also present and recalled that the baron "wore a black top hat, had a cape, and carried a silver cane".[8] The three men met at the Hotel Charles in Marshfield and sat outside to discuss the German company's new waterproof plywood glue, and a new manufacturing method using a 16-foot plywood hot plate press. Hamilton admired German ingenuity and was aware that Siempelkamp made cutting-edge equipment.[9] Despite the bad economy, Hamilton took the first steps towards acquiring the groundbreaking waterproof resin glue and the enormous press, both of which were unknown in America, and which would come to play a key role in aircraft production during the war years that lay ahead.[10]

Visiting Europe and the Threat of War

Hamilton's motor tour of Europe in 1938 (see p.157) with his wife Catherine and daughter Augusta gave him the opportunity to observe the latest German-designed equipment being used in plywood factories in Great Britain and also in Germany. He would then be able to make a decision as to the type of machinery his company should purchase. The trip combined factory visits with excursions to see cultural attractions, such as attending Shakespeare plays at Stratford-upon-Avon in southern England.[11] Driving through Europe, the family also stopped in Stuttgart, Germany, where a business contact introduced by Baron von Maltitz took them to a performance of the comic operetta *The Merry Widow*. The program, which was saved in the Roddis house, is dominated by Third Reich propaganda.[12] The performance took place on September 18, less than a month before Kristallnacht, when mobs smashed the storefronts of Jewish businesses, and the Gestapo dragged thousands of innocent Jews to concentration camps. Such tragedy had not yet occurred, nor been remotely conceived of by the Roddis family.

Since concerns about Germany's aggression and the threat of war were discussed in international newspapers, the potential need for plywood for future defense purposes may have been at the back of Hamilton's mind, along with the realization that trade with Germany could soon end.[13] Hamilton bought a wide variety of equipment as a result of this trip in 1938.[14] These, plus the purchases he made back in 1931, would put the Roddis Company at the very forefront of the American plywood manufacturing industry—and eventually both maritime and aircraft plywood wartime production too.[15] Importantly, and ironically, Hamilton's newly purchased German technology would turn out to play a significant role in helping the Allies defeat Hitler.

Augusta later wrote that some of her most vivid memories from the 1930s were from this European trip: the beautiful English countryside, the delights of London and Paris, the gardens of Versailles, the charms of the Neckar Valley in Germany and the Swiss Alps.[16] Equally vivid was the war scare that suddenly flared up as they headed home: "many people crowded onto the ship ... fleeing in fear of war.... However, [Prime Minister Neville] Chamberlain signed the Munich Agreement, and the war was averted until the next year."[17]

Despite this act of appeasement, and Chamberlain's famous words "Peace in our time", Great Britain was preparing for a coming conflict. Aviation genius Geoffrey de Havilland (1882–1965) was one of many who worked feverishly to help Great Britain build up its armaments.[18] His main project was redesigning his wooden DH-88 Comet,[19] and the result of his work was the DH-98 Mosquito (fig. 142). This wooden aircraft was remarkable for its speed, its tight turning radius, and its ability to fly long range and at very low, as well as high, altitudes. The British Air Ministry had many misgivings about wooden planes, but was finally convinced after the DH-98's test flights in November 1940: orders were placed and production began soon thereafter.[20] The Mosquito, known as the "Wooden Wonder" or "Timber Terror", quickly became the most versatile warplane ever built, and it turned out to be one of the safest.[21]

The construction of the Mosquito depended on thin plywood skins of yellow birch molded as double wing skins, with lightweight woods used as core material.[22] Fortunately, Great Britain had excellent specialized woodworkers who could switch from crafting pianos and furniture to making wooden airplanes, but the nation lacked forests and specialized plywood manufacturing. The Roddis Lumber & Veneer Company, making use of Wisconsin's abundant trees, would play a large part in satisfying that need. The family firm already had experience in this area: during World War I, when the strength and lightness of wood for military aircraft

FIG. 142
DH-98 Mosquito, also called the "Wooden Wonder". Reprinted with permission from *Wisconsin's Flying Trees in World War II* (Witter Connor 2014).

construction was vital because metal was needed for other purposes, it had supplied plywood to the U.S government, and French and Italian aircraft manufacturers.[23] For the same reason, plywood for wooden planes would once again be in demand—this time on a larger scale. In an interview with his niece, historian and author Sara Witter Connor, Hamilton's son Bill explained how the Roddis Company became involved:

> *Then in about 1939 or '40, the British came to us. They had learned that we had a 16 foot press and they needed long lengths of plywood for a plane they were developing and the result was that they placed orders early on ... my father appointed me ... chief inspector.... He was actually the main force to improve the quality and set up methods so that we could produce acceptable plywood for the Mosquito.*[24]

Quality was crucial; the British government sent inspectors to the Roddis factory in Marshfield and representatives to scout out further supplies of this specialized wood in Wisconsin.[25] Hamilton and his son worked furiously to meet the specifications for the Mosquito. Bill's engineering acumen undoubtedly contributed to Roddis Lumber & Veneer Company's future lead in aviation product development.[26]

As the British struggled to fight the Nazis, President Franklin D. Roosevelt spoke to the American people in one of his fireside radio chats. He proposed a Lend-Lease agreement whereby the United States would serve as the "great arsenal of democracy", supplying the British and Allied war machine in order to help them protect themselves and America as well.[27] When Congress passed the Lend-Lease bill, war production orders took off. After the bombing of Pearl Harbor on December 7, 1941, which precipitated America's entry into World War II, the orders soared.[28]

Wood Goes to War: Life Changes on the Home Front

Wood was essential for the war effort.[29] The Roddis Company became America's largest supplier of bulkheads, frames, and fireproof doors for the Liberty and Victory ships.[30] It supplied plywood for the construction of aircraft such as the Mosquito and expendable wooden gliders.[31] In addition, the Roddis Company produced the plywood for the Hughes H4 Hercules, a flying boat conceived by Henry J. Kaiser (1882–1967), the father of American shipbuilding. This gigantic wooden airplane was devised to transport supplies over the Atlantic, avoiding the threat of German U-boat torpedoes. Soon this visionary project for the U.S. government was largely taken over by Howard R. Hughes, Jr. (1905–76), the American business tycoon, inventor, and aviator.[32] Kaiser and Hughes turned to the Roddis Company to supply plywood that was as light as, if not lighter than, that used for the Mosquito.[33] Although nicknamed the "Spruce Goose" by critics, who considered it a government folly, it was made of birch with a basswood core engineered by Bill Roddis.[34]

With particular focus on plywood for aircraft and marine use, the men and women of the Roddis Company worked round the clock during the war years. As men enlisted to fight, 250 women employees were hired to splice and iron the veneer, as well as perform other essential tasks.[35] Security was paramount, and each employee was now required to wear a badge like the one visible in the still life on p.160. By that time, the Roddis Company was the third largest plywood manufacturer in the United States,[36] and was responsible for supplying around 65 per cent of the wood shipped to Britain and Canada for the construction of the DH-98 Mosquito.[37]

As the Roddis Company cranked up production, 90 per cent of which was for the war effort,[38] the daily lives of the Roddis family were changing—as they were for all Americans. Unemployment was replaced by an acute labor shortage, while domestic help became harder to find, and more expensive, as women chose better paid jobs in factories. A letter from Hamilton's sister, Frances, expressed worry about how she would manage if she could not find a girl to help look after her Marshfield home: "I remember during the last war how we could not get help for love or money."[39] But it was rationing that had the greatest impact on everyone: sugar, coffee, butter, meat, tinfoil, metals, hair pins, iron, rubber, refrigerators, automobiles, gasoline, shoes, fabrics, and paper products were only some of the items restricted through government controls, designed to ensure adequate supplies for the war effort.[40] In reality, rationing in America was light compared to the restrictions faced by Europeans, but it was painful nevertheless. Mary Roddis Connor wrote to her mother in June 1942, lamenting how she would be able to feed her family as they were accustomed. Mary was also worried by the advice of her local tailor who cautioned anyone needing clothes to "hurry up and get them" before rationing started, warning that materials were getting "shoddy", and that he had "to pay double" for them.[41]

During these early war years, the youngest Roddis daughter, Ellen, attended Wellesley College outside Boston. In a letter to her parents, she wrote that she had bought a new sweater since they too were "getting rare", and confessed "I just can't get used to this war time" [sic].[42] Another letter describes the college's practice blackout exercise, and notes that her Christmas break would have to extend until February so that the college could save fuel. Ellen also explained that most of her dates (also becoming increasingly scarce due to the draft) often had neither car nor gasoline. Socializing became expensive (70 cents for the train to Boston and an additional 25 cents for a taxi back to the dorm late at night), cutting into her meager allowance, which she dearly hoped could be increased to $35 a month.[43]

Photographs of Ellen taken in Wellesley (fig. 143) reveal that she wore her hair long, parted at the side with curls only at the ends, which was an easy-to-care-for wartime style made popular by film stars such as Katharine Hepburn.[44] Since curlers and especially metal bobby pins were in

FIG. 143, ABOVE
Portrait of Ellen
Roddis wearing a
typical wartime
hairstyle, *c.*1942.
RFPA.

FIG. 144, RIGHT
Augusta wore her
hair in a typical
1940s top roll.
Photograph taken
in Manhattan, 1945.
RFPA.

short supply, women found that the end curls of this hairstyle could easily be made using rags. Long hair also lent itself to tightly contained, upswept styles that were worn throughout the period; Ellen wore her hair like this as well.[45] A photograph of Augusta taken in New York in 1945 shows that she styled her own hair into a top roll at the front, but loose at the back— another typical hairstyle of the 1940s (fig. 144). Women who worked in factories, however, were cautioned that they should either cut their hair or wear turbans or snoods* to protect their long hair from the machinery.

Uncle Sam's Clothing Restrictions

A month before the bombing of Pearl Harbor, Ellen bought a red coat of "the new knee-length variety with a fitted waist and flared at the bottom, costing $29.95."[46] That "flare" was soon to be a feature curtailed and measured precisely to suit government regulations. In April 1942, *LIFE* magazine announced: "Uncle Sam last week assumed the role of fashion designer. Sweeping restrictions aim to save 15 per cent of the yardage now used on women's and girls' apparel through such measures as restricting hems and belts to two inches, eliminating cuffs on sleeves."[47] Also stipulated was the "sweep" (circumference) of hems depending on the size and type of garment: women's daytime dresses could have a maximum sweep of 74 inches, while evening dresses could have as much as 144 inches (about 6 to 12 feet).[48] (The U.S. government chose not to ban floor-length dresses since returning servicemen liked their homecoming evenings to be special; sweethearts wearing long dresses would signify celebration.[49]) The details of the new Limitation Order L-85[50] were explained in a War Production Board (WPB) promotion poster entitled "W.P.B. Yardstick" (fig. 145).[51]

Under these new restrictions, dresses could only utilize cloth for the most basic, slim silhouettes possible, in order "to eliminate waste, and conserve fabric, machinery and manpower."[51] The goal of L-85 was to "freeze the fashion silhouette" to the pre-war standard style,[52] reducing any unnecessary costs brought about by new fashions, such as alterations of manufacturing equipment, and the related increase in labor.[53] It would also conserve wool, leather, nylon, silk, and rubber for the war effort. H. Stanley Marcus, owner of the renowned Neiman Marcus department

FIG. 145
War Production Board poster, "W.P.B. Yardstick". Courtesy of the U.S. National Archives and Records Administration.

store in Texas, became head of the Apparel Section of the WPB. Marcus devised the new L-85 regulation, and he confessed to many sleepless nights wondering if he had decided wisely. He realized that at "that particular moment, [he] had greater fashion power than any monarch or couturier in the history of the world."[54]

For men and women, double-breasted jackets and three-piece suits were banned, and no more than two pockets and one collar or single revers* was allowed. Cuffs on sleeves and trousers were also banned on the "Victory Suits" for both sexes. Manufacturers breaking the L-85 rules could be subject to fines or even imprisonment, but violations still occurred. The impact on men's clothes was significant but bearable; they grumbled about changes such as smaller lapels and especially the ban on cuffs on trousers.[55] Women, who were accustomed to changes in fashion two seasons a year, dreaded the restrictions and questioned whether fashion would survive the freeze. As a key figure at the WPB and a leading retailer, Marcus replied optimistically: "The flame of fashion can't be quenched.... Fashion will adapt itself to the order of the day.... The order of this day is conservation...."[56] He believed that it was the patriotic duty of designers to create fashions that adhered to L-85, while simultaneously remaining stylish throughout multiple seasons.

"The flame of fashion can't be quenched.... Fashion will adapt itself to the order of the day...."

H. STANLEY MARCUS

Fashions did indeed evolve subtly. For the cause of victory *and* style, hemlines became generally shorter (sometimes well above the knee), and skirts narrower. Three-quarter-length sleeves were widely used, and jackets were shortened to 28 inches, or just 25 inches from neck to lower edge for evening jackets. This resulted in an overall more masculine, often boxy look. To allow women to give the impression of owning more outfits than they actually had in their closets, American designers emphasized the practicality of separates and coordinating components. Magazines were also filled with articles demonstrating how to change the look of a suit through the use of different accessories, and gave plenty of advice on how to care for garments to prolong their lifespan.

The black wool coatdress in the Roddis Collection, as worn by Catherine (fig. 146), has the typical slim wartime silhouette, but with added features that give it particular style and sophistication. This dress is collarless and has a small blue silk ribbon trim around the neckline, which acts as a substitute for a blouse. The slim-line skirt has a central opening with silk crêpe beneath, and a self-tie at the neck opening that wraps around the body. Very typical of the period is the elaborate appliqué and

FIG. 146, OPPOSITE
Wool coatdress worn by Catherine Roddis, 1942–6. THF 2014.24.62.

machine embroidery, known as passementerie*, in an abstract pattern on the bodice, back, and sleeves.[57]

Silk, which was so essential for making parachutes, was not available for domestic use during the war. It is therefore unusual that this Roddis dress, dating from 1942–6, has a silk crêpe underskirt and a black silk satin lining.[58] This silk lining may have come from existing stock, which was permitted, or else this dress was created when textile restrictions had been relaxed. Even before the Allied invasion of France in June 1944, the WPB, beset by complaints, had "relented to issuance of minor amendments relaxing strict design and manufacturing standards in several types of feminine apparel."[59] The L-85, however, outlived the WPB itself and was only revoked on October 21, 1946, over a year after the war's end.[60]

Most leather was reserved for soldiers, who sometimes needed a new pair of boots as often as every month, so civilians were rationed to three pairs of leather shoes per year. Family members, however, were allowed to share shoe ration coupons.[61] Augusta was sent her father's ration book to buy a pair of shoes in New York. When she sent the book back home, she wrote that she had a "terrible time" finding anything she liked, and realized that "the leather situation had definitely impaired the quality of shoes".[62] For this reason, and the ration limits, many women chose instead the unrationed styles of cork or wooden-heeled shoes, with fabric or hemp uppers, a style which had been introduced in 1935–6 by Salvatore Ferragamo (1898–1960).[63]

Women were also severely inconvenienced by the lack of silk and nylon stockings. Invented by the DuPont Company, nylon stockings were first unveiled to the public at the 1939 New York World's Fair. When they came onto the mass market in May 1940, sales went through the roof. Soon after America entered the war, however, the WPB stipulated that all of DuPont's nylon would be used exclusively for wartime needs, especially for parachutes and ropes. First Lady Eleanor Roosevelt donned black cotton stockings to demonstrate that women could do without nylon or silk stockings, but because black stockings were associated with mourning, this was hardly a boost for morale.[64] It is likely that the Roddis women joined millions of other Americans and hoarded what stockings they could prior to this shortage, which lasted until early 1946, and Catherine's superb mending skills would have been put to good use repairing old hosiery. (No Roddis letters mention that they resorted to painting their legs, as many women did, complete with fake seams drawn at the back.) The stockings shortage made the alternative of wearing trousers popular with the younger set and factory workers, but Catherine and Augusta stuck to ladylike skirts and dresses throughout their lives.

Unlike the restrictions in Great Britain, L-85 allowed women to make whatever they liked at home, so long as it was for personal use. Commercial patterns, however, largely followed government guidelines.[65] As early as 1941, the Work Projects Administration organized sewing classes across the country and produced "Sew for Victory" posters, linking sewing and

FIG. 147
Silk and rayon
dress with a cotton
bouclé plaid cape
(most likely a golfing
dress), 1940-5.
THF 2014.24.50.

reusing materials with patriotism. Although very little handmade clothing from this period survived in the Roddis house, a letter from Catherine to her son Bill in 1944 mentions the difficulty she was having with a dress she was making, and further letters also demonstrate that she was certainly sewing clothes during the war years.[66]

The white sports dress above, dating from 1940-5 was found in the Roddis attic. It was probably intended to be primarily a golf dress, and likely belonged to Catherine, who sometimes accompanied her husband onto the golf course (fig. 147).[67] The Roddis family was hardly what one would call sporty, but golf was Hamilton's favorite sport and his wife and Augusta also played; one photograph taken of Augusta on

a golf course shows her wearing a white dress with a linen visor cap on her head. The workmanship of Catherine's shirtdress* suggests that it may be homemade, and based on a purchased pattern, or possibly made by a local seamstress. The off-white fabric is an unusual complex weave of silk and rayon*, a fabric most likely manufactured before the restrictions on silk took effect. The accompanying cape is made of green, off-white, and black cotton bouclé* plaid. The addition of the cape—presumably worn when arriving and departing from the golf course, and not while actually playing—transforms the simple dress into a stylish ensemble.

A few hats from this wartime period also survived in the Roddis house. Hats were required daywear accessories for middle-class women in the 1940s, and luckily millinery was one area that was not restricted by government regulations. During World War II, the average American woman owned at least half a dozen.[68] Women felt they ought to try to look their best to keep up morale, and there is nothing like a hat to enliven a simple suit or dress. *LIFE* magazine reported in 1942 that milliners were "using enough materials so that a hat looks like a hat and not a piece of string and the industry is at last determined to make them flattering."[69] Some outlandish designs added fun to the otherwise sober world of wartime fashion. Augusta wrote to her mother about a new fur hat she had bought in New York that was "tres, tres cute ... quite dressy and frivolous ...

really very unusual, I think."[70] Augusta's mother, Catherine, also purchased a new hat in the war years; hers was from the French Room of Marshall Field & Company in Chicago (fig. 148). This was a brown fur felt hat designed by Florence Reichman (1896–1977) of New York, dating from about 1943. It was trimmed with dark brown, silk velvet ribbons, and included real and faux feathers, arranged to appear as a bird alighted on top of the hat. It was finished with a sized (stiffened) silk spotted veil. (Typically, Catherine wore this favorite hat for two decades.) Another hat of brown felt and velvet, probably belonging to Augusta, exemplifies the stylish asymmetry characteristic of millinery in the 1940s (fig. 149).

A Family Separated by War

During the four long years of wartime, when Augusta was in her mid-twenties, she lived with her sister Pickie's family on Long Island and worked as a secretary for Pickie's husband, Robert Beggs, at a subsidiary of the Roddis Lumber & Veneer Company in New York City.[71] Surviving

FIG. 150
William H. Roddis II as U.S. Navy enlistee, *c.*1944. RFPA.

playbills reveal that she spent many evenings at the Broadway theaters, enjoying performances by stars like Katharinen Hepburn. Frequent letters to her sister Ellen describe the occasional trips she made to elegant restaurants and society homes on Long Island. There were many poignant moments for Augusta as she wrote and received letters from friends and boyfriends who had joined the Army. Some cheerfully described the exhausting hours of drill and 18-hour marches while at camp. One young man was so appreciative of her letters that he wrote she might well "apply for a position in the morale department of the Army".[72] This soldier later wrote from a hospital in 1944, where he was recuperating after being wounded while fighting in Italy, admitting he would rather return to war than face the "horribly mutilated" soldiers around him.[73]

Since Augusta's brother Bill was engaged in important wartime work—maintaining quality at the Roddis plant—he did not enter the military until 1944, by which time many boys from Marshfield had been killed in the Philippines. Bill enlisted in the Navy, trained as a radio technician, and saw duty in the Pacific (fig. 150).[74]

With Augusta and then Bill away, the Roddis house must have felt very empty. Correspondence to Catherine suggests that Hamilton's health was suffering, but he always took time to write personal letters to the Roddis employees who had gone off to war. He also made sure that the factory newsletter, the *Roddis Bulletin*, was uplifting for the remaining employees and gave updates about those who were off training or fighting, now including his only son. Some comfort came in the knowledge that by supplying the Northern yellow birch plywood for aircraft, the Roddis Company was helping the American and British war effort. Even as early as 1943, *American Lumberman* magazine articulated this "dramatic contribution": "When the history of this war is finally written it will be

FIG. 151
Trouser-clad woman working with the "big clipper" machines at the Roddis Lumber & Veneer Company, *c.*1943. RFPC.

shown that the British aircraft, made principally of [American] Northern birch, was important in saving Great Britain."[75] Meanwhile, the Allies bombed the Siempelkamp factory in Germany, where Hamilton had obtained the all-important presses and glue, possibly with a Mosquito made with plywood from Marshfield.[76]

In the tense climate of war, Ellen transferred from Wellesley College to the University of Wisconsin in Madison, which was closer to home. During the summer of 1943, she worked in the Roddis factory, monitoring temperatures in the plywood curing process.[77] If Ellen had visited the factory's third floor, she would have seen what looked like large pieces of chiffon hanging by clothes pegs on lines. This was the thin veneer, cut at 1/90th of an inch which dried to 1/100th of an inch, used to make the Mosquito and H4 Hercules wing skins. It was so thin "you could see your hand through it" and was too fragile to dry in the kilns.[78] The second floor of the Roddis company barn, was home to the women who worked 4-hour shifts there, splicing out defects in the veneer, enduring extreme heat, cold, and foul animal smells from the horses below (fig. 151).[79] Every inch of space was needed for war production, so even the top of the barn had to be used.

Perhaps it was seeing all this aircraft material that inspired Ellen to decide to learn to fly, and thereby make a more meaningful contribution to the war effort as a civil pilot. (It is not known how unusual it was for women to learn to fly in the war years, but many thousands applied for the roughly 2,000 jobs in the Women Airforce Service Pilots (WASP), a paramilitary aviation organization that undertook non-combat duties.[80]) With his traditional view of appropriate activities for women, her father did not approve of this interest, just as he had objected to her majoring in mathematics at college. But Ellen was strong and independent, like so many of the other Roddis women. She reported to her sister Augusta that she was trying to cut back on buying clothes in order to save up for the flying course in Madison, and she soon signed up for it.[81]

When Ellen Roddis walked into the classroom, the instructor knew instantly that she was the woman he wanted to marry. Glenn Lempereur had failed the draft due to poor eyesight. He was a graduate of the University of Wisconsin Law School and also a pilot; teaching flying was his way of helping out on the home front.[82] Ellen and Glenn fell in love, but her parents and siblings did not feel that he was an appropriate choice, mainly due to his family's lack of education and social status, as well as their affiliation to the Catholic Church. Such prejudices were common for upper-middle-class Protestant Americans at that time. The relationship between Ellen and Glenn challenged the Roddis household. Realizing that her family were not likely to change their minds, Ellen took a drastic step: the couple eloped in March 1945. Informally dressed in day clothes, they were married at the Grace Episcopal Church in Madison with only two of their friends present. Ellen wore the green wool gabardine

FIG. 152
Ellen Roddis
Lempereur with
Glenn N. Lempereur
on their wedding day,
March 9, 1945. RFPC.

two-piece suit opposite (fig. 153) from renowned department store Lord & Taylor, and pinned up her long hair (fig. 152). The padded shoulders, small peplum, and narrow pencil skirt of her suit are features typical of the period, but the very nipped-in waist seems to foreshadow post-war fashion. The French cuffs on the sleeves would not normally have been allowed according to L-85 rules after August 1942, so this suit may have been purchased prior to that date, or else after the restrictions had been moderated in 1944.

The elopement of his youngest daughter was hard for Ellen's father to accept, especially with the added pressures of wartime. Hamilton longed for peace in his own home, where concerns about Glenn and Ellen had caused so much disruption, and also for peace in the wider world. A few months earlier, a passage in the *Roddis Bulletin* captured the hopes of Hamilton and all his workers: "... those of us who have remained here are ever hopeful for the day when calm and peace is again with us; when the drone of the saw in the Core Mill and the 'hist' of steam from the hot plates mingles with the satisfying knowledge that the material passing through our hands is peace-time goods. Peace on earth, good will towards men."[83] Meanwhile, good will did return to the Roddis household; the family soon realized that Glenn was intelligent, hardworking, and gentlemanly.

World Peace Ushers in New Styles

World peace came on August 15, 1945, and America was poised for an economic boom. There was a pent-up demand for domestic goods and new buildings, and Americans had plenty of money to pay for them with their wartime wages; during the war many had chosen to save and buy government bonds instead of spending their income. American industry never looked back.

FIG. 153, OPPOSITE
Wool gabardine
two-piece suit,
1942–5. As worn by
Ellen Roddis at her
wedding to Glenn
N. Lempereur,
March 9, 1945.
THF 2014.126.2.

Following the end of the war, many women began to move away from the tailored garments typical of wartime. *The Paris News*, an American newspaper from Texas, articulated this when it announced: "American women are going feminine with a bang after the severe silhouette of the war years. Real hoop skirts are in the fashion lineup for spring 1946, along with padded hips, sloping shoulders, accentuated bustlings (bustlines) [sic] and corsets worn in bathing suits." The article reminds the reader that after every war there is a change in fashion, and continues with quotes from leading American designers predicting the new trends: "NETTIE ROSENSTEIN ... Accentuate the bosom, minimize the waistline ... SAMUEL KASS ... Very full skirts and exaggerated fullness throughout ... JO COPELAND ... With men back to stay, women have begun to turn on the charm."[84] Clearly, the desire for femininity, extravagance, and a new style was already in the air by early 1946, well before Christian Dior presented his famous first collection in Paris in the autumn of 1947, dubbed the New Look.[85]

Dior's constricted waists and extravagantly full, longer skirts, supported by stiff crinoline*-like petticoats of tulle, were considered by many to be a subdued revival of the full-hooped skirts from the middle of the nineteenth century. Dior's New Look initially caused an outcry from feminists and women on both sides of the Atlantic who were dismayed by the extravagant amount of fabric required—the circumference of one Dior dress hem could range anywhere from 27 to 120 feet—and what they viewed as a regressive style.[86] Nevertheless, store buyers, ready-to-wear designers and sophisticated, wealthy Americans flocked to Paris for Dior and other couture showings, and this new style had a major impact on fashion in the United States. As noted above, the New Look had precedence in American fashion, and other leading French couturiers were certainly also designing along the same lines, but Dior crystalized the trend and received wide publicity. The hourglass silhouette of the New Look would set the prevailing shape for the 1950s, although normally in a far less extreme form than Dior's original designs. Just a month after Dior launched his new collection, a *Vogue* magazine saved in the Roddis house advocated various approaches to the Paris working line: "... it may be used wholeheartedly; or it may be only the token-shape represented by cut, seams, pleats for designs based on unexaggerated nature." The key elements for elegance, the article continued, were "more length, and slender shoes, and a strictness of top."[87]

American manufacturers purchased Dior and Parisian couture models to copy and sent in-house designers to visit Paris to observe the individual construction details from Dior and other couturier-designed dresses in situ.[88] Two examples of Dior's influence may be seen in the Roddis Collection. One is a taffeta tea-length (mid-calf) dress belonging to Catherine from around 1953 (fig. 154). The inverted gathers tucked into the subtle curved shape at the bust-line and the buttons above the waist are both hallmarks of Dior designs. The volume of the skirt, however, is moderated, as is the skirt of another navy dress of Catherine's from about

1955 (fig. 155). This dress also reveals a Dior heritage due to its small inset of light fabric at the collar, the cut, and the buttons on the bodice. Both of these dresses would have been worn with a petticoat underneath, and they attest to the "trickle-down" effect of Parisian fashion upon the garments sold at department stores across America.[89]

Fashions influenced by the "New" Look, and the later sheath styles designed by Dior in the early 1950s, required "old"-style undergarments to shape the female contour. To help achieve the necessary tiny waist of a typical Dior-inspired ensemble or dress, Augusta owned a longline "Merry Widow" brassiere, which dates from about 1955 and was manufactured by Warner's (fig. 156). The 11 hooks and eyes that fasten down the back, and the nine stiff stays in the seams, hark back to the corsets that were the bulwark of female fashion for the preceding four centuries, and had only just begun to be shed by liberated women of the 1920s.

Despite the renewed influence of Parisian fashion, by the end of World War II American designers had gained great confidence and international renown. Leading American designers such as Jo Copeland (1899–1982), Vera Maxwell (1901–95), Claire McCardell (1905–58), and Norman Norell (1900–72) all became widely known for their practical yet stylish mix-and-match separates designed for American women. Manufacturers

FIG. 154, ABOVE LEFT
Rayon shirtwaist dress with three-quarter-length sleeves and full skirt, c.1953. RDC 176, JBC.

FIG. 155, ABOVE
Navy silk afternoon dress with three-quarter-length shaped dolman sleeves, a false double-breast front with buttons, a white linen collar insert, full pleated skirt, and shaped self-belt, c.1955. RDC 79, JBC.

FIG. 156
Required for the nipped-in waists and strapless dresses of the period, this corselet brassiere, called a "Merry Widow", was the type of longline bra/girdle released by Warner's in 1952 and named after that year's MGM film adaption of the 1905 operetta of the same name. Worn by Augusta Roddis, c.1955. THF 2014.24.96.

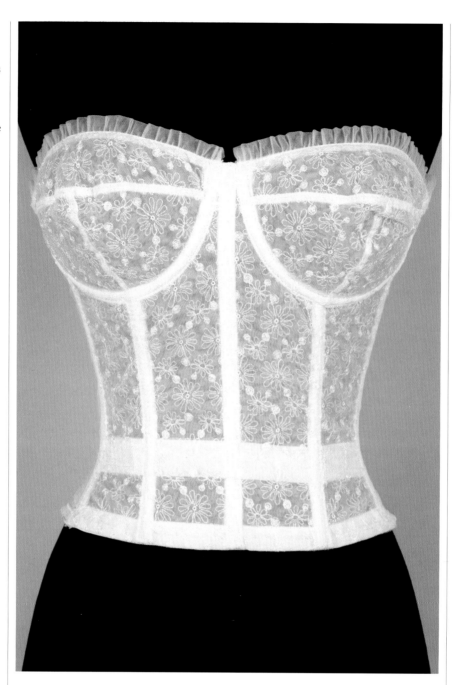

had honed their technical skills in the mass production of uniforms, and this led to significant developments in the creation of mass-market, ready-to-wear clothing. The WPB contributed by sponsoring a nationwide survey of women's measurements to create guidelines for standardized sizing—another boost for the burgeoning American clothing industry.[90]

Returning to Normality

The war and its aftermath had also changed Augusta. Talking about her life with her friend Helen L. Laird, she described the moment when she was sitting in a Long Island Rail Road car on the way to work in February 1945. Reading about the Yalta Conference Agreement in the *New York Times*, Augusta "suddenly found herself jolted by the news that the Allies

FIG. 157
Scalloped edges and long peplums were popular post-war details, as seen in this wool gabardine suit dress with a jacket, by Louise Barnes Gallagher, c.1950. THF 2104.24.63.

had agreed to the partitioning of Poland, and that Russia would be allowed to keep part of that ravaged country."[91] She revealed to Helen that "a tide of revulsion swept over her," and from then on, politics and concern for the defense of democratic countries ran hotly in her veins. This would transform her into what some would call a right-wing political "hawk" for the rest of her life.[92]

A doctor who had often written to Augusta from the Front wanted to marry her, but he couldn't convince her to accept his proposal. As for her profession, she confessed that she would have liked to become a teacher, but the dull educational training required to teach in public schools put her off. So Augusta stuck to teaching Sunday school and taking the girls who worked in her house under her wing. Through her letters, she also gave

much encouragement and guidance to her many nieces and nephews, and later her grandnieces and grandnephews too. In addition, Augusta strove to improve the quality of education in Marshfield, first as a member of the school board (a publicly elected office), and then working to upgrade the local library that her grandmother and the other members of the Ladies' Travel Class had initiated back in 1900 (see p.31). In 1948, Augusta became her father's personal secretary, a role she continued for 12 years until his death. As Augusta settled in to her new role in the family business and local community, life returned to normal for Hamilton, something he and his company had not enjoyed since the late 1930s.

Everyone was relieved when peacetime clothes began to shed the imposition of wartime restrictions. Hamilton must have welcomed the return of three-piece suits, trouser cuffs, additional pockets, and good quality wools and tweeds now available once more and suitable for cold Wisconsin winters. In 1950, he ordered the wool windowpane check suit opposite from the American branch of the highly regarded British bespoke tailoring firm, Bernard Weatherill, Inc., of Fifth Avenue, New York (fig. 158).[93] The following year he ordered more suits from this tailor, including a three-piece taupe wool suit (as seen in fig. 238) and two-piece suits in modern colors—light blue and light gray. It is not certain whether these suits were made-to-measure or entirely bespoke. Although made by a British firm, the pale colors and boxy cut of these latter suits give them an American look.

It was also in about 1950 that Catherine purchased a new brown wool gabardine dress with a jacket that was much longer than would have been allowed during the war years (fig. 157). The label on this suit dress reveals that it was the work of New York designer Louise Barnes Gallagher (1892–1972), who retired in 1949 (although her clothes were still sold under her name for a few years after that).[94] The long peplum of the jacket is similar to one seen on a suit dress attributed to Balenciaga from around 1947, suggesting that this suit may have been influenced by his designs, or that of other Parisian couturiers.[95]

The 1950s brought great prosperity to the family firm. For the rest of Hamilton's lifetime, the Roddis Lumber & Veneer Company, which was renamed the Roddis Plywood Corporation in 1948, continued to expand and increase its sales. During this decade, the family's place as economic and social leaders in Marshfield was further consolidated, along with their wealth.[96] Leading architects continued to seek out the reputable Roddis doors and paneling, and in 1951 Roddis products were even used in the redecoration of President Truman's dressing room.[97]

The era of austerity had passed; renewed prosperity allowed for new sights and new clothes. Just as the Roddis family had traveled to Europe for rest and rejuvenation after the difficult years of the Great Depression, not long after the end of World War II they returned to London and Paris once again, and also ventured further afield to South America and Africa.

FIG. 158, OPPOSITE
Windowpane check three-piece suit by Bernard Weatherill, New York, dated October 18, 1950. THF 2014.24.149.

CHAPTER EIGHT

Travel and Style
"Getting There is Half the Fun!"

In the late 1940s and the 1950s, the Roddis family had the time and the financial wherewithal to enjoy international travel on many of the most renowned ocean liners of the day. As a family of sophisticated travelers, they savored the restful environment, superb service, and exciting social life offered on board; the luxurious travel experience was as important as reaching their final destinations. For all transatlantic voyages, the Roddis family chose ships run by Cunard White Star Line, whose company motto was "Getting there is half the fun!"

Nearly every evening, the festive, elegant atmosphere of those ships required passengers to wear tuxedos* and long or tea-length dinner dresses* (a now-extinct term referring to evening dresses where the shoulders were covered and sometimes the arms as well). Dressing up formally was certainly part of the fun. A number of surviving family photographs taken during those voyages show the dresses worn by the Roddis women, and Hamilton's formal attire as well. No documentary evidence has been found to suggest that they shopped specifically for such trips, but packing for them would have required a great deal of careful planning. Life on board transatlantic crossings and cruises was akin to that of a five-star floating hotel where the inhabitants, by necessity, mixed far more fluidly than they might have on land; outfits needed to be organized in advance accordingly. Travel to warmer climates, such as Africa and the West Indies, also necessitated a different wardrobe. Yet for Augusta, it was

the opportunity to experience the transformational effect of wearing long, feminine gowns in exciting new environments that proved most exciting from a fashion perspective. Travel offered Augusta, her mother, and her sisters a break from the routine of normal life, and everyday dress.

The first major ocean trip after World War II was in May 1948 when Augusta, her parents, and her sister and brother-in-law, Mary and Gordon Connor, took a month-long Rotary Club cruise to Rio de Janeiro (for the Rotary Club International Convention) on a ship referred to as "The Darling of the Dutch".[1] Completed in 1938 as the flagship of the Holland–America Line, the S.S. *Nieuw Amsterdam* was one of the most remarkable and talked-about ships of the period, and is still regarded today by many ship enthusiasts as a particularly beautiful example of modern shipbuilding, both inside and out. Several leading modernist Dutch architects were enlisted to design the interiors, which included fine

Art Deco* touches.[2] According to the *Nieuw Amsterdam* cruise plan found in the Roddis house, the designers of the dramatic Grand Hall selected "tones of gray to enhance fully the glamorous effect of exquisitely gowned women and their escorts in evening dress."[3] A sweeping Art Deco-inspired staircase of ebony, bronze, and steel showcased the passengers making grand entrances into the Ritz-Carlton Cafe, a specialty restaurant managed by the famed, land-based hotelier (fig. 160).

Traveling to Rio aboard the Dutch national flagship was a rarefied experience. Due to the geographical location and time of year, travelers on the *Nieuw Amsterdam* had to adjust their formal attire accordingly. From family photographs, it is evident that Hamilton wore a white dinner jacket, the warm weather equivalent of the black tuxedo (fig. 161), while other passengers generally preferred the classic black version. This sartorial

FIG. 162
Menu for Assembly Dinner on the S.S. *Nieuw Amsterdam*, 1948. RFP, Courtesy of the Wisconsin Historical Society Archives Division.

finery sometimes clashed rather unfavorably with the party hats that were handed out, as illustrated here. A menu saved from this cruise depicts men in both color jackets (fig. 162).[4]

In the photograph on p.188, Augusta is wearing a full-length dress with cap sleeves, which she also wore at an evening wedding in Marshfield two years later (see pp.220–1). Additional photographs make it clear that during this cruise on the *Nieuw Amsterdam*, women were expected to wear long dinner dresses in the evenings. (As early as the 1920s, Emily Post had criticized women who wore ball dresses onboard ship rather than "semi-dinner dresses", thereby demonstrating "the worst possible taste."[5]) On the first and last nights, however, less formal attire was acceptable, since those evenings were intended for unpacking and packing. The number and variety of dresses required for evening and daywear meant that women traveling first class required many trunks and cases to contain all

FIG. 163
Catherine Roddis and her daughter Mary Roddis Connor in the Champlain Dining Room of the S.S. *Nieuw Amsterdam*, 1948. Catherine is wearing the dress opposite. RFPA.

of their clothes. Luckily, cases could be given to the liner company to hold while a passenger was traveling on land. As late as 1953, in preparation for a trip to Europe, Ellen Roddis Lempereur proudly reported that she and her husband "only [had] 4 large suitcases plus a box", although one additional formal was also being shipped to Paris.[6]

At another evening event on board the *Nieuw Amsterdam*, Catherine wisely removed her party hat before being photographed in the first class dining room (fig. 163). She is wearing the cream crêpe and silk dinner dress with an embroidered bodice and short sleeves above, the dress that she also wore to her fortieth wedding anniversary reception, given at the Roddis house that same year—1948 (fig. 164).[7] In a letter dated 1944, Catherine had mentioned what sounds very much like this dress as being her "three year old white" dress, suggesting she bought it in 1941.

FIG. 164
Crêpe and silk gauze evening dress, with a bodice of machine-embroidered silk gauze over couched cotton cording in a floral-inspired curlicue pattern, *c.*1941.
THF 2014.24.77.

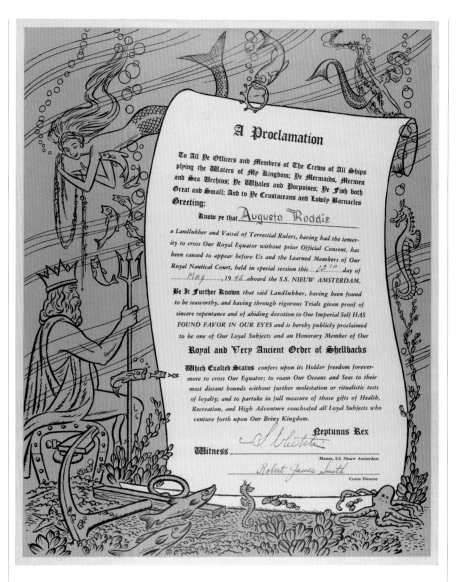

Catherine purchased dresses that were often simple and classic in design so that they didn't appear particularly dated, even after they had been worn for several years. During their engagement, she reminded Hamilton that she was not one to "splurge" on material goods (see p.92). Even in later years when her financial situation allowed far greater expenditure, she remained frugal.

Life on board the *Nieuw Amsterdam* was exciting for the 32-year-old Augusta, who attracted the ardent admiration of one of the officers, as revealed in his later letters to her. When the ship crossed the Equator, the customary "Crossing of the Line" ceremony broke the monotony of shipboard life, with a welcome interlude consisting of dressing up as well as high-spirited behavior, including "dunkings" of some passengers in the pool.[8] Presiding over the crowd was a large man decked out as King Neptune. Augusta joined the procession of passengers dressed as odd characters (she chose to appear in a white nun's habit). A proclamation signed by King Neptune confirming the day she crossed the equator was carefully saved (fig. 165). This tradition of marking the Equatorial crossing with festivities lasted well into the 1950s;[9] further notices from Neptune to Hamilton and Catherine on their trip to South Africa in 1954 also survive.[10]

Other activities were similar to those Hamilton and Catherine had experienced when they had traveled by ship to the Holy Land two decades earlier, in 1928, but now on a much grander scale. These forms of entertainment included "movies ... amateur and professional shows ... [a] costume party, the Captain's carnival dinner, as well as church services" and more.[11] Family movies show clips of Augusta on deck, looking well-dressed in a poolside ensemble, consisting of bandeau top and what appears to be matching shorts with an open jacket, topped off with a peaked cap to shield her face from the bright sun. This outfit does not remain in the Roddis Collection, unlike two of her bathing suits by Jantzen and Catalina, important Californian manufacturers that promoted

FIG. 166
Printed cotton bathing suit by Catalina. Labels: "Catalina, a California creator"; "Styled for The Stars of Hollywood, Los Angeles, Calif.", *c.*1948. THF 2014.24.9.

their links to Hollywood (fig. 166).[12] By the early 1940s, fashion magazines encouraged women to have a varied wardrobe of swimsuits to suit different occasions.[13] The condition of these two swimsuits is good, suggesting that Augusta may have saved them for "best", perhaps for lounging beside the pools onboard luxury liners. The Roddis Collection includes Augusta's Polaroid sunglasses, as seen in the still life on p.186.

Perspective through Travel

Augusta had enjoyed visiting Europe back in 1938, so in 1949 she joined a group of young women on an organized trip aboard the M.S. *Batory*, a Polish ocean liner that was far less glamorous than the *Nieuw Amsterdam*. A typewritten sheet entitled "What to Bring", which was found with other travel documents, appears to have been the advice of this trip's chaperone.[14] "Post-war travelers do not seem to be at all dressy," was one of her observations, and "Slacks are rarely worn abroad." Hats and gloves were still important accessories in urban America, so the question of how many to bring while traveling was addressed: "HATS—Take only one, if any, as you'll be sure to buy at least one hat in Paris. We travel bareheaded most of the time. The girls did not even bring one [on our trip] last year." The trip leader continued to recommend "only one pair" of gloves since she knew "where to get good ones at wholesale [prices] in Paris" and intended to stock up. This sheet of what appears to be sound advice suggests growing informality, even internationally, in the late 1940s, while making it clear that middle-class young American women were still keen to shop for hats and gloves when they found themselves in Paris. A letter from Catherine to her daughter while on this trip reveals that Augusta had bought a new hat before her departure, and had taken care to pack the right clothes.[15]

The comment about slacks being "rarely worn abroad" hints that by 1948 this previously considered masculine garment had become more common for women in the United States than in Europe. In both America and Great Britain, women had taken to wearing trousers during World War II, and photographs of trouser-wearing movie stars like Katharine Hepburn and Marlene Dietrich were common even before the war, but it appears that this new fashion took greater hold in America.[16] Based on photographs and family recollection, by the 1950s Augusta's sisters all wore slacks for sport and leisure activities, but the conservative Augusta was never known to wear them, except perhaps for sports at college, and she only wore shorts at poolside, as mentioned above. She and her mother Catherine seemed more comfortable wearing dresses and skirts.

When Augusta traveled to Europe that year, her observations extended far beyond whether Europeans were wearing trousers or hats. She was delighted by visits to historic landmarks, but what she discovered in London also involved clothing—and the effects of war. When Augusta first arrived at her London hotel during that 1949 trip, she met a British relative. Her curious cousin inquired about the voyage, and Augusta mentioned the poor standard of food onboard ship. The lady's immediate response was: "All I'd want to know—was there enough?" Coming from a woman she viewed as being in the same economic and social bracket as herself, Augusta was shocked at this concern regarding a lack of food.

"Practically no one looks well fed in England today and nearly everyone is incredibly shabby."

AUGUSTA RODDIS

Having already walked through parts of the city, Augusta "felt really jolted" by how Britain's need to ration food as well as clothing, in addition to enforcing heavy purchase taxes, had taken a huge and visible toll on the population compared to her memory of them from her last visit only a decade before.[17] "It was like going to a play and seeing exactly the same setting," she wrote, "but with a new cast of characters and a new play."[18] Although she may have been exaggerating to make a point during a talk she gave later that year about her trip, Augusta claimed that: "Practically no one looks well fed in England today and nearly everyone is incredibly shabby."[19] In the written script for that talk, Augusta describes the moment when she gave her relative a gift of chocolate and cigarettes; she was stunned by the Englishwoman's reaction of thrill and gratitude, and of her cousin's awe as she observed the American suits and blouses spread out on the hotel bed:

> Everything I wore was just too marvelous to her. My nylon blouses were just out of this world, my suit was so pretty, and so on. It really made me feel guilty to think that the things I was able to take for granted were such a source of wonder and admiration to her. And it brought home to me rather forcibly that just as it seems like fairyland to an American to go to Europe and see all the wonderful old castles, and cathedrals and historical sites, it is just like fairyland to Europeans, and more particularly the British, to see a well-dressed, well-fed American who had been eating all he wants and can buy anything he wants in the way of clothes.[20]

The Protestant ethic, long practiced in the Roddis family, encouraged everyone to be thankful for everything they had, in both the material world and also their personal life. Augusta's trip to London reinforced her gratefulness. After that trip, even her nylon blouses took on new meaning and became worthy of appreciation, and she determined that she would bring one for her cousin when she returned to Britain the following year.

Life and Dress on Cunard White Star Line Ships

Augusta could not face the return trip on the bargain-price ship selected by the tour organizers, so at the last minute she bought a first class ticket on the Cunard White Star Line's R.M.S. *Queen Mary*, and cabled the news home to her parents.[21]

The *Queen Mary* and her sister ship the R.M.S. *Queen Elizabeth* were the world's fastest and largest ocean liners respectively in the late 1940s.[22] From this period through the 1950s, ocean travel enjoyed its peak in terms of the size, speed, and amenities offered by the luxury liners.[23] Many Cunard ships were populated with actresses, celebrities, and even royalty, providing ample opportunity for people-watching.[24] Augusta once described the way elegant women would sweep into the first class dining rooms, making a dramatic entrance that reminded her of actresses appearing in films in this manner.[25]

On board, women traveling first class changed their clothes several times a day. For luncheon at one o'clock, women would don chic day dresses. The restaurant manager would then take on the challenge of seating single women with a suitable unattached gentleman. This seems to have been the case when Augusta, while traveling alone, was photographed with an Englishman as they were lunching on the *Queen Mary* in September 1949 (fig. 167).

In this photograph below, Augusta, seated with her luncheon partner, is wearing a distinctive rayon* and cotton dress by Samuel Kass. This American designer, although popular in the mid-1940s, has been almost forgotten today (fig. 168 and see p.206) Augusta's dress is the same model designed by Kass for an advertisement to promote a new Venezuelan

FIG. 168, OPPOSITE
Printed day dress by Samuel Kass, New York, 1945. The cotton-rayon fabric of this dress was made by the Onondaga Silk Company, known for collaborating with artists to create textile designs. THF 2014.24.59.

FIG. 167
Augusta Roddis with Mr. Desmond Tuck of London, England, in the first class dining room of the R.M.S. *Queen Mary*, September 1949. RFPA.

Photographed on board
R.M.S. "QUEEN MARY."

FIG. 169
Advertisements
from Cunard White
Star Line, 1950s.
JBC.

perfume, called *Tuya* ("For You Alone" in Spanish; see fig. 175).[26] These words, in both languages, are included as part of the printed fabric design, which was designed and produced by the prestigious Onondaga Silk Company.[27] This type of sportswear dress began in California in the early 1930s, and was characterized by exuberant and playful, almost child-like, fabric design. The design seen here closely resembles the work of Marcel Vertes (1895–1961), a Hungarian–French artist known for his graphic art, and for his illustrations to advertise perfumes by Elsa Schiaparelli (1890–1973).[28] In addition to using distinctive printed fabrics, Kass was known for his adept use of tucks and folds, such as the complex cut and the elaborate pleating seen on the sleeves of this dress. A label inside the dress reads: "Weathered Misses Shop", a division of Martha Weathered, an exclusive dress store on Michigan Avenue in Chicago where Augusta must have purchased it (see p.240).

Augusta remembered these trips on the great ocean liners with fondness, and her sister Mary also enjoyed them tremendously: Cunard's motto seems to have rung true for both of them (fig. 169). Judging by a 9-page letter from Mary Roddis Connor to Augusta about her recent trip to Europe in 1950, that was almost entirely focused on the sea passage, including who she socialized with on the S.S. *Caronia* (listing the guests at each nightly cocktail party), and sometimes what she wore for dancing during the "very gay" nights, it seems that "getting there" and back was certainly the highlight of her trip.[29]

The *Caronia*, dubbed the "Green Goddess" due to her distinctive green and white exterior, was a splendid moderate-sized, ultra-luxury ship, purpose-built for year-round cruising, with a hand-picked Cunard staff that provided the highest level of service.[30] Hamilton and Catherine had traveled on the *Caronia* only a few months earlier.[31] Other loyal passengers tended to be from Park or Fifth Avenue in New York, or enclaves such as Greenwich, Connecticut, so the atmosphere on board was rather like that of an exclusive country club,[32] and Mary observed "multitudinous furs".[33] Besides the society on board, Mary raved about the crew's attention to detail: "Service is hard to beat the English on! Gordie's steward hung out his dinner clothes and brushed them as a matter of course each evening, had his patents and hose all ready, etc.—over and above the fine service everywhere else along the line."[34] Even wealthy Americans seldom had valets and maids in attendance to help them dress, so to be treated with such consideration was like stepping back into a bygone era—quite different from the down-to-earth customs back in Midwest America. As early as 1929, this particular part of the experience was promoted in a Cunard advertising leaflet entitled "The New Art of Going Abroad", which enthusiastically claimed that the transatlantic voyage would be "a week that will leave you feeling like a duchess or a millionaire, or a favorite of the gods...."[35]

Passengers from all backgrounds would develop their own routines on board, choosing from the many activities on offer. A typical morning might consist of a promenade on deck after breakfast, a game of ping-pong, and perhaps enjoying a good read while sitting on a reserved deck chair sipping bouillon served at 11 o'clock in the morning. Hamilton and Augusta enjoyed playing shuffleboard, as can be seen from a photograph taken on an earlier trip (fig. 170). Luncheon and teatime filled much of the

FIG. 170
Augusta Roddis with Hamilton Roddis on the S.S. *Manhattan* playing shuffleboard, a game they also played on Cunard ocean liners a decade later. August 1938. RFPA.

FIG. 171

From left: Henry Stewart Jones, Sara Roddis Jones, Catherine and Hamilton Roddis, on the R.M.S. *Queen Elizabeth*, May 1950. RFPA.

Photographed on board.
RMS. QUEEN ELIZABETH

afternoon, along with a choice of a movie, lecture, or concert. Dinner was considered the highlight of the day.

By the 1950s and 1960s, men continued to wear tuxedos on these ocean liners, while women often wore tea-length or cocktail dresses*, considerably shorter than the full-length dresses worn on the *Nieuw Amsterdam* in the late 1940s. A brochure from a Swedish ship, saved by Catherine and Augusta in the 1960s, explained exactly what to expect: "Ladies Apparel; Most evenings on board will find you in semi-formal dress; in dinner or cocktail dresses, attractive and suitable for dancing—short evening gowns adapt themselves well to shipboard wear and take little space for packing."[36] When Catherine, Hamilton, their daughter Sara Roddis Jones and her husband Henry Stewart Jones traveled first class on the *Queen Elizabeth* in 1950, Catherine wore gold-strapped evening sandals with the tea-length dress opposite (fig. 172). The designer of this dress was David Gottlieb, known as Gothé—another nearly forgotten designer rediscovered through the Roddis Collection. He enjoyed such a high profile at that time that he created two inaugural gowns, as well as other dresses, for First Lady Eleanor Roosevelt (see p.208). Purchased around 1948, this dress is a style consisting of a fitted bodice and the new full skirt that first began to appear in American fashion in 1946, but is most often associated with the influential Paris designer Christian Dior (see p.180). One of its distinctive features is the lace overdress. According to a popular American book of etiquette in 1941, lace was "a great boon to a traveler": it holds its shape in any climate, requires little or no pressing, and assures the wearer of "never-failing

FIG. 172, OPPOSITE

Dress with lace overdress by Gothé, *c.*1948. The overdress is made of double-layered machine-made synthetic lace underlined with net. The skirt is stiffened with a cotton crinoline to create volume. THF 2014.24.60.

elegance". Consequently, this book argued that a woman should never travel without a lace dress—"What a comfort and convenience is a lace gown!"[37] Worn on this transatlantic voyage as well as to a family wedding in 1958, Catherine's lace dress appears to have been one of her favorites. When wearing it to a wedding where a head covering was appropriate, she completed her ensemble with a matching Alice band* of pleated silk organza with a veil (see p.303).[38]

> "I think it was after the transatlantic ships stopped running in the late Seventies that everything started to go downhill."
>
> IRIS APFEL, *VOGUE*, 2012

End of an Era

By the mid-1950s, when planes could make the flight from New York to London nonstop in about 10 hours, air travel threatened the exclusive world of the ocean liner. Yet Hamilton and Catherine remained loyal to this leisurely and comfortable means of overseas travel, as did many people in their social circle. By the mid-1960s, however, the jet airplane had triumphed over the transatlantic liner. The large ocean boats that could not make the transition to holiday cruise ships were sold off, and most ended their days in the scrapyard.

The demise of the ocean liner had a profound effect on fashion, a fact noted by the unique nonagenarian fashion icon and businesswoman Iris Apfel (b.1921). In a 2012 *Vogue* article, she wrote about what she saw as the decline of American fashion: "I think it was after the transatlantic ships stopped running in the late Seventies that everything started to go downhill."[39] American women, including those in the Roddis family, no longer had this special venue where they might wear semi-formal eveningwear. Once they did not have to wear a different dress for nearly every evening on board, their need to purchase such a wide array of garments was reduced. Compared to twenty-first-century travelers, however, even on domestic and international planes, travel in the 1950s and 1960s continued to be associated with style and taste. A family film of this decade shows Augusta and her sister Ellen disembarking from the Roddis Company plane in Marshfield wearing trim suits and hats (see p.225).

Dressing for Travel to Warm Climates

Augusta always paid particular attention to the appropriateness of her wardrobe while traveling. A popular style in the early 1950s was the sundress; Augusta owned a particularly attractive example with spaghetti straps suitable for cruise and vacation wear. Along with a matching jacket, it was most likely purchased in the 1950s (fig. 173). In 1952, Augusta was invited to a friend's wedding in Jamaica. While on a stopover in Miami she bought the summery cotton strapless evening gown opposite, presumably for one of the evening events (fig. 174). This dress with a "Beautime" label was forwarded to her in Jamaica. Upon its arrival, much to her dismay, Augusta discovered that the store had failed to send the matching shawl, which she was depending on to cover her "bony shoulders", and she sent a letter to the store berating them for their omission.[40] The shawl was finally delivered to her in Marshfield, where she instructed her dressmaker to attach it to the front edges of the strapless bodice in order to create a swag at the back. This was yet another example of the long tradition in both the Roddis and Prindle families of cleverly adapting a dress.

> *"This is one summer when you escape the charms of the berry patch, the peas, the canning and freezing, with great glee, no doubt."*
>
> MARY RODDIS CONNOR

Other clothes worn by Augusta would have been suitable for Marshfield summers, as well as travel to warmer climates. One family film shows her wearing a tailored brown linen dress at Victoria Falls, Zambia, in 1954 (see p.299). While visiting an ostrich farm on this African trip, film footage shows Augusta wearing a sober suit and pillbox hat—even while riding an ostrich. Clearly, for the Roddis women, decorum counted in all circumstances.

Travel abroad was a form of escapism to Augusta, offering her a welcome break from life back in Marshfield and an opportunity to wear a broader range of clothes. During the hot summer of the late 1940s when she was traveling in Europe, Augusta's older sister Mary Roddis Connor wrote to her, wryly commenting: "This is one summer when you escape the charms of the berry patch, the peas, the canning and freezing, with great glee, no doubt."[41]

Travel also reminded Augusta of how lucky she was in many ways, as she experienced in post-war London in 1949. Her love of history, alongside her enjoyment of discovering other societies and meeting new people, all while taking in museums, theaters, and stores, was formative, perhaps even transformative. Travel also gave Augusta, and the Roddis family as a whole, the chance to widen their perspective on life. They would use their experiences abroad to gain a greater understanding and appreciation of their small Midwestern hometown of Marshfield—and the wider realm of America.

FIG. 174, OPPOSITE
Cotton organdy evening dress with green embroidery, by Beautime, 1952. Re-styled with a gathered shoulder swag by a seamstress using the matching shawl.
THF 2014.24.79.

REDISCOVERED DESIGNER
SAMUEL KASS

FIG. 175, LEFT
Advertisement for "Tuya" perfume from *Seventeen* Magazine, Nov 1945. Matching fabric gloves were a fashion trend in the 1940s. EMC.

FIG. 176, BELOW LEFT
Samuel Kass dress label from 1945. THF 2014.24.59.

FIG. 177, ABOVE
Samuel Kass, passport photo, 1924. U.S. Passport Service.

FIG. 178, OPPOSITE
Detail of printed rayon/cotton day dress by Samuel Kass, designed for "Tuya" perfume, with finely pleated and scalloped shoulder decoration, and self-ties stitched into side seams. THF 2014.24.59.

BORN: 1891, Varena, Poland/Lithuania.

DIED: 1987, New York City.

EARLY CAREER: Immigrated to the United States in 1911. His mother tongue was Polish. Started his fashion business in 1922 in New York City, working with his designer wife, Ruth Rubin. Became naturalized U.S. citizen in 1924. Commissioned in 1925 to create the inaugural gown of the first female governor of Texas, Miriam Amanda Wallace "Ma" Ferguson. Became a director of the prestigious Fashion Originators' Guild of America in 1938.[42] Began selling his designs nationwide by the late 1930s.

PEAK OF CAREER: Advertisements for Samuel Kass designs appeared in hundreds of newspapers across the country throughout the 1940s. His name was as well known as other top designers, including such luminaries as Jo Copeland (1899–1982), Nettie Rosenstein (1890–1980), Adele Simpson (1903–95), and Pauline Trigère (1912–2002).[43] Kass was among the earliest dress designers to work closely with Philip A. Vogelman, director of the Onondaga Silk Company, who created and produced fashionable textiles for couturiers, designers, and dress manufacturers.[44]

CLAIM TO FAME: In 1945, Kass contacted Bess Myerson, then Miss New York, with an offer to create a complete wardrobe for her entry into the Miss America Pageant that year. Myerson would later write: "I was introduced to this distinguished, dark-haired man ... impeccably dressed ... surrounded by many models and seamstresses who were so wonderful and welcoming to us. My heart was pounding; I thought I was meeting royalty.... God bless that wonderful Mr. Kass."[45]

ALSO NOTABLE FOR: In 1946, a Wisconsin newspaper described a fashion show in which Kass embellished the glazed chintz of full skirts for his crêpe-topped evening gowns—an unusual combination of materials, and an expansive use of fabric that foreshadowed Christian Dior's radical New Look.[46] Hired leading designer Emmet Joyce (1900–72) to design for his company.[47]

BIBLIOGRAPHY: Susan Dworkin, *Miss America, 1945: Bess Myerson and the Year That Changed Our Lives* (Newmarket Press, 1998).

"He was the first person I ever met who really understood that even a pretty girl can't make do with a potato sack."

BETH MYERSON, MISS AMERICA, 1945

REDISCOVERED DESIGNER
DAVID E. GOTTLIEB, "GOTHÉ"

BORN: 1897, Warsaw, Poland.

DIED: 1966, New York City.

EARLY CAREER: David E. Gottlieb immigrated to the United States in 1909. He enlisted as a soldier in World War I. He began his career as an assistant in the New York fashion industry. When he established his own firm in 1934, his chief designer, Czech-born Irene Zerner (1906–89), worked closely with him and produced a number of designs that were patented under the company name in the early 1940s. Gottlieb and Zerner made semi-annual trips to Paris to experience each new season and returned brimming with ideas.

PEAK OF CAREER: In the 1940s and 1950s, the name Gothé became synonymous with elegant evening attire. Advertising campaigns for Cadillac and Chrysler featured ladies wearing sumptuous Gothé gowns. The Gothé name appeared in hundreds of newspapers from Texas to Maine and Florida to California during this period.

CLAIM TO FAME: Dressed First Lady Eleanor Roosevelt for the presidential inaugurations of 1941 and 1945 (the latter ball canceled because of the war).[48] Mrs. Roosevelt also wore a Gothé gown to an event at the Mayflower Hotel in Washington in 1945.[49]

ALSO NOTABLE FOR: Patented a design for a retractable dog leash in 1940. Gothé designed for *Vogue* patterns and then for *Simplicity* patterns in the 1950s. Well traveled, and known as a raconteur, he married Irene Zerner in 1956. He was often enlisted as a judge for costumes worn to local historic celebrations in rural Pennsylvania where he owned a farm. His gowns were featured in the New York Couture Group shows at the New York World's Fair in 1964.

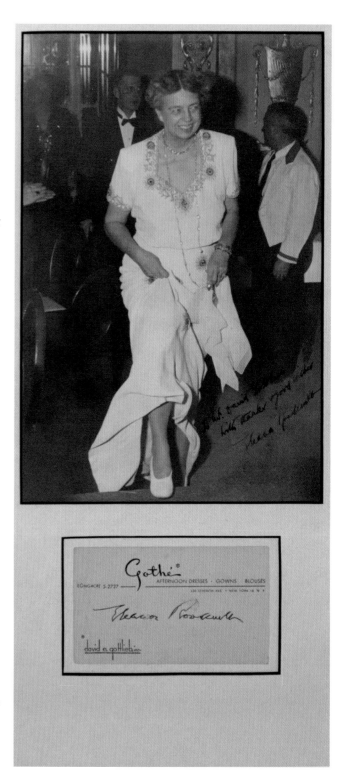

It Can Enrich Your Whole Life...

... when you take possession of your first Cadillac car. And we say this, not out of conjecture, but out of our own experience with many of the fine men and women who own and drive the "car of cars". For they tell us that their Cadillac adds so much to their pride and happiness . . . and to their pleasure and contentment . . . that they regard it as an indispensable part of their daily lives. And certainly, the motorist who discovers the joys of Cadillac ownership *this* year will find this to be *especially* true. For in beauty . . . in luxury . . . in performance . . . in economy . . . in every way that a motor car can contribute to its owner's personal happiness . . . this is the greatest Cadillac ever to travel the world's highways. We invite you to visit your dealer soon—to spend sixty minutes at the wheel—and to verify this for yourself. You will be most welcome at any time you find convenient. CADILLAC MOTOR CAR DIVISION • GENERAL MOTORS CORPORATION

FIG. 180, TOP LEFT
Gowns by Gothé featured in a Cadillac advertisement, *Saturday Evening Post*, 1957. JBC.

FIG. 181, ABOVE
David E. Gottlieb, *c*.1953. Collection of Elaine Greenstone.

FIG. 182, LEFT
Gothé New York dress label, *c*.1948. THF 2014.24.60.

FIG. 179, OPPOSITE
First Lady Eleanor Roosevelt wearing a Gothé dress of white velvet with beaded neckline ornamentation. Photo autographed to the designer, David E. Gottlieb, 1945. Collection of Elaine Greenstone.

SCORE

uS galS vOtS TRowIN
dis ShiNDig

dELpHiNE   HOneY
peGgY   ⱯLLen
JeANnE   dOtTy
        aUGuSTa

xMaS NitE, 1936

Our
SECOND
Formal
Brawl

Order of Dancing

A MERRY CHRISTMAS

CHAPTER NINE

What Shall We Wear in Marshfield?
Hometown Social Functions and Daily Life

After a glimpse at what the Roddis family wore while traveling, their attire for social occasions and for everyday wear in their hometown of Marshfield can now be examined. A number of surviving photographs, as well as family recollections, offer some insight into the formality of the clothes worn by Roddis family members to cocktail or dinner parties and weddings. Their style, not unlike those found in larger, more sophisticated urban environments, was marked by restraint, and fit with the accepted fashions of the day.[1] The Roddis family always sought to dress appropriately. Daily life involved everyday practical wear; their clothes reveal them to have been ready and willing to turn their attention to the task at hand, be it managing the household, picking raspberries, joining the bridge club, attending a women's club event, meeting with the school board, going to church, hosting a ladies' tea, heading to the golf course, or simply having a Sunday midday meal with family and friends.

Over the last century in this small town, there was an accepted level of formality in the clothing worn to social events. Chapter 1 detailed how even W.H. Roddis was a little bemused in 1902 to find that his new hometown was "becoming quite dressy", with more and more men attending the "Married Peoples dances" wearing swallowtail suits*. Despite the informality of the dance programs, with their use of rustic materials and amusing display of intentionally misspelled words (visible in the still life opposite), the two "Formal Brawl" Christmas Night dance parties of

FIG. 183, PAGE 210
Clockwise from top left: demitasse cup and saucer with spoon; Hamilton Roddis's card game score sheet with attached pencil, hand-drawn playing card; decorative holly; Christmas decoration, 1930s; Formal Brawl dance program, 1937; evening dress, c.1948; Christmas postcard; copy of a dance card in the Roddis archive, c.1936; Formal Brawl dance program, 1936.

1936 and 1937, discussed in Chapter 6, were undoubtedly formals—the American term used at that time for formal dances where young women would have worn full-length dresses ("formals"). By the 1950s, however, evening attire began to change, and long dresses became less dominant.

Cocktail and Dinner Parties

A population shift to the suburbs, combined with the climate of post-war affluence, resulted in the cocktail party developing into an American institution in the 1950s. Hamilton and his wife and daughter Augusta were nearly teetotalers, possibly due to Catherine's Methodist upbringing (see p.106), but they attended some of these early evening parties hosted by friends. As a hostess in later years, Augusta certainly served wine and non-alcoholic beverages at social gatherings of both men and women.[2]

> *"The real masterpieces of American design are the cocktail dresses, the cocktail being the symbol par excellence of the American way of life."*
>
> CHRISTIAN DIOR, 1957

The 1950s cocktail party was a catalyst for the development of a particular niche in the American fashion industry: the cocktail dress*. Christian Dior, who reputedly first coined this term, observed in his autobiography of 1957: "The real masterpieces of American design are the cocktail dresses, the cocktail being the symbol par excellence of the American way of life."[3] Cocktail dresses generally reached just below the knee during the 1950s, and although some had thin shoulder straps, the majority had short, three-quarter-length, or long sleeves. They were in much demand with middle- and upper-class American women.

Two of Augusta's sisters, Sara and Pickie, lived in Marshfield for most of the 1950s, at the height of the cocktail party's popularity. Pickie's daughter Ann Rauff recalls that her parents often attended cocktail parties: "Some of my parents' neighbors were quite cosmopolitan for a small town like Marshfield." Particularly memorable was a "quite elegant" neighbor, Bess Miller, who wore a chic cocktail dress by leading American designer and retailer Hattie Carnegie (1880–1956).[4]

The Roddis Collection includes the silk chiffon and cotton lace cocktail dress opposite, owned by Augusta and dating from about 1948 (fig. 184). The label reveals that it was "Made Exclusively for Frances Brewster", a retailer who opened a store in Lake Placid in 1920 and later specialized in resort-style fashions in Palm Beach, Florida.[5] The Roddis women frequented this store while on vacation, and during this period Augusta probably wore it while on holiday, as well as to cocktail parties in Marshfield.

FIG. 184, OPPOSITE
Silk chiffon and cotton lace cocktail dress, made exclusively for Frances Brewster, c.1948.
THF 2014.24.23.

FIG. 185
Detail of dress
on the previous
page, *c.*1948.
The gathered hip
decoration draws
attention to the
waist and hips.
THF 2014.24.23.

Given her love of lace, which she shared with her mother and grandmother, as well as her fondness for this particular shade of blue, this dress perfectly suited Augusta's taste.

A noteworthy detail seen on this cocktail dress is the draped chiffon swag on the left front, near the waist. Sometimes referred to in the post-World War II fashion world by the unfortunate moniker "rape drape", cocktail dress features such as these were considered most suitable for the sophisticated, experienced woman in her thirties and over. Here the draped effect is used decoratively in the context of a structured, fitted dress. This swag may have been inspired by the popular dress designs of Dorothy O'Hara (1911–63) of Los Angeles, who was well known in Hollywood and throughout California, or else it may have been influenced by images of similar designs worn by Hollywood stars in film magazines.

FIG. 186
Silk floral and velvet
ribbon afternoon or
cocktail hat, c.1953.
THF 2014.24.115.

A hat and a pair of gloves were integral components of every cocktail ensemble at that time. Augusta may have worn this lace dress with one of her blue floral hats (fig. 186) and a pair of silk embroidered gloves, one of many that she purchased in Paris in 1949 (see p.252).[6] There were rules, not always adhered to, governing semi-formal cocktail party attire in mid-twentieth-century America. For example, gloves were worn by female guests but not by the hostess; the hostess never wore a hat inside her own home, regardless of the formality of the occasion; however, female guests were expected to travel to a party wearing a cocktail hat, often with a veil. (Veils were widely popular in the 1940s, and their use continued well into the next decade—see pp.302–4 for examples of hats with and without veils.) Once indoors, female guests usually removed their headgear, although this convention was not universally followed—one successful book of etiquette from the mid-1950s does not mention it, but rather refers to women retaining their hats. Evidently custom varied.[7]

Perhaps the most luxurious item of clothing found in the attic is a black silk velvet, ermine-trimmed evening coat with hood (fig. 187). Catherine handed this coat down to her third daughter, Pickie, who is known to have worn it to cocktail and dinner parties in Marshfield in the early 1950s. It dates from the late 1930s, possibly purchased in Europe during her mother's trip there in 1938.[8] (American women frequently removed garment labels prior to disembarking in order to avoid the severe customs duties on what were considered luxury purchases made abroad.) Ann Rauff still recalls what a stunning impression her mother made in this coat when she set off to the home of a neighbor—looking as if she could be dressed to attend a reception in Paris.[9] Among certain social classes of American women, like those in the Roddis family, overdressing was to be avoided at all cost, so it is significant that Pickie could arrive in such a glamorous coat without appearing out of place, even in this small town.[10]

Formal Socializing and Wedding Clothes

In the Roddis household, ladies' afternoon teas were frequently given for organizations such as women's club events, or to present visiting female relatives. Mixed gatherings were also held in the evenings. Whatever the time of day, Roddis parties involved carefully pressed, ornately embroidered tablecloths, laden with platters of cakes, cookies, or savory foods, and delicate china tea or coffee cups. Silver teapots were set out, and a silver samovar coffee urn was always placed on the dining table.

Augusta and her parents were also invited to the homes of other Marshfield residents who entertained in a similarly formal manner. One such occasion, captured in photographs in 1950, is the evening wedding reception of Barbara Quirt, daughter of Mr. Howard Quirt, the publisher and editor of the *Marshfield News–Herald*.[11] (Weddings after 6 pm, which required guests to wear evening dress, were apparently considered "correct and fashionable" in the South, West, and Midwest of America, although a popular book of etiquette, published in 1941, comments snootily that they were not the custom of "Smart New York people".[12]) A photo taken at the Quirts' home shows Hamilton wearing a tuxedo*, while the father of the bride wears a plain dark suit (fig. 189). Both of these men's suits constituted appropriate dress for a wedding after 6 pm in the early 1950s. Catherine appears in a navy silk crêpe dress that probably dates from the late 1940s, along with a floral corsage and her favorite cameo pinned at the neck. Distinctive components of this dress include the Carrickmacross lace* seen on the yoke* and sleeves, and the 29 self-covered buttons and cloth loops at the center front closure (fig. 188).

In another photo taken at the same wedding reception (fig. 190), Catherine sits at the head of a table to serve coffee to the guests, just as she or one of her daughters would have done at her own parties. (Catherine

FIG. 187, OPPOSITE
Ermine-trimmed silk velvet evening coat with hood, *c.*1939. This coat belonged to Catherine Roddis, and then to her daughter "Pickie", who wore it to local dinner parties in the early 1950s. THF 2014.24.18.

FIG. 189
Wedding reception
held in the home of
Mr. and Mrs. Howard
Quirt of Marshfield,
1950. (Hamilton
Roddis, center,
wears a tuxedo, and
Catherine Roddis,
to his right, wears
the dress opposite).
RFPA.

was one of four friends who were asked by the bride's mother to assist her as hostess, a more intimate approach than hiring outsiders to undertake such tasks.[13]) This photo also shows Augusta wearing a silk satin dinner dress*, the same one she was wearing in a photo taken on their cruise to Rio de Janeiro in 1948 (see p.188), which probably dates from that year (fig. 191). With its fitted bodice and flared skirt panels, this dress is simple and restrained yet flattering. (For a 1950s gown of similar coloring and cut, see p.299.) Augusta is also seen wearing elbow-length white kidskin gloves, probably one of her favorite pairs by Dior. As was the convention at that time, Augusta peeled back the hands of these gloves in order to sample the buffet food. For a seated dinner, however, she would have removed them, as may be seen in the photo of her wearing the same dress taken while dining on the S.S. *Nieuw Amsterdam*.[14]

These modest dresses worn by Augusta and Catherine were chosen based on a clear awareness of the prevailing views on dress codes, or perhaps simply thanks to their understanding of what was appropriate. A contemporary book of etiquette by Frances Benton, published in 1956, considered women's full-length evening clothes to be of "two kinds". The first were dinner dresses, which covered the shoulders with cap or long sleeves and were considered appropriate when the invitation specified black tie.[15] (Black tie meant that men would be expected to wear tuxedos or, sometimes, dark business suits with white shirts, although the latter was not always considered "correct".) The second variety were evening dresses, which were advocated when the invitation specified white tie* or decorations*, and in that case, bareness and rich fabrics and colors were fully acceptable.[16]

Photos of Roddis family weddings demonstrate the persisting tradition of wearing full-length or tea-length dresses on such occasions.

FIG. 188, OPPOSITE
Silk crêpe evening
dress or "dinner
dress" with
Carrickmacross
lace, which belonged
to Catherine, c.1948.
THF 2014.24.75.

Catherine wore her Gothé lace tea-length dress to a niece's wedding in 1958, while at the same wedding Augusta wore a full-length yellow gown, which she once suggested had been made by her mother (see p.299).[17] To attend another family wedding in the early 1960s, Catherine chose a celadon green silk chiffon gown with a lace bodice (see p.300), while Augusta wore the same spotted pink gown mentioned above. In 1974, Augusta wore a long, turquoise, permanently pleated gown with a high ruffled collar to the wedding of her nephew Douglas Lempereur to Janice Richardson; this dress was a favorite for years to come, and was worn for other important events in the mid-1980s (see p.276).[18]

What to Wear to Church, at Work, and at Home

In contrast to the formal dresses discussed above, the Roddis Collection also contains a wide range of clothes worn on a daily basis. The everyday dresses worn by Augusta and Catherine are typical of their era, and they may be viewed in the context of the prevailing opinions that the so-called Dress Doctors espoused from the early 1920s into the 1960s (see p.156).

FIG. 190
A second photo of the wedding reception held in the Quirt home, Marshfield, 1950. Catherine Roddis assists with serving while Augusta, wearing the dress opposite, takes refreshments. RFPA.

FIG. 191, OPPOSITE
Silk satin evening gown, c.1948.
THF 2014.24.70.

These advisors stressed how important it was to dress in a manner suitable for the individual, as well as the given occasion. "In the first place, your clothes should be suitable," stated one such book of etiquette. "This means, they should flatter *you* regardless of whether they are copies fresh from new Paris collections, or whether they are five years old...."[19]

What to wear to church was one of the many issues discussed in the etiquette guides of the time. As one home economist observed, church was "not the place for a style display". Instead, a simple and unrevealing dress or suit that did not distract others—or preoccupy the wearer—was all that was required, and for most Protestant and Catholic churches, a hat too.[20] An advertisement for the Roddis Company in *Newsweek* features a woman dressed in the appropriate fashion for church (fig. 194).[21]

FIG. 192
Silk shantung day dress, made expressly for Frances Brewster, *c.*1956. THF 2014.24.30.

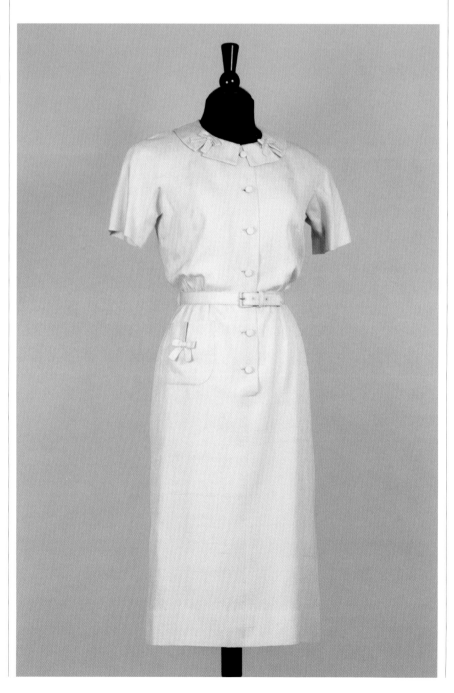

Seating made of Roddis Timblend
helps this new church get started

These pews built of Roddis' man-made board, Timblend, provide beauty, strength and durability — and saved the church $3,125.00!

Like so many today, this parish started out with a *temporary* church. Later when funds permit, this structure will be converted to other uses and a permanent church will be erected.

One early problem was to obtain pews for this temporary church that would be attractive and serviceable . . . yet relatively inexpensive.

Cathedral Craftsmen of Waukesha, Wisconsin, had the answer. They manufactured these pews of Timblend, Roddis' unique man-made board. Timblend has all the properties they were looking for . . . strength, durability, warp-resistance and paintability.

Most important, total cost was considerably lower than could be attained with lumber or plywood. *$3 per lineal foot lower, as a matter of fact!*

Economical Timblend is versatile, too. It has proved itself in everything from book shelves to boat decks . . . from school desks and fine furniture to roof sheathing and walls. It may be of value in your product or process. To find out how, read the complete Timblend story. Write: Roddis Plywood Corporation, Marshfield, Wisconsin.

Roddis does such wonderful new things with wood.

Roddis

Craftwall wood paneling • Custom panelings • Wood Doors • Plywoods • Tigaclad-protected genuine woods

Augusta might have worn the pink shantung, short-sleeved day dress opposite to St. Alban's Episcopal Church in the mid-1950s (fig. 192). She may well have accessorized this with the floral embroidered handbag (purchased in Rio de Janeiro in 1948), and matching floral hat above, by Therese Ahrens (fig. 193).[22] Ahrens was a milliner known for her light, delicate creations, decorated with flowers, butterflies, leaves, and jewels; these were sometimes called "hatlets" or "whimsies" and were designed for those women who did not want to cover their expensively coiffed hair.[23] (By the mid- to late 1960s, bouffant hairstyles, along with the sleeker, more minimal fashions, finally ended the reign of hats for women.[24])

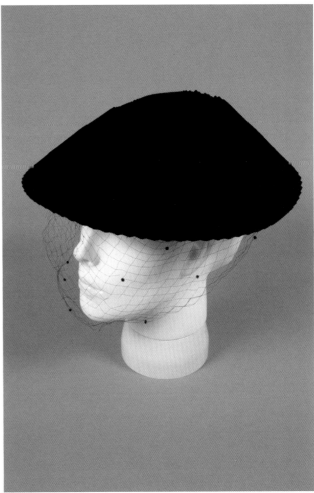

FIG. 195, OPPOSITE
Black and white wool
hounds-tooth suit,
Gunther Jaeckal,
New York, c.1954.
THF 2014.24.91.
"A good wool or
tweed suit is the
backbone of most
women's wardrobes.
A suit is expensive, so
buy fairly classic ones
that are perennially
correct." Frances
Benton's *Complete
Etiquette*, 1956.

Practical and well-cut suits were another mainstay of daily wear for Catherine, and for Augusta and her sisters. As her father's private secretary, Augusta would have often worn suits to work. Likewise, most American women would have chosen to wear them to the office and to meetings, to ladies' teas, church, and bridge club sessions, and to travel, and go shopping as well. A 1936 issue of *Vogue* (saved in the Roddis attic) identified this trend more than a decade earlier: "Clinging or no, you'll spend half your waking hours in a suit. Perhaps a tailored one, but never so relentlessly mannish as to confuse you with your brother...."[25]

Examples of Roddis suits with clearly defined feminine lines include the black and white wool hounds-tooth suit opposite, c.1954 (fig. 195). Augusta wore this suit at a family gathering, and when disembarking from the Roddis Company private plane at about the same time. The label identifies it as being from Gunther Jaeckal, an exclusive woman's dress and fur shop in New York.[26] The nipped-in waist and full skirt reflect the influence of post-war styles, including Dior's New Look.

Another practical but feminine ensemble is the brown and white hounds-tooth pattern suit with white linen removable (but attached) collar above, which was purchased at Saks Fifth Avenue in about 1952 (fig. 196). A more masculine suit, most likely worn by Catherine and dating from the same

FIG. 196, ABOVE LEFT
Brown and white
hounds-tooth pattern
suit with white linen
removable, attached
over-collar, Saks
Fifth Avenue, c.1952.
THF 2104.24.93.

FIG. 197, ABOVE
Fur felt hat with
pleated moiré
silk ribbon and
short veil, Bonwit
Teller, c.1950.
THF 2014.24.124.

year, is the wool gabardine suit above by designer Anthony Blotta (1888–1971) (fig. 198).[27] This suit's clean lines and defined shoulders epitomized the style popularized in the 1940s, and promoted by such renowned Hollywood designers as Adrian and Irene. Appearing in many films, this style became a "war horse" of the sophisticated woman's wardrobe following World War II.

The Roddis Collection also includes a number of typical cotton dresses that would have been worn around the house or while running errands in town. American home economics teachers and clothing advisors instructed women to wear attractive but practical housedresses. They did not approve of women who were "frumps in the privacy of their own homes."[28] It was suggested that housedresses should be "suitable for morning wear at home. Usually of gaily printed, washable cotton fabric

... smartly made and trimmed."[29] Catherine and her daughter Augusta wore just this sort of dress on a daily basis. A cotton floral day dress of Catherine's, which dates from *c.*1952, bears a Frances Brewster label, along with another label for the internationally renowned Liberty of London fabric—a favorite of the Roddis women (see p.298). There are several of Augusta's everyday dresses in the Roddis Collection, including an Abercrombie and Fitch cotton floral print dress, *c.*1960 (fig. 200), as well as a sleeveless floral print dress that may be slightly earlier in date (fig. 201). Another example is the blue floral print cotton dress below (fig. 199), which was made expressly for Frances Brewster, *c.*1957. The sophisticated trim of grosgrain ribbon makes it dressier than the other examples, but it was still an everyday sort of dress. Cotton fabric was comfortable to wear and

FIG. 199
Detail of dress, with pearlized buttons and a flat grosgrain bow decoration, *c.*1957. RDC 47, JBC.

easy to wash, and the short sleeves and flared skirts of these housedresses allowed ease of movement, while the floral prints were cheerful and feminine. The photo of Augusta in her living room on p.11 shows her in one such floral dress worn with a cardigan; this was her typical appearance at home from the 1950s right through the 1980s.

Always in classic good taste, Catherine and Augusta's Marshfield attire was perfectly suited to every occasion, but never showy. Various social events in the town were remarkably formal, and the Roddis women dressed in a ladylike fashion accordingly. To dress well—simply and appropriately—was the key message stressed by American dress advisors; as their clothes show, this concept was thoroughly ingrained, and adhered to, in the Roddis household.

FIG. 200
A typical dress worn at home by Augusta Roddis, often with cardigans handmade in London, this cotton print day dress is by Abercrombie and Fitch, *c.*1960. THF 2104.24.21.

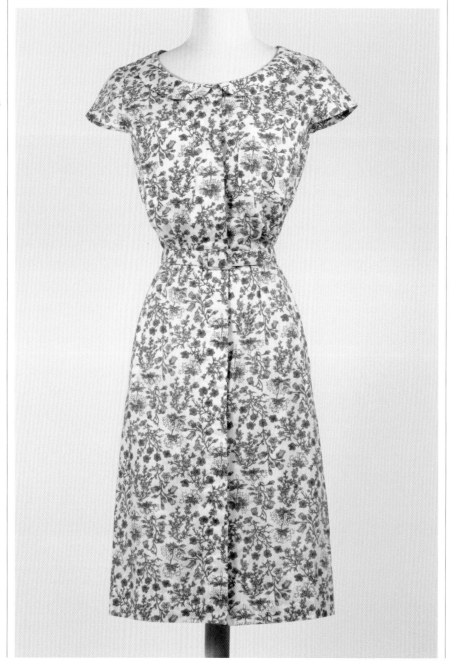

FIG. 201, OPPOSITE
Cotton day dress, *c.*1958. RDC 55, JBC.

GLOVES

le gant topaze

DIRECTORY
SHOPPING PAD

CHAPTER TEN

Let's Go Shopping!
The Quest for Good Clothes

The fine workmanship and design associated with the clothes in the Roddis Collection demonstrate that the family members, while never big spenders, valued high-quality clothing. With the exception of early dresses undoubtedly made by seamstresses for Sara Roddis, a dress made for Augusta's sister Ellen Roddis Lempereur in Paris, and possibly the presentation gown made there for Jane Prindle Gammon in about 1880, none of the women's dresses in the Collection are custom-made. Instead, they are either ready-to-wear or homemade clothes. In addition to the clothing, letters written by Augusta, in particular, and some of her surviving shopping receipts, offer insights into her personal goals and priorities while shopping.

Clothing labels were introduced before the middle of the nineteenth century, and have remained a clear source of attribution in the long history of American retail. By following the trail of the labels found in the Roddis garments, it is possible to trace where family members shopped, and also rediscover several fashion salons from the 1950s that were well-known in their time but have now been nearly forgotten or neglected in American retail histories. Research into the ways in which these stores (and several department stores), whose labels are found on clothes in the Roddis Collection, treated their customers reveals a shopping experience from a bygone era. A study of the use of store labels versus designer labels, as seen on Roddis clothes, also sheds light on retail trends not widely discussed elsewhere in current fashion histories.

FIG. 202, PAGE 230

Clockwise from top left: receipt for gloves from a shop on the Rue de Rivoli, Paris; hat purchased at Best & Co., New York; postcard sent to clients by Roy H. Bjorkman, 1960; *Vogue*, August 15, 1948; gold wrapping ribbon inscribed "Clothes of Distinction by Evelyn Barton Brown" from her shop; card from *le gant topaze*, Paris; embroidered gloves; Bonwit Teller store directory; wool suit purchased at Russeks, New York, 1941.

As explained in previous chapters, most of the sources for the men's clothing are known. This is because the clothes, suits, waistcoats, and shirts bear the name of the tailoring and manufacturing firms where they were made. In addition, some accessories, such as the derby* hat that belonged to W.H. Roddis, or the leisure-wear Haspel suit of Hamilton's, are clearly marked as having been made exclusively for department stores (in these cases, for Marshall Field & Company in Chicago). The suits of W.H. Roddis were most likely made-to-measure rather than entirely custom-made, as explained in Chapter 2, whereas the suits ordered by Hamilton Roddis in the 1950s may well have been bespoke (see p.185).

By contrast, the majority of the clothes worn by Roddis women dating well into the 1940s do not have labels, so their origins are unknown. Notable exceptions of several pre-1940s garments include the presentation gown from Mon. A. Angla, Paris, dating from about 1880; the brown walking suit from the New York department store Franklin Simon & Co., dating from about 1908; the French lace dress bearing the label of Adair, House of France, from the mid-1920s; and the mink-trimmed, wool evening coat purchased at Carson Pirie Scott in Chicago in about 1940 by Augusta's sister Mary Roddis Connor (see pp.83, 89, 125 and 298). The majority of the women's clothes in the Roddis Collection are from the 1950s, and nearly all of these have store labels, which provide a rich source of information about the shopping habits of Catherine and Augusta. Mother and daughter visited specialist fashion salons known for their well-selected, well-made clothes, as well as leading department stores. In addition, surviving purchases from Paris hint at their penchant for shopping abroad.

Together, the Roddis family clothing and personal letters reveal how many family members over several generations sought out the very best clothes they could afford, or ones that they felt were of sufficiently fine quality to justify the expenditure. Indeed, making wise choices was certainly important to Catherine and her daughters, and usually required shopping in cities far from Marshfield. Although the Roddis family shopped for clothes in many places, including Paris, New York, Washington, D.C., Minneapolis, Madison and Milwaukee, Wisconsin, Boston, and Palm Beach, Florida, it was inevitable that Chicago, the most significant metropolis near Marshfield was the most favored. The family also shopped in the Chicago suburb of Evanston, Illinois, where they had relatives. In 1958, Augusta Roddis wrote to her old school mate and close friend Ellen Sexton: "I feel quite gay getting down to Chicago so often these past few months, and I certainly enjoyed my latest jaunt down."[1] To make shopping easier, it appears that the Roddis women charged nearly all their purchases to their store accounts, and the clothing was later sent directly to their homes. They paid by sending checks in the mail.

This tradition of stores delivering or sending purchases dates back to the early 1900s, when it was felt that no lady should be expected to carry around bundles, even for the smallest purchases. It also has links to mail-order businesses started as early as the 1870s by Sears & Roebuck, and other similar enterprises. Marshall Field & Company, then the leading retailer in Chicago and worldwide, introduced the first free delivery service to its customers. Marshall Field's delivery vans were a common sight on Chicago streets up until the late 1970s,[2] while out of the city deliveries, such as to the Roddis homes in Marshfield, were made using the public mail service. With its extravagantly domed atriums,[3] lavish seasonal displays, superb service, and fine quality clothing, Field's was certainly a favorite of the Roddis men and women for many decades. Items in the Roddis Collection purchased there date from 1914 to the late 1950s.

> ## "I feel quite gay getting down to Chicago so often these past few months, and I certainly enjoyed my latest jaunt down."
>
> AUGUSTA RODDIS

Marshall Field & Company was also one of the first department stores to offer a "money-back guarantee", another convenience for customers who lived both far and near. In the early years, as was the case with many department stores, registered customers did not have to pay with hard currency.[4] As historian Jan Whitaker explains, in the early twentieth century women simply gave their name and their purchase would be added to their store account.[5] Even as late as 1941, Ellen Roddis, aged 18, was slightly surprised that she was able to ask the sales clerk at Carson Pirie Scott to put a formal dress on her mother's account, without having to offer any proof of identity; they must have thought she had "an honest face".[6] Store account cards were created to promote customer loyalty and improve service.

The idea of charge cards existed as early as 1914, when Western Union issued metal identification plates, dubbed "metal money", which allowed preferred customers to operate under a carefully controlled credit system.[7] In the late 1920s, a company in Boston was the first to introduce the charga-plate, a small metal plate on which the customer's name and address was embossed, rather like a soldier's dog tag, with a cardboard signature card on one side.[8] These charga-plates were mainly used by individual department stores, such as Marshall Field's.[9] In the late 1940s or early 1950s, however, cities such as Brooklyn, Philadelphia, and Portland, Oregon, formed cooperative agreements allowing a customer to use one plate in a variety of local stores.[10] Catherine had one such metal card contained in its own leather case, with a signature card on one side marked "Charga-plate Stores of Minneapolis". This charge plate most likely dates from the late 1940s or early 1950s (fig. 203). The plate would have been laid onto a machine with a roller and an imprint was made on

FIG. 203

"Charga-plate Stores
of Minneapolis":
an early example of
a charge card that
could be used in
more than one store,
probably late 1940s.
THF 2015.96.1.

a paper docket; this metal card was the forerunner of plastic credit cards, the first of which was the Diners Club card, launched in 1950.[11] The use of such embossed cards continued for several decades.

For Catherine and her daughters living in Marshfield, shopping expeditions had to be specially organized, and were important events, since they involved travel by car, train or plane, and often included hotel reservations (if they did not stay with friends or relations). Like all women of decorum seen on city streets throughout the first half of the twentieth century, the Roddis women would have undoubtedly dressed in smart town clothes while out and about shopping, which for most of this period included hats and gloves.[12] By 1952, Amy Vanderbilt's *Complete Book of Etiquette* stated that for the "country dweller ... a good dress hat ... will carry you smartly into town on your occasional sorties into the more sophisticated world of clothes."[13] A few years later, when hats were "fighting a losing battle", another etiquette book admitted that a well-dressed woman could go without wearing a hat, except in church.[14] Even so, wearing a hat could help a woman "get better service", but it is unlikely that the Roddis women needed to resort to this ploy.[15] They probably continued to wear hats while shopping in big cities as late as the early 1960s.

Clothing Budgets and Careful Purchasing

In order to understand Augusta's attitude to shopping in the 1950s, a closer look must be taken at her family's particular point of view towards spending. As described in Chapter 5, in 1929, letters suggest that Mary Roddis was allowed to splurge on new clothes for her trousseau* and honeymoon to Europe. This was certainly uncharacteristic for the Roddis family. According to Augusta, her father Hamilton was rather "tight-fisted with money". He also believed that individuals should keep track of their spending as an accountant would in a business environment. (Catherine kept every household receipt filed in boxes by year in her closet,[16] and, as previously noted, the eldest girls were required to itemize their spending down to the last pencil while at boarding school.) During the Depression, Hamilton and Catherine instructed their unmarried children never to buy clothes without their permission. When Pickie was at boarding school in 1930, for example, she felt she simply had to "invest" in a new formal and therefore disobeyed, writing to her parents later: "Bawl me out when you get down here, but you'll be crazy about it when you see it."[17] Even when the economy had picked up in 1941, Ellen was still required to inform her parents of any clothing purchases she made while at college,[18] and Augusta was well aware of the trouble she would probably get into for her latest extravagance while shopping in New York. She wrote to her sister Ellen: "I shot my wad on one outfit but I still think it was worth it. Perhaps when I get the bellyache from home I will change my mind."[19] It seems that parental approval of Augusta's expenditure still continued to be a concern even when she was 34 years old. Augusta described the ensemble that cost so much (fig. 205):

> *I finally got the suit dress that I liked so well in the advertisement in* Vogue. *I found it at Russeks in the soft shade of light olive green and in a material that has rabbit's hair in it and which is much prettier than any of the materials we saw the dress in at Saks in Chicago. I feel quite pleased with myself ... although am still a little guilty over spending so much on one dress. However, you should see it with my sable, and the little fur hat I got to go with it. Really, I think it is quite elegant. The fur hat is mink but looks pretty good with the sable, anyway I think so (this may be rationalization) and it (the hat) goes perfectly with my coat with the mink trimming so I feel sumptuously outfitted now.*[20]

Augusta's description reveals that she studied *Vogue* for ideas about what she would like to buy. (This magazine's influence on the Roddis women is also demonstrated by Ellen's comment in 1943 that a dress she thought was outstanding looked "like it is right out of *Vogue*".[21]) The earthy color and slightly rough texture of Augusta's suit fabric, as well as the feminine, nipped-in waist with its draped detail, no doubt appealed to her. With its combination of fur and feathers, the hat she purchased at Best & Co. (fig. 204) to compliment this suit dress picks up the town and country mixed mood of the ensemble (both this hat and suit are visible in the still life on p.230). The quote from Augusta's letter above also illustrates the care she took when choosing that suit. Both her limited budget and her family's traditional emphasis on moderation reinforced her natural instinct to select her wardrobe with conscious deliberation.

From a retail perspective, this purchase also demonstrates that Augusta was able to see the same model of suit in a wide variety of materials and colors in a number of leading department stores—in this case, Saks Fifth Avenue in Chicago and Russeks on Fifth Avenue in New York (now defunct, but known for women's wear at that time). Her words "any of the materials we saw the dress in at Saks" imply that this department store had bought the suit in a variety of fabrics and colors, apparently differing from the fabric of the same suit at Russeks. It appears that a customer in 1941 was offered more fabric options for one design than is customary today.

Augusta certainly enjoyed searching for the perfect outfit. In 1942, she was asked by her best friend Ellen Sexton to be maid of honor. She was given *carte blanche* to purchase whatever she wanted for herself, without having to consider what would suit the other bridesmaids. Augusta relished shopping for her new dress: "I am having a delightful time weighing all the possibilities and visualizing this and that. Everything is as amorphous as a cloud now though."[22] No photographic evidence has been found to attest to Augusta's choice of gown, but she wrote to Ellen suggesting that it was a good one: "… my dress was a great success, and everyone was so complimentary about it & how I looked that I felt quite sensationally beautiful."[23]

Both of Augusta's comments suggest that shopping was "a lot of fun", as she wrote in her letter, but also a task to be taken seriously.[24] Her emphasis on judicious shopping may be seen in her advice to her sister Sara in 1953: "P.S. If you shop for a formal, don't settle for anything less than a real addition to your wardrobe."[25] This approach had been inculcated by their discerning mother Catherine and was precisely what had been long preached by American advisors on dress: women were encouraged to "choose good design" and select clothes that are "neither commonplace nor conspicuous".[26] Wearing an old but good dress was also typical of Catherine Roddis, who debated in a letter whether she should wear a six-year-old dress or a three-year-old one. New dresses were not usually bought merely for the sake of owning something new; they were purchased only if they were believed to be useful and attractive additions to an existing wardrobe.

> *"... my dress was a great success, and everyone*
> *was so complimentary about it & how I looked*
> *that I felt quite sensationally beautiful."*
>
> AUGUSTA RODDIS

Just as the Prindle women had written to each other about their clothing choices, so too did Augusta and her sister Ellen. Even after Ellen was married, they still corresponded about such topics as whether a sweater or pearl choker might look better on the other. Things were not to be left unused and thrown into a drawer if they could be worn by another family member.[27] These sisters were willing to help each other out; in one of Ellen's letters from 1947, she asked Augusta to buy her some spectator pumps* while shopping at Saks Fifth Avenue—shoes that were apparently not available in the Boston area, where she lived. Her letter even included a simple sketch of this feminine version of the two-tone man's Oxford shoe with perforations (see p.163), rather like their mother's sister Miriam Prindle illustrated her own letters in the early years of the century.[28]

"A bit out of fashion"

Augusta clearly enjoyed shopping, but she was sometimes indecisive and from time to time returned her new purchases. This was much to the frustration of her sister Mary, who often went shopping with her in Chicago, and encouraged her to acquire some more fashionable outfits. One item that Augusta returned is as revealing as what she purchased and wore. A receipt from the New York store Gunther Jaeckal, dated January 22, 1953, reveals that she returned a recently purchased suit by Adrian (1903–59), which had cost $265 (the equivalent of $2,225 in 2016).[29] Adrian was not only a household name but one of the foremost designers in the country. Famous for costume

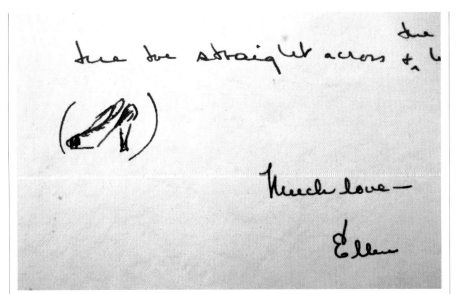

designs for such Hollywood films as *The Wizard of Oz* (1939), he had his own fashion company and was particularly well known for his iconic suits. Of course, one can only speculate as to why Augusta returned that Adrian suit. Based on family lore and memory, and her personal comments in numerous letters, it is probable such "fearful extravagance" may have bothered her "conscience", just as it had when she purchased a mink coat in 1955, as she confessed in a letter to her sister Ellen (they often discussed quality versus price in their letters).[30] Perhaps Augusta felt that the suit was too formal for her life in Marshfield: "We really have so little occasion for dressy clothes here", she writes just a few years later.[31] Then again, she may have decided that the design of the suit was not to her taste.[32] Possibly Augusta felt the Adrian suit would not age well. She would undoubtedly have agreed with Frances Benton, who wrote *Complete Etiquette* at about the same time: "A 'high-fashion' or very dressy suit is, on the whole, an extravagant buy. It isn't versatile enough to be worth in wear what it costs."[33]

Correspondence reveals that Augusta and Ellen, in particular, were well aware of current fashion in the 1940s. In a letter describing her latest clothing purchases in full detail, Ellen admits that she bought an "irresistible white wool dress. White wool is *in*, so I got that too."[34] Although Augusta always admired "pretty" clothes, in her later life she never wanted to look like she was trying to be fashionable. In the mid-1960s, she commented to a niece: "I usually don't wear a dress when it is new. I like to keep it in the closet for a few years and wear it when it is a bit out of fashion."[35] This comment is most likely rooted in Augusta's familiarity with the novel *The Age of Innocence* by Edith Wharton, one of her favorite authors. In this novel, female characters in conversation among themselves criticize other women who "flaunt abroad their Paris dresses ... instead of letting them mellow under lock and key." One character recalls how in her youth, "it was considered vulgar to dress in the newest fashions ... in Boston the rule was to put away one's Paris dresses for two years" but in New York "one season" would suffice.[36] This concept of letting new clothes season in one's closet may have resonated with Augusta. Ultimately, despite her admiration for the most attractive garments in the stores she visited, it was probably the fear of overdressing or appearing to be too fashionable in her middle age that Augusta most wanted to avoid. This was especially the case in her milieu of school board meetings and ladies' club get-togethers, where it was recommended that women should "dress down rather than up for a special appearance."[37] In her later years, Augusta dressed as she pleased and cared little for what was the latest fashion trend. In this way, she would have been applauded by American designer Elizabeth Hawes, author of *Fashion is Spinach*, who categorized American women into three groups: the rare chic women (mostly of international origin), the women who followed fashion trends slavishly, and finally those women who "dress as they please ... use high collars when only low necks are being worn, and generally defy the demon Fashion with the best possible results."[38] Augusta would undoubtedly have been placed somewhere in Hawes's final category of American women.

Specialty Fashion Salons and the Growing Presence of Designer Labels

Although top department stores were certainly visited by the Roddis women, the majority of surviving garments in the Roddis Collection from the 1940s onwards were mainly bought in specialty dress salons. A few of the floral printed cotton dresses discussed in Chapter 9 were purchased at the Palm Beach, Florida, branch of Frances Brewster, while Augusta's afternoon dress, worn on the R.M.S. *Queen Mary*, bears the label of the designer Samuel Kass and that of the exclusive Chicago store Martha Weathered. This was one of Chicago's most exclusive fashion importers, whose stores on Michigan Avenue attracted wealthy customers from 1922 until 1971.[39]

What distinguished the specialist fashion salons from other clothing stores was the level of service and comfort they provided, as well as the pre-selection of garments that they offered. Some examples of Roddis

FIG. 207
Postcard of the 28 Shop, Marshall Field & Company, Chicago, opened in 1941 as the place to shop for haute couture in Chicago, and be "the fashion center of mid-America". EMC.

FIG. 208, OPPOSITE
Checked wool day dress belonging to Augusta Roddis, from Saks Fifth Avenue, *c.*1957. THF 2014.24.40.

clothing that belonged to Catherine and Augusta, unfortunately in poor condition,[40] are from Marshall Field's 28 Shop—an exclusive women's salon opened in 1941 and named for the address of its private elevator entrance, 28 East Washington Street, as well as the 28 dressing rooms that radiated off the central salon. Field's was known for its superb customer service, but at the 28 Shop the highly trained staff did everything possible to ensure the satisfaction of its customers. Women shopping there could sit in elegant, comfortable chairs and even lunch while watching live mannequins model the clothes (fig. 207). Stock was not put on display; instead, a saleswoman would bring out dresses, furs, and even shoes after discussing what sort of outfit a customer was seeking.[41] Although not of the same level, a high degree of service could also be found in certain sections of department stores, especially Saks Fifth Avenue. Helen O'Hagan, a longtime Vice President of Public Relations at Saks, New York, recounts that in the 1950s "even in the [Saks] ready-to-wear department, most of the clothes were kept in a back stockroom, rather than on racks." Customers waited for garments to be brought out by saleswomen for viewing.[42] O'Hagan adds that even in these ready-to-wear areas, amenities such as tea stands and beautiful furniture for sitting were also available.[43] The store labels in surviving garments in the Roddis Collection indicate that Augusta shopped at Saks for a number of hats and dresses, including the checked wool day dress with Parisian design components, from around 1957 (fig. 208). Its fitted sheath style, and the horizontal band at the hip, suggest the influence of designs by Balenciaga and Dior.[44]

Another top favorite hunting ground for Catherine and Augusta was the Marshall Field's millinery section called the French Room. France, and Paris in particular, was associated with the ultimate in hats, hence the name. One example of a hat that must have belonged to Augusta is a cream wool beret with a pair of crystal-covered spheres, dating from about 1960. This hat has two labels set side by side: "Mr. John" and "The French Room/Marshall Field & Company" (figs 209 and 210). Mr. John was one of America's most famous milliners from the 1930s through the 1960s, and was noted as the designer of the hats worn by Vivien Leigh in the 1939 film *Gone With The Wind*. For a further example of a hat from the French Room, see p.303.

One of Catherine's favorite salons was the elegant, multi-level store, Roy H. Bjorkman (see pp.258–9), in Minneapolis—a city that Catherine and her daughters sometimes visited in order to attend performances of New York's Metropolitan Opera on its annual tour through the Midwest. A postcard with a painted image of the Arc de Triomphe in Paris and a printed message on the reverse, hand-addressed to Catherine Roddis, is evidence that Bjorkman reached out directly to his regular customers. Dated May 23, 1960, and entitled "Greetings from Paris!", Bjorkman writes: "Selecting the latest styles, the newest inspirational ideas from the great couturiers and fourreurs [furriers] in Paris, Rome and London."

FIG. 209, LEFT
Wool beret with
crystal-covered
spherical buttons
by Mr. John, c.1960.
RDC A19, JBC.

FIG. 210, BELOW LEFT
Detail of the labels
in the hat on the
left, c.1960.

He asks that Catherine come in to "give us the privilege and pleasure of showing them"[45] (see p.259). A grayish-blue rayon* taffeta dress, dating from about 1953 and undoubtedly worn by Catherine, bears the label of "*le petit salon*/Roy H. Bjorkman", so she must have been one of his customers for seven years at least. The V-neck fitted bodice and skirt have soutache* braid, machine-embroidered in a pattern of curlicues and stylized floral motifs (fig. 211). This dress is reminiscent of a 1953 design by Cristobal Balenciaga (1895–1972) (fig. 212).

From the 1920s until the 1950s, copies of Paris originals dominated the American ready-to-wear market; this is illustrated by several of Catherine's dresses, including this example, and two mentioned in

FIG. 212
Silk cocktail dress
with soutache
braid embroidered
trim by Cristobal
Balenciaga, 1953.
Owned by Elizabeth
Firestone, this dress
may have been
the inspiration for
Catherine's dress
opposite. Musée
des tissus et des
arts décoratifs de
Lyon, France. Photo
courtesy of Beverley
Birks and Francesca
Galloway.

Chapter 7 (see p.180), all of which have an obvious French influence, rather than being the work of independent-minded American designers. Although Bjorkman's store was renowned, especially in the 1950s and 1960s, it has now been largely forgotten.

At least nine suits and dresses in the Roddis Collection, all belonging to Augusta, are from Ruth McCulloch—another fashion salon that has been largely forgotten, at least outside the Chicago area, yet is a prime example of the type of shop frequented by the Roddis women and others like them (see pp.260–1). In the 1950s, there was a mass migration of the middle classes from American cities to the suburbs. Leading department stores followed their clientele, setting up small branches in shopping centers that

FIG. 211, OPPOSITE
Rayon taffeta cocktail dress with soutache braid, machine-embroidery trimming, and self-corded belt. Label: *le petit salon*, Roy H. Bjorkman, c.1953. THF 2014.24.52.

catered specifically to wealthy suburban women. Ruth McCulloch never had premises in Chicago itself, but chose to set up her exclusive fashion shops in the Chicago suburbs of Evanston and Hubbard Woods, as well as the Northbrook Court shopping center.[46] Her salons featured classic and well-made clothing for the American woman in her thirties or over. "Spacious, hushed rooms ... furnished with French Provencal sofas and chairs upholstered in satin damask" is how one magazine article described the establishment in Evanston. According to a hostess who presided at the Northbrook Court store, the atmosphere was "dignified": a "salesgirl" seated customers to discuss what they were looking for (sportswear was *not* on offer—this was a store for "ladies"). Then, several choices would be brought out and displayed. If one was chosen, it was fitted for the customer and, if possible, altered before her departure.[47]

For Augusta, the curated selection offered by the McCulloch fashion salon allowed her the opportunity to indulge in what she called "fast shopping", which improved the chances of a "successful expedition".[48] The clothes Augusta purchased there became the mainstay of her wardrobe during the 1950s and 1960s. One of the more striking examples is a gray linen day dress with white linen panels, complete with heavily corded and embroidered black trimming set onto the bodice. Dating to around 1952, this dress combines decorative trimming on an otherwise minimalist outfit, which may well have appealed to Augusta's appreciation of detail and sense of decorum (fig. 213).

The typical style of Ruth McCulloch's designs is evident in two dresses with matching jackets that Augusta purchased in the late 1950s: one of cranberry-colored bouclé* wool (fig. 214), and the other of blue silk (fig. 215). Augusta wore the former ensemble to family get-togethers and for a photo used for one of her publicity flyers when she stood for election to the Marshfield School Board. (When appropriate, Augusta may have perked up this suit dress with her hat embellished with miniature artificial apples, leaves, and green velvet ribbon, an element of which is just visible in the still life on p.280.)

McCulloch's signature label was elegantly hand-stitched into every garment (see McCulloch box, p.260). Of all the many Ruth McCulloch dresses and suits in the Roddis Collection, only one from the 1960s also includes the original designer's name. This white two-piece suit bears

FIG. 213, OPPOSITE
Detail of dark gray and white linen sleeveless day dress, *c.*1952. Label: Ruth McCulloch, Hubbard Woods. The machine embroidery on the bodice is inspired by traditional "Hungarian" motifs that were popular at the time. THF 2014.24.38.

FIG. 215
Peau de soie
afternoon or
cocktail dress
with jacket,
*c.*1958. Label:
Ruth McCulloch,
Hubbard Woods
and Evanston.
THF 2014.24.64.

FIG. 214, OPPOSITE
Wool bouclé and
silk dress with
matching jacket,
belt, and self-
covered buttons,
*c.*1959. Label:
Ruth McCulloch,
Hubbard Woods
and Evanston.
THF 2104.24.67.

both the McCulloch label and also that of the American designer and manufacturer Davidow (1880–1973) (fig. 217). By the 1960s, Davidow was producing copies of the classic suit styles of Coco Chanel (1883–1971), as exemplified by this collarless, button-up, bouclé wool jacket, with a fitted skirt, and metallic buttons.[49] Augusta wore this suit, with a hat and her favorite embroidered gloves from Paris, to attend the wedding of her niece Ellen Beggs and Thomas Everson in 1968 (fig. 216).

In the mid-1960s, Ruth McCulloch allowed the labels of certain well-known designers to remain in the clothing she sold, as an undated document from the McCulloch archive reveals. In addition to those of Davidow, she instructed her staff to retain the labels of other prominent American designers including Adele Simpson (1904–95), Pauline Trigère

FIG. 216, ABOVE
Augusta Roddis,
wearing the Davidow
suit to the right of the
photo, and a pair of
embroidered gloves
(purchased in Paris
20 years earlier),
with her sister Ellen
Roddis Lempereur
on the wedding day
of their niece Ellen
Beggs to Thomas
Everson, March 30,
1968. RFPA.

FIG. 217, TOP RIGHT
White wool bouclé
two-piece suit, with
metallic gold buttons,
c.1964. Labels:
Davidow (designer,
manufacturer) and
Ruth McCulloch,
Hubbard Woods
and Evanston
(fashion salon).
THF 2014.119.5.

(1912–2002), Ceil Chapman (1912–79), and Geoffrey Beene (1927–2004).[50] It appears that McCulloch was certainly not alone in realizing the value of designer labels for her customers. The president of Saks Fifth Avenue, Adam Gimbel, had taken a similar action in about 1964, when he rescinded the long-standing practice of asking most designers to ship garments to Saks without their personal labels.[51] As demonstrated by the range of women's clothes in the Roddis Collection dating from before the 1960s, previously department stores and dress salons predominantly used only their own labels; it was felt that it was their company names that had the "chief pulling power".[52]

Other Roddis dresses and accessories were purchased from the North Chicago branch of Blum's. The label of this leading department store, known for its high-quality merchandise, appears quite prominently on Augusta's silk print dress dating from c.1953 (fig. 218). However, discreetly tucked away at the waist is another label—that of Nettie Rosenstein, an Austrian-born designer who began designing clothes in the 1920s when imported fashions by named French couturiers were considered the best to be had in America. According to an article about her in *TIME* magazine in 1942, for much of her early career, Rosenstein's designs were sold under the particular department store's own label, although customers were apparently told that the dresses were in fact by Nettie Rosenstein.[53] In later years, Rosenstein earned name recognition and her personal label gained much prestige, as did that of other designers, in line with the retail trend noted above.[54]

The label "Christian Dior New York" is in a ready-to-wear day dress Augusta purchased in about 1959 (fig. 220). Augusta may have bought it directly from the Dior store that opened on Fifth Avenue in New York in 1948, but in later years models with this label were sold by a number of leading department stores as well, so its origin is uncertain. Given the date, however, this dress was certainly designed by Yves Saint Laurent (1936–2008), who had taken over the House of Dior upon the death of its founder in 1957. Its design includes hints of the A line* shape that would

FIG. 218
Silk print dress by
Nettie Rosenstein,
*c.*1953. Labels:
Blum's – North
Chicago, and Nettie
Rosenstein.
THF 2014.24.27.

FIG. 219

Augusta Roddis wearing the Christian Dior dress opposite during a Caribbean cruise on board M.S. *Kungsholm* with family and friends, 1966. Mary Roddis Connor (center) is wearing a dress by Irish designer Sybil Connolly, purchased in Dublin, *c.*1962. RDC 189, see p.300. RFPA.

come to exemplify the dress styles of the 1960s. Augusta can be seen wearing this dress in the photo above on a Caribbean cruise aboard the Swedish Line M.S. *Kungsholm* in 1966 (fig. 219).

Shopping in Paris

When Augusta and other members of her family traveled to Paris, they shopped there too. Mary Connor Roddis summed up the general Roddis view when she wrote to her father in 1929: "Of course I couldn't come to Paris and not buy one or two things in the way of clothes."[55] In 1953, Augusta warned her sister Ellen that the cultural attractions, and certainly the shopping, were indeed a huge temptation: "When you get to Paris you are going to wish you could stay a month...."[56]

Augusta's particular Parisian passion seems to have been to shop for gloves. For centuries, decorated gloves have symbolized refinement, and the finest silk embroidery on gloves was still the specialty of Paris workshops in the mid-twentieth century. In 1953, Augusta wrote to Ellen, advising her where to find the best: "A lot of glove shops on the Rue de Rivoli have embroidered gloves, but I found more that I like at the Gant Topaze."[57]

Receipts from that store (also located on the Rue de Rivoli) dated 1949 reveal that she bought more than a dozen pairs of gloves there. Some of those gloves may have been purchased as gifts, but Augusta kept many of them and they survive in remarkably good condition (figs 221 and 222). A letter from her sister Mary demonstrates that she must have received one pair from Augusta for Christmas. Mary wrote to her sister after the New Year that she was "charmed" with her gift: "The black suede gloves from Paris are so elegant I am almost afraid to carry them. Shall have to get a glove fastener* for my purse."[58]

FIG. 220, OPPOSITE

Silk tweed two-piece afternoon dress by Christian Dior New York, *c.*1959. THF 2014.24.45.

le gant topaze

194 BIS, RUE DE RIVOLI
PARIS - 1er

FIG. 221, ABOVE
A selection of gloves, many purchased at *le gant topaze* in Paris. The finest silk embroidery on gloves was still the specialty of Paris workshops in the mid-twentieth century.
THF 2014.24.110; RDC A112, JBC; RDC A68, JBC.

FIG. 222, TOP RIGHT
Receipt from *le gant topaze*, 194 bis Rue de Rivoli, Paris, which was Augusta Roddis's favorite glove shop.
THF 2015.10.71.1. From the Collections of The Henry Ford. "A lot of glove shops on the Rue de Rivoli have embroidered gloves, but I found more that I like at the Gant Topaze." Letter from Augusta to her sister Ellen, 1953.

It is believed that while in Paris in 1950, Augusta also purchased a mohair and wool bouclé suit that bears the label "Jeanne Lanvin/ Castillo/PARIS".[59] Antonio del Castillo (1908–84) was a Spanish-born designer who took over the House of Lanvin after the death of its founder Jeanne Lanvin in 1946 (figs 223 and 224).[60] Up until his departure in 1962, the salon continued to be known for the elegant clothes he created. Several elements seen in this suit are typical of Castillo designs: the two front pockets, the curved shoulder panel into which the back is gathered, and the use of the distinctive carved buttons are all recognized hallmarks. These wooden buttons were made to compliment the texture of the mohair and wool suit.

Augusta's sister Ellen Roddis Lempereur traveled with her husband to Paris in 1953. The Lempereurs had just had their third child and were finally in a financial position to visit Europe for three months and take the honeymoon they had never been able to enjoy. Ellen's husband encouraged her to have clothes custom-made, and a fine dress salon (name unknown) was recommended to her by the Hotel Continental, where they were staying. Ellen had a magenta and pink printed floral silk shantung dress made into an off-the-shoulder summer cocktail dress* (fig. 225). She was photographed a few years later wearing this dress (fig. 226).[61] Additional garments made for Ellen in Paris included a swing coat lined with floral silk, which unfortunately has not survived.

An American Stereotype Refuted

In his autobiography, first published in 1957, Christian Dior wrote that America:

... represents the quantitative over the qualitative. Men and women both prefer buying a multitude of mediocre things to acquiring a few carefully chosen articles.... The American woman prefers three new dresses to one beautiful one.... She does not deliberate on her choice ... the dress she is in the process of buying will be jettisoned very soon.[62]

This may have been increasingly the trend in America in 1957, especially in the large cities that Dior visited. However, this view of American attitudes towards clothes is in sharp contrast to the sage advice given in numerous books by American home economists and dress and etiquette advisors. In particular, it contrasts with the approach of the Prindle and Roddis women, as can be seen in the examination of their surviving garments as well as their personal comments about clothes over more than a century.[63]

The clothing of the Roddis Collection, viewed in the context of letters written by the wearers, clearly contradicts this stereotype of the

FIG. 226
Ellen Roddis
Lempereur wearing
the dress opposite,
mid-1950s. Portrait
by Bradford
Bachrach, Boston.
JBC.

big-spending American men and women with little taste and interest in good design. It also refutes the notion that the majority of Americans were willing to discard clothes after only a short time. The clothing of this particular extended American family was not quickly "jettisoned", but worn for many years, and subsequently saved for decades. What survived in the Roddis attic offers a unique insight into, and a different perspective on, the shopping habits and attitudes towards clothes of this Midwestern family, and of many Americans in the twentieth century.

REDISCOVERED FASHION SALON
ROY H. BJORKMAN

FIG. 227, LEFT
Portrait of Roy H.
Bjorkman, c.1935.
Courtesy of Betty
Bjorkman.

FIG. 228, BELOW LEFT
Label from the
dress on p.244
(fig. 211).
THF 2014.24.52.

FIG. 229, BELOW
Roy H. Bjorkman
hat box, with
printed wood veneer
pattern, c.1950s.
THF 2014.24.183.

FIG. 230, OPPOSITE ABOVE
Postcard of the Arc
de Triomphe, sent
by Roy H. Bjorkman
to special customers
from Paris in 1960.
THF 2015.10.66.

FIG. 231, OPPOSITE BELOW
Grand opening
of Bjorkman's
new building in
1948 with a 1920s
car representing
the twenty-fifth
anniversary of the
company. JBC.

BORN: 1893, Lincoln, Nebraska.

DIED: 1984, Minneapolis, Minnesota.

EARLY CAREER: Opened his first dress store in Lincoln, Nebraska, in 1923. A year later, he purchased the Martha Weathered store in Minneapolis, a 30,000 square foot store that carried an exclusive line of ladies' apparel and accessories. He expanded his business from dresses, shoes, and hats to include furs.

PEAK OF CAREER: Was the most prominent source for ladies' elegant clothes in Minneapolis for more than 40 years, and was highly successful during the period of World War II.[64] Was involved in supporting the unions in the dressmaking industry in New York and elsewhere in America. He made several trips a year to Paris and New York to secure the best designs for his clients in the Midwest. When he retired in 1968, his son Roy E. took over the fur business, while his son Edwin ran the dress business. The firm closed in 1989.

CLAIM TO FAME: The Roy H. Bjorkman building, designed by the prominent Minnesota architectural firm Lieberberg and Kaplin, on Nicollet and Tenth in Minneapolis, opened in 1948. This elegant store, which included a group of rooms called *le petit salon* (see label opposite) consisted of special areas for gowns, day dresses, hats, shoes, and the outstanding furs that had made the company famous since it was established in the 1920s.

ALSO NOTABLE FOR: After retirement, Bjorkman pursued philanthropic causes, and became involved in the Salvation Army and the American Indian Community, and was also active in the Minnesota State Historical Society (of which he became a life member in 1945).

BIBLIOGRAPHY: Roy H. Bjorkman, *Northwest's Most Exclusive Women's Specialty Shop: Through 25 Years, 1923-1948* (Bjorkman Company, 1948).

> "[Bjorkman] was famous for such sales techniques as throwing an expensive fur coat on the floor ... it was just a little flair, a bit of showmanship.... The customer would gasp and buy the coat. A good salesman must inspire the customer.... Too many newcomers don't understand that in selling, you must feel the joy of being needed."

BARBARA FLANAGAN,
MINNEAPOLIS STAR (VARIETY PAGE), MARCH 1, 1973

REDISCOVERED FASHION SALON
RUTH MCCULLOCH

BORN: August 9, 1900.

DIED: 2007, Florida.

EARLY CAREER: The daughter of immigrant parents (Austrian father and French mother), Ruth McCulloch was born Emma Ruth Dobler, the middle child of six siblings. She attended the College of St. Catherine in St. Paul, Minnesota, and married Bruce McCulloch, a Nebraska native, in 1924. By 1930 they were living in Detroit, where Ruth was a buyer of ladies' dresses. Following her divorce in 1935, she opened her first dress store in the North Shore Hotel, Evanston, Illinois, in April 1937, retaining her married name for business reasons. Ruth McCulloch, Inc. was incorporated in 1946 and dissolved 42 years later. She had two other stores, one in Hubbard Woods, and one in the newly established shopping center, Northbrook Court, in Northbrook, Illinois.

PEAK OF CAREER: "The only word to describe the atmosphere at Ruth McCulloch's dress store is 'genteel'. Although Ruth McCulloch advertises [see photograph of her well-known playing cards], word-of-mouth is considered the primary means of publicizing the store—and that usually means mothers passing the word to daughters...."[65] Her own distinct label, a lady in a bonnet with flowing ribbons, was prominent in all of the clothes and many of the hats she sold. In her Evanston store, there was a millinery room where ladies could buy a hat to go with the outfit they had just purchased and had fitted.

CLAIM TO FAME: Her store was considered the most exclusive dress store on the North Shore, the string of affluent suburbs north of Chicago, Illinois, bordering on the shore of Lake Michigan.

ALSO NOTABLE FOR: In 1953, Ruth was on a softball team of professional grandmothers—"the Galesburg Merchanettes"—and was highly successful.[66] She was active in the league until 1963.

FIG. 232, TOP
Photo of Ruth McCulloch in her salon, *Business North Shore*, March 1964, p.89. Courtesy of Evanston History Center, Evanston, Illinois.

FIG. 233, ABOVE
Ruth McCulloch label from the dress opposite, woven with stylized figure with leg-o'mutton* sleeves and a large hat, with characteristic stitching, c.1958. THF 2014.24.64.

CHAPTER ELEVEN

End of an Era and Looking Back
Augusta and Dressing Up

By the late 1950s, Hamilton Roddis's eyesight and health were failing, yet he remained President of the Roddis Plywood Corporation, assisted by Augusta as his private secretary. But the end of an era was looming: soon Augusta would be left to live alone in the Roddis family home in Marshfield, and her grandparents' old house next door would burn down.[1] Augusta cherished all the family clothing, letters, photographs, and ephemera that were stored on her top floor, and on special occasions would wear some of the dresses that had belonged to her mother and grandmother. Dressing up in these old-fashioned clothes was amusing, but it also allowed Augusta to savor the fine workmanship of the garments, and reminisce about family members and their history, both in the Midwest and further afield.

Augusta had a very close relationship with her parents, and was pleased by two major events in their lives that took place in the late 1950s. On July 7, 1958, Hamilton and Catherine Roddis celebrated their fiftieth wedding anniversary. All their children and grandchildren gathered for the celebration, which was held in their home, decked out with flowers, newly polished silver, and the finest family linens. Hamilton wore an understated contemporary taupe-colored suit;[2] Catherine wore her original princess-line* wedding gown (fig. 238).[3] Her attire harkened back to the life and times of the young woman who wore this dress for her wedding, and for the lavish reception 50 years ago, given by Hamilton's parents in the garden next door (see pp.36 and 95–6).

FIG. 237, PAGE 262
Clockwise from
top left: Catherine
Roddis wearing
an Italian folk
ensemble, 1900;
unknown girl and
William H. Roddis II
(Bill) dressed up as
George and Martha
Washington, c.1928;
iridescent bronze
leather high button
shoes, c.1890; shot-
silk taffeta blouse;
Palestinian headgear
worn as part of
Arabian costume;
lace dickey, c.1900;
Augusta and Ellen
Sexton playing dress-
up, c.1928 ; all resting
on a Palestinian robe
worn in Nativity
plays, 1928.

FIG. 238
Catherine and
Hamilton Roddis
on their fiftieth
wedding anniversary,
standing in the living
room of their home,
July 7, 1958. RFPA.

Exactly one year and a day later, the couple attended a special luncheon in the presence of Queen Elizabeth II, who had scheduled a stop in Sault Ste. Marie, Ontario, during her trip across Canada to celebrate the opening of the St. Lawrence Seaway.[4] As well as the many timber-cutting agreements Hamilton had made to expand his holdings across North America, he also obtained a license from the British Crown to harvest some of its extensive crown lands in Canada.[5] To process this timber, he built a sawmill in Sault Ste. Marie. It is likely that his business there resulted in the invitation for Catherine and him to join this luncheon. His attendance seems fitting, however, for a man who had indirectly helped Great Britain achieve victory over Germany in World War II (see Chapter 7), although there is no evidence that this connection was acknowledged that day. A gold spoon presented by the Sault Windsor Hotel to commemorate the queen's visit is the only remaining ephemera from this event.[6] Although only Mr. Hamilton Roddis's name appears on the guest list, a family member confirms that the couple arrived on the company plane to attend the luncheon.[7] Another relative recalls that Catherine mentioned to her that she wore a print dress and matching hat to this reception, but sadly these have not survived.[8] The silk dress and floral hat below, which belonged to Catherine, offer a sense of the type of ensemble she would have worn to such an important occasion (figs 239 and 240).

In the late 1950s, it is not certain whether Catherine continued to make any clothes for Augusta (see p.220 for a discussion of her yellow gown), but her great love was practical needlework. In the photograph visible in the still life on p.266 (fig. 241), she is pictured completing a needlepoint seat cover for a rocking chair in her living room. She also stitched a complete set of chair seats for the family dining room.

At the same time, despite his failing health, Hamilton, a devoted businessman, maintained his old habit of going to work every day, and returning home for a midday break to enjoy the main meal of the day with his family. By this time, his company had reached annual sales of nearly $60 million, and he remained vigilant of its progress;[9] Hamilton continued his regular routine of going into his office right up until the last few months of his life (fig. 242). He also maintained his prominent role in both his church duties and civic activities.[10] During his last years, when his eyesight was failing, he enjoyed listening to Augusta read aloud his favorite classics, particularly Victor Hugo's *Les Misérables*.

FIG. 239, BELOW LEFT
Floral afternoon hat by Ruth McCulloch, *c.*1959. Catherine most likely wore this hat with the dress below, as the colors are so similar. THF 2014.24.121.

FIG. 240, BELOW
Floral print silk afternoon dress (no label, possibly made by a local dressmaker), *c.*1959. THF 2014.24.42.

FIG. 241
Clockwise from
top left: pattern in
McCall's Magazine,
January 1936;
Catherine Roddis's
dressmaking book,
1931; young Bill's
buster suit, most
likely made by
Catherine, *c.*1920;
photo of Catherine
embroidering a
rocking chair seat,
*c.*1955; assorted
buttons and
sewing materials
from Catherine's
collection; sewing
machine, 1939.

By the time of Hamilton's death in March 1960, the Roddis Plywood Corporation had expanded its sales and extended its influence into the American Northwest, Northeast, and the South, and even Canada. In the summer of 1960, the family firm was merged with Weyerhaeuser, another major lumber company that had originated in Wisconsin. Although no longer privately owned by the family, the former Roddis Plywood Corporation continued to be a major employer in the town.[11] Catherine and Augusta carried on living much as they had before, but Hamilton's absence was keenly felt.

In 1964, Catherine died quite suddenly. Augusta was distraught, and it was only in the afternoon before the funeral that she suddenly realized she had nothing to wear that she deemed worthy for this solemn occasion. She announced to one of her nieces that she would *have* to borrow her Pierre Cardin suit from Paris.[12] Even at such times, clothes mattered.

Augusta was left to live alone in the large Roddis house that was filled with so many personal and family memories. She had become a moderately wealthy woman, thanks to the sale of the family company, and her ownership of Weyerhaeuser shares. She never changed her life-long frugal ways, however, except for the occasional flight of fancy, such as when she bought an antique Chinese lacquer sewing table, or an exact copy of her favorite French painting—a self-portrait by Louise Élisabeth Vigée Le Brun (1755–1842).

Up in the attic, clothes that had belonged to her grandparents, as well as members of her mother's family, the Prindles, were now joined by suits of her father and dresses her mother had worn from the early 1900s up to the present, along with artifacts, photographs, and letters belonging to all of these relatives (fig. 243). Her mother's more recent dresses remained hanging in closets downstairs: Augusta could not bring herself to give them away. She felt that, like all the old clothes, they were not merely keepsakes but valuable for "the historical record,"[13] and became "increasingly interesting with each passing year."[14] Augusta must have realized that all the preserved clothing would potentially become an intimate record of her family's past. She also knew they would be useful when period costume was needed for dress-up occasions.

FIG. 242
Hamilton Roddis, typically wearing a bow tie, examining sheets of veneer in his factory, c.1955. RFPC.

FIG. 243
View of a corner
of the playroom
on the top floor of
the Roddis house.
Behind the wall
was the "attic", the
walk-in closet where
the earliest family
clothing was stored.
Photo by Gillian
Bostock Ewing, 2011.

Costume and Historic Dress

Both the Prindle and the Roddis families enjoyed dressing up, as a number of photographs, documents, and garments bear witness. The photograph opposite, dating from the mid- to late 1880s is almost certainly linked to *Mikado* characters—"the Three Little Maids from School" (fig. 244). *The Mikado* was a comic opera by Gilbert and Sullivan, first performed in England and America in 1885, and thereafter continuing to be a top choice for amateur productions—sparking a fad for all things oriental.[15] Taken in a photographer's studio in Milwaukee, this portrait shows three women, probably Roddis friends or relatives, wearing homemade kimonos, which were probably used for a party or an amateur production.[16] Indeed, Roddis family members participated in theatrical productions themselves: in September 1929, for instance, several family members appeared in a "musical extravaganza" at the local theater to raise money for their church guild. Augusta dressed as a "Japanese Maiden" and a "School Girl"; her sister Pickie as a "Dancing Bride"; and Hamilton as a "Blind Beggar" (his sister Frances was in charge of the props, possibly including the parasol, fig. 95, as seen on p.114).[17]

In addition to oriental-inspired dress, various letters and photographs reveal the Prindles' interest in European regional dress, as well as the Roddis family's interest in American historical costume. In 1900, the already fashion-conscious Catherine Sarah Prindle, aged 17, was photographed (probably by her brother Richard),[18] wearing an Italian folk costume. This may have been a gift from her aunt, Mary Prindle Newton, who also sent her photographs of Italian women in traditional dress.[19] One of the photographs taken of Catherine in this costume is visible in the still life on p.262, along with another photograph of her young son Bill, taken in the 1920s, when he was about 11. Wearing a wig and what appears to be a professionally made historic costume, he was dressed as "George Washington", according to an inscription on the reverse of the photograph, and stands beside an unidentified classmate dressed as Martha, Washington's wife.[20]

Further surviving evidence of dressing up is a simple, long, cotton robe with small paper pumpkins attached to it, suggesting that the Roddis

FIG. 244
Women in Japanese-inspired costume, photograph taken in Milwaukee, Wisconsin, c.1885. RFPA.

family also enjoyed wearing costumes at Halloween. Augusta spoke more than once of her delight in donning a new identity for one exciting Halloween night.[21]

"A Trip to Never-Never Land"

Augusta seemed to understand that even if enjoyed for one evening, one performance, or only an hour in the attic, dressing up could be a powerful experience. By shedding one's normal appearance and feeling the otherness of an historic or foreign costume, the imagination is triggered, even more so perhaps than a disguise of pure fantasy. For Augusta, wearing antique clothing transported her to the past, as seen in this extract from a letter written in 1963:

> *The other day we started delving into an old trunk of Aunt Frances's that contained some of Grandmother Roddis's choicest dresses that Aunt Frances had saved. It was like a trip to never-never land. The lace and embroidery and ruffles are really breath-taking. I really began to feel that I was missing something in life not to be able to swish around in silks and laces more! Living was an art in those days, and getting dressed must have been a real ritual with all the countless hooks and eyes to be fastened up.*[22]

The emotional connection felt when wearing the clothing of a revered ancestor or a close older relative could be powerfully evocative for Augusta, cementing the familial bond in a way that no other activity could quite accomplish. Just as Edith Prindle could summon the memory of Aunt Jennie when she posed in her presentation dress* from around 1880 (see p.9 and p.83), Augusta, in turn, enjoyed trying on that particular dress for the same reason. Years later she enthusiastically handed it to her niece Jane so that she too could experience the thrill of wearing such a gown and connect with her namesake (see p.8).

Celebrating History Through Dress

Dressing in the treasured clothes stored in her attic was as important to the grown-up Augusta as it was when she was a child. She recalled fondly how she and her friend Ellen Sexton had enjoyed dressing up in the old-fashioned dresses when they were 12 years old (as seen in the photograph of them in the still life on p.262; see also p.117). In later life also, she enjoyed wearing some of the period dresses and sharing them with others in her community and beyond. Reflecting that this activity was perfectly natural, Augusta recorded this observation in a letter:

> *When I had the Centennial Tea last summer and quite a few of us dressed up in old-fashioned clothes, I thought, "Women never really change; this is the sort of thing I was doing more than forty years*

ago, and here we all are, still doing it." Actually, I do think love of pretty clothes is one of the deepest of feminine instincts, and basically a healthy one if it doesn't degenerate into self-centered vanity.[23]

For these groups of local women, dressing up was more than mere frippery. The Colonial Revival of the late nineteenth century revitalized a sense of heritage and pride by remembering the American Revolution. The wearing of century-old dresses brought this celebration to life. These were the same underlying reasons behind Augusta's participation in the historic fashion shows and other events in Marshfield designed to celebrate patriotic institutions, such as the Daughters of the American Revolution (DAR),[24] as well as local, family, and national anniversaries.

Augusta's local chapter of the DAR, of which she was a long-time member, often wore old-fashioned dresses to celebrate both national and Marshfield anniversaries. Back in 1947, Augusta enthusiastically joined other DAR members to celebrate their town's seventy-fifth anniversary. A photograph survives of these local ladies, including many of the most important citizens of the community, posing for a group portrait, several of

them wearing old-fashioned dresses. One woman, Mrs. L. Dressendorfer,
even appears in native costume typical of the Seminole tribe in Florida in
the 1940s (fig. 245).[25]

The Marshfield Centennial (1872–1972) was an even more important
occasion. As part of those festivities, Augusta hosted historic dress-up tea
parties at her house, when she and her guests wore family garments that
were stored in their homes. Reporting on the DAR centennial tea given by
Augusta in June of 1972, a local newspaper wrote: "Attics, closets and trunks
yield a wide variety of styles of former days...."[26] At this event, Augusta
wore one of the dresses that had belonged to her grandmother Sara Roddis
(fig. 246; see also p.33). A further dress-up event was held in 1981, when
Augusta's sister Pickie, and various nieces and grandnieces, all attended and
wore dresses from the Roddis family collection (fig. 247). On the occasion
of this photograph, taken with Pickie and her grandnieces, Tempe and Ann
Everson, Augusta is wearing the black two-piece dress opposite that had
belonged to her mother around the time of her parents' marriage in 1908
(fig. 248). Since Augusta was a member of the local chapter of the P.E.O.
Sisterhood, a philanthropic society dedicated to expanding educational
opportunities for women, she also unveiled some of her historic clothes for
events associated with that organization.[27] As she wrote in 1970, "I do use
some of these clothes for DAR and P.E.O. programs."[28]

FIG. 249, BELOW
Two programs
for The Confederate
Pageant, Natchez,
Mississippi, as
attended by
Augusta Roddis,
1941 (left), RFPA,
Courtesy of WHS
Archives Division;
1976 (right).
THF 2015.96.11.

In 1976, Augusta accepted an invitation to an event that sounded to her "like pure frivolity and fun": she would be required to visit Natchez, Mississippi, and "receive [sic] with the Mississippi DARs at their ante-bellum mansion which is on the Natchez Garden Tour."[29] There she attended "The Confederate Pageant" which comprised a series of tableaux based on historical themes, "to present in a bright fleeting moment," as the program states, "the charm of a gracious past" and the "days of stately bows, of rustling silks, of fluttering fans...."[30] Augusta had attended one of these pageants in 1941, so she was familiar with the highly romanticized portrayal of history that she would encounter there (fig. 249).[31] She quickly turned her thoughts to how she should dress: "Everybody wears an ante-bellum costume, and I thought it would be a great excuse to try to put together the dress in the attic" (Augusta is referring to the crinoline* dress belonging to her Aunt Jennie, see pp.78–83).[32] Augusta succeeded in having its unpicked skirt reassembled, and she wore it proudly in Natchez. This delicate dress was taken out of the attic again in 1988, when Augusta narrated a period fashion show for the eightieth anniversary of the DAR of Marshfield, at which nineteenth- as well as early twentieth-century clothes were modeled.[33]

The reconstruction of this crinoline dress illustrates how an occasion such as this event in Natchez helped to breathe life into the Roddis Collection stored in her attic. Similarly, Augusta had long harbored

Step Into The Past With Natchez!

Confederate Ball
10th Annual Pageant of the Original
Natchez Garden Club
March 22 - April 6 - 1941

Step Into the Past With Natchez!

The Confederate Pageant
1976

a desire to have two of the oldest and most appealing dresses restored, not only for the sake of preservation, but also to enable them to be safely worn for these special dress-up events honoring the past.[34]

The nation was preparing for the United States Bicentennial in 1976, and many women wondered what to wear for the festivities. Augusta and a number of local Marshfield women owned historic dresses, but most Americans hoping to dress up for the patriotic events had little access to any authentic historic clothing, or even any remotely accurate replicas. Recognizing this problem, Joan Severa, Curator of Costume at the Wisconsin Historical Society (WHS),[35] agreed to launch a project to take patterns from original garments (1830–1900) and to have them made into full-scale dress patterns in three modern sizes. (This work was undertaken by Edward Maeder, by then a specialist in historic dress patterns.[36]) Convinced of the importance of such a project, Augusta supported it financially, and eventually thousands of these historically based patterns were sold internationally.[37] Augusta felt that to support dressing up in historic costume was to feed an interest in history, and thereby a reverence for America's past.

"Everybody wears an ante-bellum costume, and I thought it would be a great excuse to try to put together the dress in the attic."

AUGUSTA RODDIS

A Few More Pretty Clothes

Augusta observed that part of the attraction of dressing up was simply "the love of pretty clothes".[38] She felt that many antique dresses, such as those belonging to her grandmother, were far more exquisite than contemporary women's wear. Even so, especially when she was young, Augusta enjoyed dressing up in attractive current fashions for special events in Marshfield, dances at Northwestern University, Mardi Gras balls in New Orleans, and aboard luxury ocean liners too, as discussed in earlier chapters.

As Augusta aged, the clothes that she wore in real life were of increasingly less interest to her. Still, a few of her later purchases that survive in the Roddis Collection reflect her taste for what she considered to be feminine and well-designed attire. In about 1968, she chose a silk jersey dress by Florence-based designer Averado Bessi, whose clothes resemble those by Emilio Pucci (fig. 250). In her later years, one of Augusta's trusted stores, named after the proprietor, Evelyn Barton Brown, was situated in a suite in the Mayflower Hotel, where Augusta stayed when she visited

Washington, D.C., for the annual DAR convention. (Jackie Kennedy was also a customer, according to Brown's niece Cynthia Barton Kasten.[39]) Evelyn Barton Brown maintained the former tradition of store owners like Ruth McCulloch and only included her store label in her dresses, rather than the designer name, so she was definitely the source of Augusta's turquoise permanently pleated dress (fig. 251). The high ruffled neck and long sleeves, in addition to the fact that it hardly required pressing, made it an attractive and practical choice for Augusta in her later years. As she mentions in the letter quoted above, ruffles were a detail she loved in historic costume, so here her delight in the old was fused with decorative detail on a contemporary gown.

Augusta's love of a rich blue color, and her eye for good cut, is demonstrated by one of the more recent dresses in the Roddis Collection: a wool, bias-cut dress by Louis Féraud (1921–99), a French couturier

FIG. 252, OPPOSITE
Wool bias-cut
dress by Louis
Féraud, *c.*1985.
THF 2014.24.43.

who also had a line of ready-to-wear clothing (fig. 252). This dress, from around 1985, was made in Germany, but by this time store labels were less common so where it was purchased is not known. The most recent item of clothing in the Collection is a multi-colored, checked rayon*, cotton and silk bouclé* suit by Cynthia Sobel for Herbert Grossman (see p.301). Sobel (active 1978–2000) was the leading designer for Grossman. Like other designers of the day, she created suits in the popular style of Coco Chanel. Sobel herself dates this particular suit to about 1995.[40] Altogether, while these garments purchased late in Augusta's life show a certain attention to design, practicality, and quality, they demonstrate no lasting interest in current fashion for its own sake. Augusta continued to wear some of these later purchases while she was still well enough to attend functions.

Luckily, the clothes in Augusta's attic largely escaped the terrors of scissors wielded by an enthusiastic and well-meaning descendant preparing for a fancy dress ball. The normally locked door to the attic closet certainly helped. The only dress that underwent truly significant alterations was Catherine's wedding dress, the waist of which was slightly enlarged and a new lining inserted so she could wear it for her fiftieth wedding anniversary. Besides this understandable exception, and the unwitting destruction of a civil war-era dress by the local dry cleaner, the integrity of the original garments remained intact—a tribute to Augusta and all the other women in the family who saved the family clothing.

Towards the end of her life, Augusta was no longer able to climb the stairs to the attic. Thus, buried in trunks and crowded into closets, the Roddis Collection remained largely untouched, protected by benign neglect and just waiting for all its secrets to be revealed. It was only after Augusta's death that anyone knew the extent of what was tucked away in the Roddis house.

Excellence In Education
Without Extravagance

Augusta Roddis

LIFELONG RESIDENT   For

H EDUCATIONAL STAN
SPENDING OF YOUR
EFFORTS THROUG
COMBAT DRUG

April 6th. W

by Augusta R

AMMON THEOLOGICAL SEMINARY, ATLANTA, GA.

Forestry
Futures
and
Conservation
Misconcepts

MARY RODDIS CONNOR

WIN WITH
JONES
JONES

The
GOOD
That
PROHIBITION
Has
Done
The
United
States

BY
MARY RODDIS

American Style and Spirit

As rich as the Roddis Collection seems on the surface, what was saved in the attic represents only a small fraction of the total number of clothes owned and used by this family. Clothing associated with special events tended to be treasured and kept. Some of the existing garments in the Collection may have survived simply by accident, while others were saved for historical interest. Augusta in particular found all the clothes "increasingly interesting" as the years passed and they no longer represented the current fashion of the day. Sadly, other items that were intentionally saved were later lost, either through loans for theatrical productions that were never returned or by accidental destruction.

Nevertheless, the Roddis Collection is cohesive enough to reflect the spirit of its age over several generations. Like most garments, the ones found in the Roddis attic share characteristics with the prevailing fashions of their time and place. But since these clothes are all from one extended family, and their context is revealed by family photographs and the personal observations of the wearers in their letters, diaries and other documents, as well as more general research, they provide further insights into the way these Americans viewed their clothing. One can even glean a sense of what we call the "American spirit" behind the Collection.

There is nothing radical or eccentric about the Roddis clothing. A sufficient number of the men's suits and shirts survive to demonstrate that W.H. and his son Hamilton were "well dressed" according to the standards of their time (W.H. Roddis was faithful to the British inspired

FIG. 253, PAGE 280
Clockwise from
top left: afternoon
hat, c.1954; Ruth
McCulloch dress
with jacket, c.1959;
book by Mary Roddis
Connor, 1947;
photograph of DAR
campaign billboards
for Sara Roddis
Jones, c.1974; cover
of booklet by Mary
Roddis, 1928; DAR
pin; Lumberjack
Steam Train at Mrs.
Connor's Camp Five
Museum, Laona,
Wisconsin; postcard
of the Gammon
Theological
Seminary; Augusta
Roddis's campaign
flyer when running
for local school
board, April 6, 1971.

cutaway suit, whereas Hamilton, although also a conservative dresser, adopted a more modern American look).

Evaluating the written evidence, it is apparent that the Roddis women, as well as their Prindle relatives, were interested in, but not obsessively enthralled by, whatever was the latest fashion. Rather than being chic in the French sense, or "fashionistas" beholden to ever-changing trends, these women had a sense of personal *style*. What was of simple, harmonious design and in "good taste" mattered; clothes should suit one's own coloring and physique; and appropriate outfits were needed for the occasion to which they were worn.

Shopping was certainly fun for the family members, yet as an activity it was limited to special days spent away from their Midwestern homes. Like other middle-class American women, the Roddis ladies maintained tight control over their annual wardrobe budget. Quality was important, not quantity, and wearing a dress, hat, or pair of gloves carefully purchased years earlier was perfectly acceptable, even desirable. If budget or availability prevented them from finding what they wanted, some of them were trained in the art of dressmaking and made clothes for themselves and other family members. By understanding their personal style and not succumbing to short-lived fads, these women displayed a high level of self-confidence. While regarding clothing as an essential element in self-presentation both in and outside the home, they also appear to have viewed good, suitable clothes as merely the first step on the path towards achieving more important things in life. This was a viewpoint also preached by countless American home economics teachers and retail advisors up to the 1960s.

Beyond their fundamental focus on family, the Roddis women were dedicated to civic activities and other interests. These included funding a seminary for African-American men, working for women's suffrage, running for election to local school boards, promoting education for women, taking a keen interest in politics and government policy, establishing a heritage museum to expose summer tourists to lumber industry history and forest management, and encouraging awareness of American history. Many of them also shared more domestic interests, such as sewing, embroidery, needlepoint, gardening, and flower arranging.

This book, and the exhibition it has inspired, offers the modern reader a glimpse into the lives of the Roddis family and their relations, both at home and in the world at large. Through their clothes and their letters, the Roddis Collection frames almost a century and a half of American style and spirit, offering a unique perspective on fashion, travel, war, leisure and, above all, family and daily life.

Notes

Chapter One

1 Augusta Roddis to Jane Lempereur, Feb 12, 1973. RFPC.
2 Frances Leddell (1808–73). Sara's grandfather, William Leddell (1746–1827), was born in Mendham, NJ, and played a significant role in supplying the continental army during the American Revolution.
3 According to the 1850 U.S. census, the births of Sara and her older siblings, Frances Augusta (1839–1901), Mary Esther (1841–1909), and John (1843–99), were registered in NJ.
4 Heatly Dulles 1890, pp.31–2.
5 A "normal" school was a state school created to train teachers, and establish teaching standards or norms, hence its name.
6 Edward Austin Sheldon (1823–97) was president of the Oswego Normal School and instrumental in bringing object training to the U.S.
7 Swiss pedagogue Johann Heinrich Pestalozzi (1746–1827) set up a school in Switzerland with an unorthodox curriculum. His motto was "learning by head, hand and heart".
8 E.A. Sheldon, "Address of Welcome", in Oliphant 1888, p.35.
9 Ibid.
10 Ibid., p.250.
11 Milwaukee, WI, City Directory, 1873/1874.
12 W.H. Roddis was the son of Thomas Roddis, who was born in England.
13 W.H. Roddis to Sara Denton, Aug 15, 1874. RFP, WHS, Box 8, Folder 23.
14 This comment is taken from a caption written by Augusta Roddis in the multiple family albums she created for her relatives in the 1960s.
15 Chemises and drawers were light and loose-fitting garments of white linen or muslin* which extended below the knee and were worn underneath corsets to keep the corsets clean and away from the skin.
16 See Chapter 4 of this book for further details.
17 Receipt for purchases made on the account of Rev. Jonas Denton. RFP, WHS, Box 7, Folder 13.
18 Hamburg edging (so-called as it was imported into the U.S. through the German port of Hamburg) was based on broderie anglaise*.
19 *New York Times*, Jan 27, 1873, p.7.
20 Hamilton Roddis (1875–1960); Frances Mary (named for her mother's mother and her father's sister, Mary Roddis), (1877–1952).
21 The information here is from the executor's petition concerning the estate of W.H. Roddis in Aug 1921, pp.3–7. RFPC.
22 As dictated by Augusta Roddis to Jane Bradbury in 2008.
23 See Schnitzler 1997, p.3.
24 Laird 2006, p.17.
25 William H. Upham was the elder statesman of Marshfield. In 1878, He established the first sawmill in Marshfield. He was well connected socially and politically, and apparently knew W.H. Roddis in 1894. They became close friends for the rest of their lives, as did their wives, Mary and Sara.
26 Schnitzler 1997, p.4.
27 Jones et al 1923, p.180.
28 Huston 1972, p.2.
29 Schnitzler 1997, p.3; Laird 2006, p.18.
30 In 1894, the Wisconsin Central Line (later called the Soo Line) scheduled a train that left Milwaukee at 11.35 am and arrived in Marshfield at 7.00 pm.
31 Augusta Roddis, *A Few Random Notes on the Social History of Marshfield*, an informal lecture given by Miss Roddis to the local Chapter AJ of the P.E.O. Sisterhood, date unknown, p.1.
32 In the Addenda of Upham's unpublished account at the North Wood County Historical Society in Marshfield, WI, Mary Upham added: "When boardwalks came into fashion we felt very proud and ceased carrying shingles when we walked about." Paving of Marshfield's Central Avenue began in 1914. See Schnitzler 1997, p.13.
33 Schnitzler 1997, p.2.
34 Ibid.
35 See Laird 2006, p.18.

36 *Die Demokrat* (published 1885–1921); *Wochenblatt* (published 1921–6).
37 Laird 2006, p.18.
38 "Club Members Knew Their Stuff", *Marshfield News – Herald*, Nov 28, 1994.
39 Schnitzler 1997, pp.230 and p446.
40 Ladies' Travel Class Program for 1905–6. RFP, WHS, Box 8, Folder 1.
41 Laird 2006, p.26.
42 Roddis 1 (undated), p.2.
43 Blair 1988, p.62.
44 Family tradition dictated that the paper from London was the *Times*. A set of *The Century* magazine was also found in the Roddis house and may have belonged to Sara (now part of the collection at THF).
45 "The Shakespeare Tea", *Marshfield Times*, Mar 28, 1902, p.4.
46 Blair 1988, p.119.
47 Jones et al 1923, p.219. See also Schnitzler 1997, p.230.
48 The earliest public library was in the home of Mary Upham. This book collection was then moved to various places and maintained by the Women's Christian Temperance Union for 20 years.
49 Laird 2006, pp.26–7.
50 Schnitzler 1997, p.230.
51 See Matthews 2003, pp.14–23, especially pp.14–17. See also Blair 1988.
52 See *Marshfield Times*, Nov 4, 1908, p.1.
53 *Wisconsin Alumni Magazine*, Vol. 13, No. 5 (Feb 1912).
54 *Marshfield Times*, Sep 11, 1902, p.6; *Marshfield Times*, Jul 25, 1906, p.1.
55 William H. Roddis and his fellow leading lumberman, William Henry Upham, held controlling interests in the First National Bank of Marshfield. See Laird 2006, p.17.
56 Sara to W.H. Roddis, Mar 11, 1901. RFP, WHS, Box 7, Folder 20.
57 *Marshfield Times*, Oct 3, 1902, p.7.
58 This hairstyle was made popular through the graphic art of Charles Dana Gibson (1867–1944).
59 "Roddis Family Enjoys Long Stay Across the Sea", *Marshfield Times*, Jul 9, 1913, p.1.
60 It must have been a favorite of Sara's at any rate: when the dress was restored in 1975, the silk lining was virtually in shreds, partly as a result of the metal salts used in the dye baths for the silk taffeta, but possibly due to frequent use as well.
61 Frances to Catherine, Apr 12, 1908, p.2. RFP, WHS, Box 5, Folder 14.
62 See Myers 1892 for a guide as to the number of dresses a woman like Sara would have owned: a bride "moving in a modest circle socially" would require in her trousseau "two woolen street dresses, as many silk or dinner dresses, one evening dress at least … two simple and pretty house dresses and a heavy and lighter wrapper or tea gown."
63 Early dress reformers include Amelia Jencks Bloomer (1818–94).
64 Annie Jenness Miller (1859–death date unknown) was an outspoken advocate of artistic reform in women's dress. See Cunningham 2003 and Newton 1974.
65 Julia C. Brown to Mary Roddis (younger), Jan 15, c.1897 (date illegible). RFP, WHS, Box 7, Folder 19.
66 Augusta Roddis left this dress to her niece, Sara Witter Connor; it is in her collection.
67 Upon the request of Augusta Roddis, Edward Maeder replaced the bodice lining and the upper part of the skirt lining from 1973–5.
68 The British Aesthetic Movement included an attempt to return to the medieval world as viewed idealistically by the Pre-Raphaelites.
69 Green 1983, p.27.
70 *Marshfield Times*, Aug 12, 1908, p.7.
71 From an original newspaper clipping, source unknown. THF 2015.10.33.
72 W.H. Roddis was not by nature a politician. He was elected mayor in 1908, but resigned before the end of his one-year term in 1909.
73 Roddis 1 (undated) (see pp.8–9 of transcript).
74 Ibid. (see p.9 of transcript).
75 Obit. of Mrs. W.H. Roddis, *Marshfield Daily*, Jun 23, 1926, p.1.
76 See Lauren Whitley in Steele 2010, pp.213–15.
77 Executor's petition: the estate of W.H. Roddis, Aug 1921, pp.3–7. RFPC.
78 Taylor (1983) 2009, pp.124 and 128.
79 Ibid., pp.237–8.
80 See Veblen (1899) 2009, pp.111 and 119.
81 Augusta Roddis to Jane Lempereur, Feb 12, 1973.

Chapter Two

1 In the City Directories of Milwaukee, W.H. Roddis is listed as book keeper in 1869, 1879, 1885; active in real estate and loans in 1872, 1892.
2 Huston 1972, p.2.
3 Augusta Roddis to Jane Lempereur, Nov 17, 1973. RFPC.
4 W.H. Roddis to Sara, Apr 1, 1894. RFP, WHS, Box 7, Folder 19.
5 "Roddis Family Honored Guests of Rotary Club: 50th Anniversary of Roddis Factory Observed", *Marshfield News – Herald*, Oct 1, 1940, p.7.
6 Cheese boxes were large containers for processed raw milk curds to cure and store the cheese. See Schnitzler 1997, p.12.
7 Rutkow 2013, p.108.
8 Ibid.
9 Nesbit 1989, p.308.
10 Ibid., p.114.
11 Ibid., p.297.
12 Rutkow 2013, pp.115–20.
13 *Marshfield News*, Mar 29, 1894, p.1.
14 See www.marshfielddoors.com/who_we_are/history_page.html
15 Huston 1972, p.2. See also www.marshfielddoors.com/who_we_are/history_page.html
16 Roddis 2 (undated), p.1.
17 *Marshfield Times*, Nov 20, 1896, p.4.
18 Mary Roddis to W.H. Roddis, *c*.1896. RFP, WHS, Box 7, Folder 19.
19 Mary Roddis to W.H. Roddis, Apr 26, 1897. RFP, WHS, Box 7, Folder 19.
20 *The Centralia Enterprise and Tribune*, Apr 24, 1897, p.6.
21 "I am glad you are going to rebuild. You have some of your father's pluck." Mary Roddis to W.H. Roddis, May 15, 1897. RFP, WHS, Box 7, Folder 19.
22 Roddis 2 (undated), p.1.
23 *Marshfield Times*, Jun 4, 1897, p.14.
24 Parish of St. Alban's Episcopal Church, est. 1890. W.H. Roddis helped to finance the building of a Gothic-style church in 1898.
25 Roddis 2 (undated), p.2.
26 Schnitzler 2000, p.586.
27 *Sterling Laminated Flush Veneered Doors*, Catalog D, Roddis Lumber & Veneer Company, undated but *c*.1913, p.1. RFPC.
28 See Green (1983) 2003, p.107.
29 Thanks to Charles Sable, Curator of Decorative Arts at THF, who analyzed interior photographs of the W.H. Roddis home, Nov 26, 2014.
30 Information told by Augusta Roddis to Jane Bradbury in 2008.
31 Huston 1972, p.4.
32 See Karamanski 1989.
33 Huston 1972, p.1.
34 Laird 2006, p.20.
35 Usually, only specialized collections devoted to shoes contain any kind of representational chronology of fashionable footwear. Moreover, shoes also were often simply worn out and discarded, meaning their inclusion within a dress collection is especially exceptional.
36 W.H. Roddis's house was occupied by his daughter Frances and later his grandson W.H. Roddis II after his marriage to Marilyn Hodgert.
37 W.H. Roddis to Frances, Jan 19, 1902. RFP, WHS, Box 3, Folder 11.
38 The labels in this suit and waistcoat read: "Wilkie & Sellery / Chicago / Mr. W.H. Roddis / DATE: 3/24/20."
39 Visual elongation mattered to W.H. Roddis, who was 5 ft 6¾ in. tall.
40 G. Bruce Boyer in Mears and Bruce Boyer 2014, p.18.
41 Whitaker 2006, p.49. See also Boorstin 1973, p.99: the proportion of ready-made compared to customized clothing was "nine tenths".
42 See a heavy ribbed, cream silk waistcoat with mother-of-pearl buttons, Dec 1, 1913, by Carver & Wilkie & Carroll McMillen Inc., Chicago.
43 Four years later, a gray and white vertically striped, ribbed silk waistcoat had the label "Wilkie & Sellery, Tailors, Chicago, 11/30/[19]15".
44 See Laura Roberts, *The Telegraph*, Oct 6, 2010.
45 Chenoune 1993, p.130.
46 A cane has a curved handle and was originally made of cane; a walking stick is straight with a handle attached on the same plane.
47 W.H. Roddis alludes to traveling with his sticks in a newspaper article about his trip to Europe: *Marshfield Times*, Jul 9, 1913, p.1.
48 This fob is now owned by one of the descendants of W.H. Roddis.
49 The Phillips-Jones Company, NY, printed the date "16AU11" and "Fraternity" on the lower left side of the front shirt. RFPC.
50 The stamped label of the surviving collars worn by W.H. Roddis read: "Arrow, Cluett, Peabody & Co. Inc. U.S.A." (style: "Tuxara").
51 Chenoune 1993, p.92.
52 See "The Collar", *Gloucester Citizen*, Jul 19, 1906, p.4.
53 Mary Roddis to W.H. Roddis, Apr 13, 1896. RFP, WHS, Box 7, Folder 19.
54 A version of the safety razor was introduced in 1847, but it was not universally accepted until 1903.
55 Huston 1972, p.6.
56 From a letter dated Feb 19, 1908. RFP, WHS, Box 5, Folder 12.
57 W.H. Roddis was mayor of Marshfield from 1908–9.
58 *Roddis Doors*, Catalog G, 1929, front page. RFPC.
59 *Sterling Laminated Flush Veneered Doors*, Catalog D, Roddis Lumber & Veneer Company, undated but *c*.1913, pp.10 and 12. RFPC.
60 Obit. of W.H. Roddis in the *Marshfield News*, Nov 11, 1920.
61 W.H. Roddis to George W. Ogden, Nov 7, 1912. RFPC.
62 See Matt Gross, "Lessons From the Frugal Grand Tour", *New York Times*, Sep 5, 2008.
63 Mary Roddis to her son, Apr 19, 1898. RFP, WHS, Box 7, Folder 19.
64 *Marshfield Times*, Mar 8, 1901, p.1.
65 Roddis 2 (undated), p.3.
66 Information based upon executor's report to the court of Wisconsin concerning the estate of W.H. Roddis. RFPC.
67 *Roddis Flush and French Doors*, Catalog F, *c*.1923, p.4. THF 2014.115.1.
68 The funeral announcement and a black-bordered photo of W.H. Roddis is prominent on p.1 of the *Marshfield–News*, Nov 11, 1920.
69 E. Clark of the Minneapolis, St. Paul & Sault Sainte Marie Railway Co. to Hamilton Roddis, Nov 8, 1920. RFP, WHS, Box 4, Folder 22.
70 Hamilton Roddis, speaking about his father W.H. Roddis at a 1940 Rotary Dinner, *Marshfield News Herald*, Oct 1, 1940, p.7.

Chapter Three

1 U.S. Census, Chicago, IL, Jul 19, 1870, p.280.
2 Inscribed on the reverse of the photo: "Isabella Arents Hedenberg. This photo was taken at the age of 21, the year before her marriage to Jason R. Prindle, 7/28/1871." RFPA.
3 "Grand Presidential Party at the White House, 1862", Frank Leslie's *Illustrated Newspaper*, Feb 22, 1862.
4 From the diary of Isabella A.H. Prindle, Feb 22, 1873. RFPC.
5 Ibid., *c*.Jan 1872. RFPC.
6 Ibid., Apr 10, 1873.
7 Ibid., Dec 5, 1873.
8 U.S. Census, Chicago, IL, 366 Jackson Street, Jun 1880, p.22.
9 Jason's occupation is listed differently in more than one U.S. Census: "clerk" in 1878; "salesman" in 1880; and "real estate" in 1900.
10 From the diary of Isabella A.H. Prindle, Dec 5, 1873. RFPC.
11 Miriam Elizabeth, b.1873; Edith Isabella, b.1879; Catherine Sarah, b.1882; Lucy Adelaide, b.1885.
12 The card includes an annotated musical waltz phrase and a dedication to her mother, Nov 23, 1887. RFP, WHS, Box 8, Folder 12.
13 *Daily News* (of Chicago or Evanston) held a competition for public school children for the best Christmas stories and illustrations. Miriam was awarded second prize, winning $5. RFPC.
14 *Lullaby*, music with illustration, was published by *Music, A Monthly Magazine*, Vol. V, Nov 1893 to Apr 1894.
15 Isabella Prindle to her sister-in-law Jane Prindle Gammon, explaining that Miriam received a Church scholarship thanks to her illustrated lullaby (see endnote 14). RFP, WHS, Box 8, Folder 23.
16 See *The Arrow of Pi Beta Phi*, Wisconsin Alpha, Madison, WI: Miriam spent 3 months in the Chicago School of Illustration.
17 *Northwestern University, College of Liberal Arts, Entrance Statistics*, Sep 19, 1899, states her father was a lumber merchant, that she attended Evanston Township High for 4 years and did not seek a college degree.
18 Snowden 1897, pp.354–71.
19 Edith to Catherine, Mar 25, 1902. RFP, WHS, Box 5, Folder 9.
20 A photo of Edith wearing her Aunt Jennie's dress is dedicated on the reverse: "To Richard, Christmas 1918, Edith". RFPA.
21 One reason Edith may have not married is that married women frequently had to give up their jobs. See Gordon 1990, p.5.

22 John Wesley Hedenberg (1820–1902).

23 The list of names and their meanings in Isabella's handwriting from a later date specifies that Catherine meant "pure" and Sarah meant "princess". RFP, WHS, Box 5, Folder 12.

24 Isabella to Miriam Prindle, Apr 25, 1898, p.3. RFP, WHS, Box 8, Folder 12.

25 Arents Legore, b.1875; Richard Hedenberg, b.1877.

26 A portion of letterhead reading "A.L. Prindle, Teacher of Banjo, Mandolin, and Guitar, 1622 Wesley Ave. EVANSTON" with a date in pencil "1895" is pasted into Isabella's scrapbook. RFPC.

27 Richard later became a businessman, breeding pedigreed Belgian hares from his farm near Richmond, Virginia.

28 Evanston High School, Catherine Prindle, Feb 1897; Modern Languages, Spelling 94, Mythology 92, Latin 93, Drawing 85, English History 95. RFP, WHS, Box 5, Folder 9.

29 See Taylor (1983) 2009, p.136. See also the "Mrs. Ralston Answers" column in The Ladies' Home Journal, Vol. XXV, No. 7, Jun 1908, p.76.

30 The family lived beforehand in Chicago, Evanston, and Kirksville.

31 Catherine's notebook and workbook from the Armour Institute are at THF: 2015.10.8 and 2015.10.9.

32 RFP, WHS, Box 5, Folder 9. The certificate is number 6694.

33 Mary Prindle married Don Carlos Newton (1832–93) on Oct 27, 1853, the same year her sister Jane married Norman Colton.

34 Catherine received a "First Methodist Episcopal Church Scholarship for the year 1903–4" and again in 1904–5 from the church in Batavia. RFP, WHS, Box 5, Folder 10.

35 Yearbook entitled SYLLABUS, Northwestern University, 1906, Catherine Sarah Prindle is listed as being involved in the Classical Course. Y.W.C.A., Alethenai Literary Society, President Y.W.C.A. and alongside her photo is the inscription: "Is she not passing fair?"

36 Gordon 1990, p.1.

37 Isabella Challacombe Hedenberg (1827–92) born in Devon, England.

38 Letter of condolence written by Susan B. Anthony of the National American Woman's Suffrage Association to Cecelia Hedenberg, Isabella's sister, Dec 1, 1892, p.3. RFP, WHS, Box 8, Folder 25.

39 The latter quote is from a clipping featuring part of her address, "The Solitude of Self", given before the U.S. Senate Committee on Woman Suffrage, Feb 20, 1892, by Elizabeth Cady Stanton.

40 For an example of the predominance of men over women at American universities, the Northwestern University Annual Commencement, Jun 11, 1896, includes Miriam Prindle's name along with 32 other students, only seven of whom are women, as those receiving a BA. RFPC.

41 Edward Clarke wrote an article listing many ailments, including "haovaritis, prolapsus uteri, hysteria, neuralgia", which he claimed resulted from college training for women. See Clinton 1984, p.131.

42 "You educate a man; you educate a man. You educate a woman; you educate a generation" (attributed to Brigham Young, 1801–77).

43 Gordon 1990, p.2. Her data also shows that women made up 35.9 per cent of the total students enrolled in 1890, and 39.6 per cent in 1910. See also dig. ref. Snyder 1993.

44 See Clinton 1984, pp.131 and 145.

45 E.g. Isabella to Catherine, Oct 14, 1904. RFP, WHS, Box 5, Folder 10.

46 Miriam to Catherine, Dec 4, 1902, p.1. RFP, WHS, Box 5, Folder 11.

47 Miriam to Edith Prindle. RFP, WHS, Box 8, Folder 7, p.7: "Mrs. B. is … very 'dressy' looking.… She has on a black silk skirt with a tail a yard long, & a waist of magnificent lace … & a fold of chiffon around her neck with a fine diamond in front."

48 Various letters from Edith to Catherine Prindle mention her waists of different colors. Only white versions survive in the Roddis Collection.

49 The 1911 Marshall Field & Co. employee book stated that all women employees must wear shirtwaists with black skirts. See Goddard 2011.

50 Frances Roddis to Sara Roddis, Jan 2, 1897. RFP, WHS, Box 8, Folder 1.

51 Belmont Davis 1908, p.9.

52 Fogg 2013, p.195.

53 The Modern Priscilla, Vol. XXI, No. 11, Jan 1908, p.11.

54 Kidwell and Christman 1974, p.145.

55 These panels are at THF (THF 2014.24.104).

56 Miriam to Catherine, Nov 28, 1906. RFP, WHS, Box 5, Folder 11.

57 Miriam to Edith Prindle, RFP, WHS, Box 5, Folder 11.

58 Miriam to Edith Prindle, 1902. RFP, WHS, Box 8, Folder 7.

59 It was not unusual then for a mother-of-the-bride to wear black, even if she was not in mourning. See dig. ref. Hoppe and Taylor (1983) 2009, p.258.

60 Green (1983) 2003, p.100.

61 Ibid., p.82.

62 "Department of Needlework", Ladies' Home Journal, Vol. XXIV, No. 8, Jul 1907, p.43.

63 Gould Woolson 1874, pp.93–4. Also see Brown Blackwell 1874, p.181.

64 Elizabeth Cady Stanton to the Dress Reform Convention, Jan 8, 1857, published in The Sibyl, Feb 1, 1857, Vol. 1, No. 15, pp.119–20.

65 Green (1983) 2003, p.83.

66 To this day, a family tradition remains to pass down to succeeding generations a pin that had belonged to Aunt Jennie; it is given to a descendant with the first or middle name Catherine.

67 Words reputedly spoken by Elijah Gammon after suffering damage to his voice from bronchitis, as quoted by Augusta Roddis in the 1960s.

68 Gammon gave up the ministry in 1858 due to poor health. In 1864, he secured the rights to sell and distribute the Marsh Reaper, and formed a partnership with William Deering. Gammon used his fortune to promote the Christian message and help those most in need.

69 Quarterly Bulletin, Gammon Theological Seminary, Vol. III, No. IV, Feb 1893, p.8. RFPC.

70 "Elijah H. Gammon: A Memorial Address", Quarterly Bulletin, Gammon Theological Seminary, Dec 23, 1891, p.9. RFPC.

71 Quarterly Bulletin, Gammon Theological Seminary, Vol. III, No. IV, Feb 1893, p.2. RFPC.

72 www.bataviahistory.org/historian-vol-26-51/the-batavia-historian-vol-43/volume-43---volume-3.aspx

73 This attribution was made by a leading painting restorer in Boston, MA. George P.A. Healy was one of the most prolific and popular painters of his day, and his sitters included Abraham Lincoln.

74 The frame has printed on the inside frame: "Genuine Union Case. Improved, Peck's Patent, Oct. 3d, 1854—Halverson's Patent Aug. 7, 1855. Assigned to S. Peck—Peck's Patent, Feb 4, 1856."

75 See the "Procession" Shawl, attributed to Pin Fils & Clugnet (France, Lyon), c.1867, Los Angeles County Museum of Art. Gift of Dr. David Bloom (M.86.236).

76 The Gammon Theological Seminary in Atlanta, GA, still thrives today.

77 Held between May and Nov 1878, this was the third Paris World's Fair.

Chapter Four

1   Isabella to Catherine, Sep 20, 1907. RFP, WHS, Box 5, Folder 12.

2   Announcement, Elkhorn City Schools, 1906–7, High School Teachers, Catherine S. Prindle, Latin and German. RFP, WHS, Box 5, Folder 11.

3   Marshfield Times, Apr 3, 1907, p.7.

4   See Vanderbilt 1952, pp.99–100.

5   Roddis 2 (undated), page unknown.

6   Marshfield News – Herald, Obit. of Hamilton Roddis 1875–1960, pp.1, 6.

7   Roddis 2 (undated), p.3.

8   Hamilton to Catherine, Apr 8, 1907. RFP, WHS, Box 5, Folder 12.

9   Hamilton to Sara Roddis, Sep 9, 1907. RFP, WHS, Box 1, Folder 8.

10 Hamilton to Catherine, Sep 16, 1907. RFP, WHS, Box 5, Folder 12.

11 Hamilton to Catherine, Sep 20, 1907. RFP, WHS, Box 5, Folder 12.

12 Account Book of Isabella A.H. Prindle. RFP, WHS, Box 11, no folder.

13 Catherine to Edith Prindle, Sep 9, 1907. RFP, WHS, Box 11, no folder.

14 Hamilton to Catherine, Oct 21, 1907. RFP, WHS, Box 5, Folder 12.

15 "I love you" in German. Catherine to Hamilton, Oct 10, 1907. RFP, WHS, Box 4, Folder 20.

16 Letter from the principal of Elkhorn School to Catherine, accepting her resignation, Oct 22, 1907. RFP, WHS, Box 5, Folder 12.

17 Catherine to Hamilton, Oct 8, 1907. RFP, WHS, Box 4, Folder 20.

18 Hamilton to Catherine, Sep 16, 1907. RFP, WHS, Box 5, Folder 12.

19 Hamilton to Catherine, Nov 22, 1907. RFP, WHS, Box 5, Folder 12.

20 Frances to Catherine, Sep 12, 1907. RFP, WHS, Box 5, Folder 12.

21 Catherine to Isabella, May 15, 1908. RFP, WHS, Box 8, Folder 9.

22 Catherine to Hamilton, Jan 10, 1908. RFP, WHS, Box 4, Folder 20.

23 The term "kimono" here refers to a loose-fitting, Japanese-inspired garment that was worn casually. It had been in fashion in the U.S. since the 1880s through Gilbert and Sullivan's Mikado, set in Japan.

24 Catherine to Edith, Nov 24, 1907. RFP, WHS, Box 8, Folder 9.
25 Catherine used the word "crinoline" in this letter to refer to the nineteenth-century fashion term as it was used in an early twentieth-century context, when it simply meant a particularly full skirt.
26 Catherine to Edith, Nov 24, 1907. RFP, WHS, Box 8, Folder 9.
27 Ibid.
28 Cotton velvet was rich-looking and practical.
29 Catherine to Edith, Mar 17, 1908. RFP, WHS, Box 8, Folder 7.
30 Catherine to Edith, Apr 14, 1908. RFP, WHS, Box 8, Folder 7.
31 For the background of the trousseau, see pp.25, 85 and 91.
32 Catherine to Edith, Apr 14, 1908. RFP, WHS, Box 8, Folder 7.
33 Catherine to Edith, Oct 8, 1907. RFP, WHS, Box 8, Folder 7.
34 Ibid.
35 A catalog from Bloomingdales, dated in the 1880s, lists a deluxe "Bridal Set" costing $148.79. See dig. ref. Aiello 2012.
36 Various women's magazines offered advice for the housewife on topics such as monogramming, including *Godey's Lady's Book*, *Peterson's Magazine*, and *Harper's Bazaar* (first spelled *Bazar*).
37 Identifying initials could be transferred to cloth using copper stencils or carved wooden blocks.
38 U.S. *Vogue*, Apr 23, 1908, p.612.
39 This set was bought from Barber Bros. of Hastings, MI, in June 1908. The Morris chair cost $10.50 and the entire set totaled $75.75. RFPC. The set was moved to the library of their new house in 1914, and the receipt dated 1908 was kept. RFPC.
40 Catherine to Edith, Apr 14, 1908. RFP, WHS, Box 8, Folder 7.
41 Catherine to Hamilton, Jan 22, 1908. RFP, WHS, Box 4, Folder 20.
42 Receipt from Marshall Field & Company, dated Jun 1, 1908, was found in the Roddis house in 2011.
43 Catherine to Hamilton, Oct 2, 1907. RFP, WHS, Box 4, Folder 20.
44 Ibid.
45 Hamilton to Catherine, date illegible, 1908. RFP, WHS, Box 5, Folder 12. Methodism and the Episcopal Church are both Protestant.
46 Catherine to Edith, date illegible. RFP, WHS, Box 8, Folder 7.
47 This tradition is still maintained today: after 6 pm, weddings are formal.
48 From original article cut out from unknown local newspaper, now at THF.
49 Sara Frances Roddis (1909-75); Mary Isabella Roddis (1909-2000); Catherine Prindle Roddis (1911-86).
50 Gus A. Krasin was born in Volyna, Russia, in 1885, and immigrated to the U.S. in 1892. The Roddis house, on Fourth Street, built in 1914, is the earliest surviving example of his work.
51 "The local paper noted that the modern mansion contained 12 rooms and cost in excess of $13,000." *Marshfield Times*, Jan 27, 1915, p.5.
52 Hamilton to W.H. Roddis, Aug 9, 1894. He paid $65 for this bicycle.
53 An Arco Wand Vacuum Cleaner was hooked up with pipes to suck dust from the rest of the house. See Bostock 2011.
54 See dig. ref. Hailey 2009.
55 Augusta Denton Roddis (1916-2011).
56 William Henry Roddis II (1917-2008).
57 An undated handwritten note in Catherine's handwriting, including the words "Whole set", was found inside a brochure entitled *Medical and Health Publications for the Layman*.
58 See p.165 for the Roddis Company military contracts in World War I.
59 "Tango at last invading Marshfield", *Marshfield Times*, Jan 7, 1914, p.1.
60 Catherine to Hamilton, Mar 17, 1908. RFP, WHS, Box 4, Folder 20.
61 Augusta to Jane Prindle Lempereur, Mar 2, 1970, p.2. RFPC.
62 Frances Roddis to Sara, Mar 13, 1912. RFP, WHS, Box 8, Folder 2.
63 Joseph Maklary (c.1881-1989) emigrated from Hungary to America, 1903.
64 The Wiener Werkstätte* (Vienna Craft Workshops) was a production community of visual artists in Vienna, Austria, that began in 1903 and expanded into textile and fashion.
65 See Blanke 2002, p.108.
66 Schnitzler 1997, pp.13 and 23.
67 German organizations in Marshfield raised money to ship food and clothing to German widows, orphans, and wounded soldiers.
68 Augusta Roddis to Jane Bradbury, May 2, 1988. RFPC.
69 Augusta Roddis to Jane Prindle Lempereur, Apr 15, 1978. RFPC. See also Roddis for Bostock c.1995-6, p.4.
70 Schnitzler 1997, p.16.
71 Aldcroft 2012, p.12.

Chapter Five

1 Laird 2006, p.18: in 1895, the town's population was 4,586. Schnitzler 1997, p.20: during the 1920s it increased to c.7,400 and was growing.
2 The region had many cheese makers, ice cream factories, and companies that processed milk, eggs, and chickens. Schnitzler 1997, pp.25-6.
3 Jones et al 1923, p.187; pp.191-2.
4 Ibid., p.208. See also Schnitzler 1997, p.23.
5 A receipt dated 1921 was found in the Roddis house for the purchase of a Franklin-Ritt Co. sedan for $4,090. RFPC.
6 Schnitzler 1997, p.23.
7 Ibid., pp.32 and 35. In 1923, over 37 per cent of Marshfield children were found to be underweight.
8 As detailed in *Marshfield Times*, Feb 13, 1918.
9 Mary Roddis, *The GOOD that PROHIBITION Has Done The United States* (1928). RFP, WHS, Box 7, Folder 2.
10 Schnitzler 1997, p.28.
11 Mary to W.H. Roddis, May 31, 1894. RFP, WHS, Box 17, Folder 19.
12 See Ujifusa 2012, pp.70-86.
13 Thanks to historian Steven Ujifusa, who undertook *Leviathan*-related research for the Roddis Collection Project in 2012.
14 Ellen Cecilia Roddis (1923-75).
15 Ellen Cobbins to Catherine Roddis, Jul 10, 1925. RFP, WHS, Box 6, Folder 1.
16 Jane Bradbury recollects that this book was kept on the bookstand by the door of the guest room of the Roddis house.
17 Post 1922, p.540.
18 The end of the silent film era began with the premiere of the first major film with sound, *The Jazz Singer* (1927).
19 See Lewis Allen 2010, p.144.
20 Popular historic films set in "Merry Old England" included *Little Lord Fauntleroy* (1921) and *Dorothy Vernon of Haddon Hall* (1924).
21 By the 1920s, and into the 1930s, this successful fashion house had become a center for apprentices, e.g. Madeleine Vionnet (1876-1975).
22 Lewis Allen 2010, p.151.
23 A receipt in the Roddis archives shows that the robe cost $16.50 and that it took two years for the merchant to send it to Mrs. Roddis in Marshfield. Letter and receipt, Jul 9, 1930. RFP, WHS, Box 6, Folder 3.
24 A box found in the attic with these Palestinian robes inside was marked "Nativity play costumes bought in Jerusalem 1928".
25 For example, see lot 45 from a sale at London-based Kerry Taylor Auctions, Jun 24, 2014: a couture evening coat, probably by Lanvin, c.1928-30, formed from gold and ivory Syrian brocade.
26 Pattern 7741 for "Ladies' Empire Dressing Gown or Negligee", *Pictorial Review*, 1918. 19 BWS, Commercial Pattern Archive, URI.
27 This buster suit was found in a box with a handwritten notation that it belonged to William H. Roddis II (also known as Bill).
28 Pattern for "Little Boy's Suit", Butterick 3755, 1922.71. BWS, Commercial Pattern Archive, URI.
29 Sara Denton Roddis (1846-1926); Cecilia Hedenberg Whitlock (1860-1926) was the sister of Catherine's mother Isabella Hedenberg Prindle.
30 Taylor (1983) 2009, p.174.
31 Diary of Augusta Roddis, Jan 7, 1928. RFP, WHS, Box 3, Folder 1.
32 Frances Cavanah, "The Secret of Belden Place" (two-part series), *Child Life*, Oct-Nov 1927, pp.604-6, 638-42, 699-701, 721, 730.
33 Augusta Roddis to Jane Lempereur, Feb 12, 1973. RFPC.
34 Augusta Roddis to Jane Lempereur, Nov 9, 1986. RFPC.
35 Pickie to Catherine, Dec 17, 1930. RFP, WHS, Box 6, Folder 3.
36 See U.S. *Vogue*, cover, Jul 1, 1926; see Drowne and Huber 2004, p.41.
37 The total production of cigarettes in the U.S. more than doubled between 1918 and 1928. See Lewis Allen 2010, pp.94-5.
38 According to her family, while at university, Mary and her beau Gordon Connor attended Proms and Balls in the State Capital Building, where marble floors reflected lights and glistening gowns.
39 Drowne and Huber 2004, p.109; Lewis Allen 2010, p.92; Kathy Peiss in Steele 2010, p.172.
40 "Paris Considers the Jeune Fille", U.S. *Vogue*, May 15, 1928, p.162.
41 Roddis family members recall hearing that at least one of Mary's

dresses was by Worth of Paris, purchased by her parents in 1928. This may have been one of the other dresses listed on her 1928 receipt. See endnote 56 below.

42 *La Garçonne*, meaning tomboy in French, is a term associated with a novel of the same name written in 1922 by Victor Margueritte.

43 See Clare Sauro in Steele 2010, pp.339–41; and Kyvig 2004, p.206.

44 The Charleston became popular after the 1923 Broadway musical *Runnin' Wild*. See dig. ref. Hennell-Foley 2014, pp.2–3.

45 Between 1914 and 1928, the quantity of fabric used in an average woman's outfit, known as a "costume", was reduced from 19 to 7 yards (17.5 to 6.5 meters). Herald 2006, p.49; Mintz and Kellogg 1988, p.110.

46 Beads were applied with a chain stitch, so if a thread was broken, beads would be ground into the dance floor by the dancers' shoes.

47 U.S. *Vogue*, "Paris Considers the Jeune Fille", May 15, 1928, p.160.

48 An undated letter, *c*.1924. RFP, WHS, Box 1, Folder 6.

49 In the early years of movie theaters, an announcement was made before the show began: "Ladies, please remove your hats." With the close-fitting *cloche* hats, this was no longer as necessary.

50 Miriam Prindle Waller to Edith Prindle, May 8, 1927. RFP, WHS, Box 8, Folder 7.

51 The family film of the wedding of Mary Roddis and Gordon Connor shows a dozen girls in a variety of hats. RFPC and a copy at THF.

52 Cecilia H. Whitlock to Catherine Roddis, Jan 25, 1926. RFP, WHS, Box 6, Folder 1.

53 Other labels from Adair give the address of 4 Cité Paradis. See also the Adair evening dress, Indianapolis Museum of Art (2009.564).

54 Compare with the Jeanne Lanvin (1867–1946) dress, 1923, now at the Metropolitan Museum of Art, New York (c.1.62.58.2a, b).

55 Isabella A.H. Prindle to Catherine Prindle Roddis, May 4, 1928. RFP, WHS, Box 6, Folder 2.

56 This receipt from Adèle & Cie, 83 Rue des Petits-Champs, Paris 1er, lists three dresses: one was entitled "Clairette" (meaning transparent, thin), described as "Robe mousseline rose bi-couleur" and priced at 1,000 Francs (*c*.$540–1500 in 2016).

57 U.S. *Vogue*, "Paris Considers the Jeune Fille", May 15, 1928, p.160.

58 See Laird 2006, p.20.

59 The social impact of more cars in the U.S. was enormous.

60 Melvin Laird to Jane Bradbury, Mar 7, 2011, and also Oct 12, 2011.

61 Mary Roddis to Augusta, Jun 29, 1929. RFP, WHS, Box 1, Folder 1.

62 Frances Roddis to Augusta, May 24, 1931. RFP, WHS, Box 1, Folder 2.

63 Pickie to Augusta, Jul 9, 1929. RFP, WHS, Box 1, Folder 1.

64 Roddis for Bostock *c*.1995–6, p.1.

65 A copy of this film is at THF.

66 The underdress of pink silk taffeta was shattered and replaced with a modern silk version of the same color by Edward Maeder in 2012.

67 Piña fiber was originally used in the 1830s to make knitted lace, but in the mid-nineteenth century it became increasingly popular, when combined with silk and used as fabric for crinoline* dresses.

68 Laird 2006, p.153.

69 Kyvig 2004, p.208.

Chapter Six

1 "We are a happy people—the statistics prove it. We have more cars, more bathtubs, oil furnaces, silk stockings, bank accounts, than any other people on earth." U.S. President Herbert Hoover, Mar 1929, as quoted in Roberts Compton 1980, p.414.

2 See Roddis for Bostock *c*.1995–6, p.5.

3 Ibid., p.3.

4 Hamilton's salary reached $20,000 in 1925, was cut to $7,200 at a board meeting on March 22, 1932, and increased to $9,000 in 1935. RPCR, WHS Archives Division, Box 1, Folder 9.

5 By 1933, the income of Americans had fallen by an average of 54% since 1929. See Kyvig 2004, p.209.

6 See Huston 1972, p.96; and Roddis for Bostock *c*.1995–6, p.3.

7 Roddis for Bostock *c*.1995–6, p.5.

8 Ibid., p.3.

9 Augusta to Catherine, Oct 26, 1930. RFP, WHS, Box 6, Folder 3.

10 Ibid.

11 Roddis for Bostock *c*.1995–6, p.2.

12 Ibid. See also Schnitzler 1997, pp.52 and 446.

13 Thanks to Grace Roddis, daughter of William H. Roddis II, who shared this story with Jane Bradbury in Aug 2014.

14 Schnitzler 1997, pp.43 and 54–5.

15 Roddis for Bostock *c*.1995–6, p.2.

16 Ibid.

17 Huston 1972, p.72.

18 Schnitzler 2000, p.586.

19 Ibid.

20 *Wisconsin Rapids Daily Tribune*, Aug 29, 1928, p.3.

21 *Marshfield Times*, Feb 1915, p.5.

22 Replies from Miss Virginia Vedder and Mr. Kenneth Eiche, from May 1932. RFP, WHS, Box 1, Folder 2.

23 On the back of this card, listed under "Order of Dancing", is the name Kenny, possibly referring to Kenneth Eiche, who wrote the reply mentioned in endnote 22 above.

24 See Fogg 2013, p.317.

25 Roddis for Bostock *c*.1995–6, p.5.

26 Taylor 2013, p.55. More elaborate use of ties may be seen in a dress from Vionnet's collection (*c*.1933) now in the Kyoto Costume Institute (inv. no. AC7652 92-43-2). See also Fukai 2006, p.411.

27 Toiles are fabric patterns from which a dress could be copied. U.S. department stores bought toiles from Paris to make cheap yet accurate copies of couture gowns. See Laver 2012, p.246.

28 Spanabel Emery 1999, p.247.

29 Golbin 2009, pp.295–6.

30 Whitaker 2006, p.71. See also Hawes 1938, pp.238–9: a custom-made ready-to-wear dress from New York in 1933–4 would have cost *c*.$195.

31 This is a spare copy, as there are no names inscribed in it.

32 U.S. *Vogue*, Apr 15, 1932, p.106. See Lewis Allen 1986, p.137.

33 DAR 80th Anniversary Chris Buchanan Style Show, Augusta Roddis narrator, Oct 8, 1988. Copy at THF.

34 See dig. ref. Bernstein.

35 Letter from "Del" (Delphine) to "Ellen", most probably Ellen Sexton not Ellen Roddis who was only 13 at the time, which explains the budget and the idea for the programs. RFP, WHS, Box 3, Folder 8.

36 Playful use of language and slang was a fad of that time; "P.J.s", short for pajamas, and "bra", short for brassiere, were coined in the 1930s.

37 "Anything goes ('cePtIn PHormalNeSS)" is the name of the first dance listed on the 1936 "Formal Brawl" party program. 1936 program: THF 2015.10.41; 1937 program THF 2015.10.42.

38 Melvin R. Laird to Jane Bradbury, Mar 7, 2011. RFPC.

39 Roddis for Bostock *c*.1995–6, p.3.

40 Ibid., p.3.

41 Ibid., p.1.

42 Hennessy 2012, pp.292–3. See also Jane Trapnell in Steele 2010, p.6.

43 See *The Daily Northwestern*, "Official Publication for over 12,000 Students, Evanston Illinois", Mar 31, 1937, Vol. 57, No. 60, p.1.

44 Kay Carrington was the future wife of the Broadway composer and lyricist, Arthur Schwartz. Edward Maeder owns a handwritten note by Carrington (signature visible): it is clearly by the same hand as the signature on the 1937 photographs of Augusta.

45 See dig. ref. Lodwick 2008: The film *Romeo and Juliet* (1936) was designed by Oliver Messel. For the craze for Juliet caps, see Costantino 2007, p.35.

46 See Farneti Cera 1992, p.215.

47 As told by Augusta Roddis to Jane Bradbury, *c*.2009. Augusta wrote to the New York Dress Institute to inquire if they knew anything about Gladys Parker. Augusta to Ellen Koslow, Feb 15, 1950. RFP, WHS, Box 1, Folder 13.

48 "'Flapper Fanny' Artist Designs Fashions for Zembo Parade", *The Evening News* (Harrisburg, Pennsylvania), Mar 12, 1936, p.11.

49 "Wife of Corsicana Man Turns Talents to Dress Designing", *Corsicana Daily Sun*, Feb 24, 1934, p.6.

50 A similar dress was shown at one of Parker's fashion shows in Florida in 1935: www.efootage.com/stock-footage/58568/Gladys_Parker_Fashion_Show

51 Ely 1935, p.32.

52 "Flapper Fanny And You Behold Her Artist", *La Crosse Tribune And Leader Press*, Feb 2, 1934, p.2.

53 *New York Times*, Mar 18, 1934, p.7.
54 "Junior Miss Fashions by G. Parker", *Reading Times*, Aug 31, 1934, p.5.
55 Augusta to Ellen, Nov 6, 1936. RFPC.
56 In a letter Hamilton writes to Mr. H.F. Below, dated Aug 11, 1933, he requested accommodation for 8 family members when they attend the World's Fair, Aug 28–9, 1933. RPCR, WHS Box 3, Folder 2.
57 See Jean Shepherd, *In God We Trust, All Others Pay Cash* (Broadway Books, 1991) about his impressions as a boy going to this world's fair.
58 *A Century of Progress Exposition: Official View Book*, 1933.
59 See endnote 47 above.
60 *Buck Rogers in the 25th Century: An Interplanetary Battle with the Tiger Men of Mars*.
61 *Chicago Sunday Tribune, Paris—Chicago Fashions*, Oct 1933, p.1.
62 Mears and Bruce Boyer 2014, pp.80 and 200.
63 Catherine to Augusta, Apr 9, 1935. RFP, WHS, Box 1, Folder 5.
64 *McCall's Magazine*, Jan 1936, p.73.
65 Lewis Allen 1986, p.280.
66 Cinema Fashions was a chain of shops established in 1930 by the Modern Merchandising Bureau. See Jane Trapnell in Steele 2010, p.6, Whitaker 2006, p.73, and Wilson and Taylor 1989, pp.99–100.
67 Spanabel Emery 1999, p.248.
68 Roddis for Bostock *c*.1995–6, Addendum.
69 Diary of Augusta Roddis. RFP, WHS, Box 11, Folder 1.
70 Pickie married in June 1936. Ellen was only 13 years old that year. Their garments from this period do not survive.
71 Cartier 1931, p.1.
72 Przybyszewski 2014, pp.17–18.
73 Ibid., pp.9 and 17.
74 Quoted in Przybyszewski 2014, p.15.
75 See Laird 2006, p.212.
76 See U.S. *Vogue*, Jul 15, 1940, pp.58–9 for a full-page photo of the actress Hedy Lamarr (1914–2000) in a dress by Gladys Parker.
77 *SPOT Magazine, The Entertaining Picture Journal*, May 1942, p.44.
78 *Santa Cruz Evening News*, Feb 20, 1931, p.6.
79 *The New York Times* (obit.), Apr 28, 1966, p.43.
80 Ely 1935, pp.31–2.

Chapter Seven

1 Hamilton built up the family business after the death of his father in 1920 and kept it from bankruptcy during the Great Depression.
2 Hamilton's tuxedo*, 1927, was by Jansson Bros. Co. of Chicago. His other surviving suits from the 1950s were by Bernard Weatherill, Inc.
3 These spectator shoes are labeled "Hanan's Hurdler's" (inside sole).
4 *Milwaukee Journal*, Jul 13, 1936.
5 See dig. ref. Scharf 2015.
6 The 1934 film *It Happened One Night* had a significant impact on men's fashions. See Patricia Campbell Warner in Welters and Cunningham 2005, pp.85–6.
7 Marcus 2001, p.114.
8 See Witter Connor 2014, p.147.
9 Siempelkamp Maschinen- und Anlagenbau is still located in Krefeld.
10 In 1945, a local newspaper reported that the Siempelkamp press was "one of the largest hot-plate presses in the industry". See "Total War Effort Backed by Roddis", *Marshfield News – Herald*, May 19, 1945, p.3.
11 Surviving playbills reveal that they attended *Macbeth*, *A Comedy of Errors* and *Twelfth Night* in Stratford-upon-Avon, Sep 1938.
12 The front is embossed with the Nazi eagle. THF 2015.10.97. Images in Witter Connor 2014, pp.155–6.
13 See Witter Connor 2014, p.29.
14 Ibid., p.156.
15 Ibid., pp.148–50.
16 Roddis for Bostock *c*.1995–6, p.5.
17 Ibid.
18 He was to become Sir Geoffrey de Havilland when knighted in 1944 for his contribution to Great Britain and its allies in World War II.
19 Wooden airplanes had been used since World War I, but metal planes were thought to be the only sensible option in World War II.
20 Witter Connor 2014, p.99.
21 The Mosquito was useful in multiple scenarios, as a bomber, pathfinder, day/night fighter and photograph-reconnaissance aircraft.
22 Plywood refers to a structural material consisting of thin layers of wood glued together under pressure. See Witter Connor 2009, p.19.
23 Ibid., p.17.
24 In 1939 or 1940, the British Government placed a large contract (which eventually amounted to $3 million) with the Roddis Company for aircraft plywood, causing the plant to be reorganized to ensure high standards. RPCR, WHS, Box 8, Folder 16. See also Witter Connor 2014, p.101.
25 Ibid.
26 W.H. Roddis II studied Mechanical Engineering at M.I.T, late 1930s.
27 See Kearns Goodwin 1995, pp.194–5.
28 The bill was passed on Mar 11, 1941. See Kearns Goodwin 1995, p.214.
29 See Witter Connor 2014, p.217.
30 "Total War Effort Backed by Roddis", *Marshfield News – Herald*, May 19, 1945, p.3.
31 Witter Connor 2014, pp.71–4.
32 Howard Robard Hughes, Jr. (1905–76) was a U.S. business tycoon, film producer and director, aviator, aerospace engineer, and philanthropist, known as the one of the wealthiest men in the world. See Bartlett and Steele 1979 (2003), p.118.
33 Witter Connor 2014, pp.113–23.
34 Ibid., p.120.
35 *Marshfield News – Herald*, May 19, 1945, p.3.
36 Witter Connor 2014, p.168.
37 Ibid., p.102.
38 Ibid., p.26.
39 Frances to Catherine Roddis, Apr 10, 1942. RFP, WHS, Box 6, Folder 7.
40 Coffee was scarce because the ships used to transport it were needed to carry soldiers and supplies instead. See Kearns Goodwin 1995.
41 The letter from Mary Roddis Connor to Catherine Roddis is in the Connor Family Collection and is quoted by Witter Connor 2014, p.22.
42 Ellen Roddis to her parents, Mar 19, 1942. RFPC.
43 Ellen to Hamilton Roddis, undated. RFPC.
44 Examples include Katharine Hepburn in *Woman of the Year* (1942) and Gene Tierney in *Laura* (1944).
45 Women took their own bobby pins to the salon for an "up-do".
46 Ellen to Augusta, Nov 10, 1941. LFC.
47 *LIFE*, Apr 20, 1942.
48 These details may be seen on the WPB Yardstick poster (fig. 145).
49 Przybyszewski 2014, p.120.
50 "L" standing for Limitation Order; 85 for section on clothes.
51 *Click* 1943, p.30.
52 Marcus 2001, p.115.
53 Ibid.
54 Ibid.
55 "Cuff": American term for British "turn-ups", at the bottom of trousers.
56 *Women's Wear Daily*, Apr 8, 1942, quoted in dig. ref. Stanton 2009.
57 During World War II, passementerie embroidery was used by leading Parisian designers and also became popular in America.
58 The use of silk fibers for domestic use was also severely restricted.
59 See dig. ref. Stanton 2009.
60 Although the Japanese surrendered on Aug 15, 1945, the surrender documents were not signed until Sep 2, 1945.
61 See dig. ref. Kolkman 2011.
62 Augusta to her parents, Mar 29, 1943. RFP, WHS, Box 6, Folder 7.
63 Italian designer Salvatore Ferragamo first created the wedge shoe from cork and wood due to a lack of the right sort of steel to support the arch of the foot in his shoes. See Ricci and Maeder 1992, pp.90–1.
64 See Kearns Goodwin 1995, p.316.
65 In the U.S. the responsibility of adhering to the wartime restrictions fell on the manufacturer, not the consumer.
66 Catherine to Bill, Jun 10, 1944. RFP, WHS, Box 8, Folder 5.
67 A local golf course, the Marshfield Country Club, opened in 1923.
68 Przbyszewski 2014, p.127, en 111. See Raushenbush 1942, pp.110–11.
69 "Eye-Catcher Hats", *LIFE*, Oct 5, 1942, p.77.
70 Augusta to Catherine Roddis, no date. RFPC.
71 Catherine Prindle Roddis m. Robert Thomas Beggs on Jun 30, 1936.
72 Sgt. Maurice C. Rosch to Augusta, Jul 21, 1942. RFPC.

73 Lt. Maurice C. Rosch to Augusta, Feb 28, 1944. RFPC.

74 Details given by Grace Roddis, daughter of W.H. Roddis II, in 2015.

75 *American Lumberman*, Jul 10, 1943, p.213.

76 See Witter Connor 2014, p.150: "Tell the woman that her grandfather's plywood sent to England for the Mosquito bombers bombed our archives, and we have no photos before 1945."

77 Witter Connor 2014, p.136.

78 Ibid., pp.39–40, 116 and 120.

79 Ibid., pp.42–3.

80 Apparently, over 25,000 women applied, but only 1,074 were accepted into the Women Airforce Service Pilots (WASP), formed in 1943. The accepted women all had prior experience and pilots' licenses.

81 Ellen to Augusta Roddis, Mar 26, 1943. LFC.

82 Glenn had previously taught aerodynamics to the Army Air Cadets, according to a letter from Ellen to her brother Bill, Apr 6, 1944. LFC.

83 Witter Connor 2014, p.37.

84 "Hoop Skirts for 1946", *The Paris News*, Jan 10, 1946, p.3.

85 The term "New Look" was first used by Carmel Snow, then editor of *Harper's Bazaar*, when writing about Dior's collection "Ligne Corolle".

86 Mackenzie Stuart 2012, p.145.

87 "PARIS FORM from the inside", U.S. *Vogue*, Oct 1, 1947, p.179.

88 See Jean L. Druesedow in Steele 2010, p.594.

89 See Marilyn Revell DeLong in Steele 2010, pp.321–2.

90 Laver 2012, p.255.

91 She lamented the consequent loss of freedom. Helen L. Laird, "Augusta Roddis: A Sketch of Her Life", May 11, 1999, p.4. RFPC.

92 Ibid.

93 Bernard Weatherill was responsible for the finely tailored riding and hunting suits for the royal family in Great Britain.

94 From the mid-1920s, Gallagher was running her own business producing dresses, suits, and coats.

95 See wool dress attributed to House of Balenciaga, *c.*1947, Metropolitan Museum Accession Number: 2009.300.423a, b.

96 *Marshfield News – Herald*, Jun 25, 1955, p.1: in 1946 the Roddis Company "realized sales of $9,000,000" and by 1950 sales reached $50,000,000; *Marshfield News – Herald*, Mar 28, 1960, p.1: by 1960, the Roddis Plywood company reached sales of $59,000,000 and a net worth of $20,000,000.

97 An article in the *Marshfield News – Herald*, "Roddis Veneer Used in Revamped White House", is mentioned in a tribute entitled *Miss Augusta Roddis: A Woman of Substance*, Apr 15, 2009, DAR Annual Meeting, Marshfield, WI.

Chapter Eight

1   Miller 2010 (a), see Foreword, unpaginated.

2   Dawson 2007, p.94.

3   Holland–America Line brochure for the S.S. *Nieuw Amsterdam*. THF 2015.67.10.

4   Menu aboard the *Nieuw Amsterdam*, 1948. RFP, WHS, Box 9, Folder 16.

5   Post 1922, p.608.

6   Ellen Roddis Lempereur to Augusta Roddis, written on board the S.S. *Independence*, late Apr 1953. RFP, WHS, Box 2, Folder 1.

7   *Marshfield News – Herald*, Jul 8, 1948. Original at THF.

8   A description of this cruise found in the Roddis house and written by a Rotarian mentions "King Neptune's equator dunkings". RFPC.

9   See Donzel 2006, pp.120–2.

10 Three more "Crossing of the Line" certificates survive from a cruise to South Africa in 1954. THF 2015.67.5; 2015.67.6; 2015.67.7.

11 From a description of this cruise by a Rotarian. RFPC.

12 Jantzen was the largest swimwear manufacturer in the world by 1930. Catalina was Jantzen's major competitor.

13 Susan Ward in Steele 2010, p.672.

14 "What to Bring": typewritten sheet now in the Roddis Collection (THF 2015.10.93).

15 Catherine to Augusta, Jul 12, 1949. RFP, WHS, Box 11, Folder 3, p.2.

16 Summers 2015, p. 24.

17 Rationing continued in Britain well after World War II ended (up to 1949 for clothing and 1954 for meat and foods).

18 Augusta Roddis, undated script for a talk she gave about her 1949 trip to Europe, 1949–50, p.3. RFPC.

19 Ibid., p.4.

20 Ibid., p.5.

21 Cable & Wireless Ltd. Cable sent from Augusta Roddis, Hotel Piccadilly London [sic], on Aug 30, 1949. RPF, WHS, Box 11, Folder 13.

22 The S.S. *Queen Mary* held the prestigious Blue Riband for the quickest time across the Atlantic from 1938 to 1952.

23 See Braden 1988.

24 A passenger list for the S.S. *Roosevelt*, Sep 1938, lists Eleanor Roosevelt. By her name, "President Roosevelt" is handwritten. THF 2015.67.8.

25 Recollection of Jane Bradbury talking to Augusta in the mid-1980s.

26 Advertisement for Tuya perfume from *Seventeen* Magazine, Nov 1945.

27 The Onondaga Silk Company was a leading couture textile manufacturer in New York, New Jersey, and Pennsylvania.

28 See Blum 2003.

29 Mary Roddis Connor to Augusta Roddis, May 17, 1950. RFP, WHS, Box 1, Folder 13, p.7, and entire 9-page letter.

30 Miller 2011, p.79.

31 The *Special European* Itinerary *for Mr. and Mrs. Hamilton Roddis*, Mar–May 1950. THF 2015.67.3.

32 Miller 2011, p.79.

33 Mary Roddis Connor to Augusta Roddis, May 17, 1950. RFP, WHS, Box 1, Folder 13, p.7.

34 Ibid., p.3.

35 Brinnin 2000, p.444.

36 "Ladies Apparel" for cruise members, 1966, p.6. THF 2015.67.4.

37 Wilson 1941, pp.61 and 65.

38 Catherine Roddis is shown in an archival photograph wearing this Gothé dress with the matching Alice band shown on p.303, Jan 9, 1958.

39 British *Vogue*, May 2012, pp.207–9.

40 Augusta Roddis to Richards' Department Store, Miami, FL, Jun 14, 1952. RFPC.

41 Mary Roddis Connor to Augusta Roddis, Jul 25, 1949. RFP, WHS, Box 11, Folder 13.

42 The purpose of this organization was to control design piracy in the fashion world. It was active between 1933 and 1949.

43 *The Paris News*, Jan 10, 1946, p.3.

44 See Amy Lund and Linda Waters in Welters and Cunningham 2005, pp.123–44.

45 Dworkin 1998, p.76.

46 *Racine Journal Times* (Wisconsin), Jan 13, 1946.

47 See Valerie Steele, in Kirkham 2001, p.187.

48 A letter from the White House, Nov 27, 1944, confirms the appointment for Mrs. Roosevelt in the Gothé studio for 10.45 am, Apr 7, 1944. David Gottlieb's niece (Elaine Greenstone) was present at the time and confirmed this with Edward Maeder, Mar 27, 2012.

49 Photograph courtesy of Elaine Greenstone, niece of David Gottlieb.

Chapter Nine

1   In later life, Augusta's clothing began to be increasingly old-fashioned.

2   Personal recollection of Jane Bradbury.

3   Dior 1957 (reprinted 2007), p.157.

4   Email from Ann Rauff, daughter of Pickie Roddis Beggs, to Jane Bradbury, Feb 15, 2011. She recalls that her parents' friends often gave cocktail parties, and that Mrs. Steve Miller (Bess) hung her Hattie Carnegie dress on the clothes line after a party in the early 1950s to mitigate the smell of cigarette and barbeque smoke.

5   *Syracuse Herald-Journal*, Dec 12, 1981, p.80.

6   For a cocktail dress by Sybil Connolly, purchased in Dublin *c.*1962 by Mary Roddis Connor, see fig. 219 and p.300.

7   See Elyssa Schram Da Cruz in Steele 2010, p.154, who states that hats were always removed. However, Benton 1956, p.45, states that: "Hats may also be worn to cocktail parties or luncheons...."

8   Elegant evening coats had been popular for decades but were much in fashion in the 1930s and were often featured in fashion magazines.

9   Ann Rauff told Jane Bradbury how stunning her mother looked when dressed to go out to dinner in that velvet evening coat, Feb 2011.

10   Benton 1956, p.42: "*If in doubt, wear the plainer dress....*"
11   Howard Quirt, publisher and editor of the *Marshfield News – Herald*, lived in a spacious house on West Fifth Street, Marshfield.
12   Wilson 1941, p.58.
13   *Marshfield News – Herald*, Aug 26, 1950, p.9.
14   See p.188, fig. 161.
15   Benton 1956, p.47.
16   See Benton 1956, p.46.
17   A photograph shows Augusta wearing this yellow gown on Jan 9, 1958.
18   Augusta wore this gown from the mid-1970s onwards, purchased at Evelyn Barton Brown's store in Washington, D.C.
19   Trilling and Williams Nicholas 1942. See also Benton 1956, p.41.
20   Godlove Donovan 1943, p.95.
21   *Newsweek*, Aug 15, 1960, no pagination.
22   The hat and bag almost certainly belonged to Augusta.
23   *Desert Sun*, Number 42, Sep 30, 1958.
24   See Przybyszewski 2014, pp.252–4, on the demise of the hat.
25   U.S. *Vogue*, Feb 1, 1936, p.41 (copy from the Roddis house).
26   In 1948, two old-line furriers from New York City, Gunther & Sons and Jaeckal, Inc., merged with the aim of widening their line.
27   Anthony Blotta was born in Italy and started his fashion house in New York in 1919. He designed a suit for Marlene Dietrich in the early 1930s.
28   Butterick 1926, p.108.
29   Quoted in Przybyszewski 2014, pp.103–5.

Chapter Ten

1   Augusta to her friend Ellen (Sexton Olson), Apr 10, 1958. RFPC.
2   Recollection of Janice Lempereur, shared in 2015. For deliveries, see Whitaker 2006, p.37.
3   The South Rotunda was crowned with a spectacular Fevrile mosaic dome designed by Louis Comfort Tiffany.
4   Sears & Roebuck offered mail-order service.
5   Whitaker 2006, p.37.
6   Ellen to Augusta Roddis, May 5, 1941. RFPC.
7   See Klaffke 2003, pp.22–3.
8   Garfinkel and Spafford 2002, p.611.
9   See Goddard 2011, p.63; and Soucek 2010, p.106.
10   Klaffke 2003, p.23.
11   Ibid., pp.22–3.
12   Wilson 1941, p.54.
13   Vanderbilt 1952, p.192.
14   Benton 1956, pp.44–5.
15   Shields 1991, p.89.
16   Jane Bradbury recalls many document boxes marked by year on the uppermost shelf of Catherine's bedroom closet. These did not survive.
17   Pickie to her parents, Nov 10, 1930. RFP, WHS, Box 6, Folder 3.
18   Ellen to Augusta Roddis, Mar 10, 1941. RFPC.
19   Augusta to Ellen Roddis, Feb 13, 1941. RFPC.
20   Ibid.
21   Ellen to Augusta, Nov 10, 1943. RFPC.
22   Augusta to Ellen, May 10, 1942. RFPC.
23   Augusta to Ellen, Jul 12, 1942. RFPC.
24   Augusta to Ellen, May 10, 1942. RFPC.
25   Augusta to Sara Roddis Jones, Apr 10, 1953. RFP, WHS, Box 2, Folder 4.
26   Trilling and Williams Nicholas 1942, p.465.
27   Augusta to Ellen Roddis Lempereur, Jan 28, 1958. RFPC.
28   Ellen to Augusta, May 22, 1947. RFP, WHS, Box 1, Folder 12.
29   This receipt from I. Magnin was found in the Roddis house. RPFC.
30   Augusta to Ellen Roddis Lempereur, Aug 10, 1955. RFP, WHS, Box 2, Folder 4.
31   Augusta to Ellen (Sexton Olson), Apr 10, 1958. RFPC.
32   For criticism of Adrian, see Mackenzie Stuart 2012, p.164.
33   Benton 1956, p.45.
34   Ellen to Augusta Roddis, Mar 10, 1941. RFPC.
35   Thanks to Ellen Everson, one of Augusta's nieces, for her recollection of this comment that Augusta made to her in the mid-1960s.
36   Wharton 1920 (2003), p.156.
37   Wilson 1941: "Any woman seeking to gain favor in a club would dress down rather than up for a special appearance."
38   Hawes 1938, p.129.
39   Martha Weathered also had a store in the Drake Hotel. See obit. of Frank L. Cole, *New York Times*, Dec 2, 1950.
40   Due to their poor condition, the three surviving garments (RFPC) from the 28 Shop were not included in this book.
41   Soucek 2010, pp.101–3. See also Katz Frommer 2013, p.95.
42   Ibid.
43   Katz Frommer 2013, pp.95–6. See also Hawes 1938, pp.124–5.
44   For example, see the black wool suit attributed to Balenciaga at the Metropolitan Museum of Art, New York (accession no. 2009.300.422).
45   This postcard is now in the Roddis Collection (THF 2015.10.66).
46   Northbrook Court was a prestigious shopping center in Wheeling, IL, where McCulloch opened her last store in 1976, aged 75.
47   *Business North Shore*, Mar 1984, p.89.
48   Augusta to Ellen (Sexton Olson), Apr 10, 1958. RFPC.
49   In the late 1920s in Paris, Coco Chanel used traditionally masculine clothing features when designing her woman's "Chanel suit".
50   This undated document is on Ruth McCulloch headed paper. Archive at the Evanston History Center.
51   Katz Frommer 2013, pp.96–7.
52   Whitaker 2006, p.68.
53   "No More Nettie", *TIME* magazine, Mar 16, 1942.
54   Nettie Rosenstein designed First Lady Mamie Eisenhower's dress, commissioned by Neiman Marcus for the 1953 Inauguration Ball.
55   Mary Roddis Connor to Hamilton Roddis, Sep 9, 1929. RFP, WHS, Box 5, Folder 3.
56   Comments by Augusta to Ellen Roddis Lempereur, undated but 1953. RFP, WHS, Box 4, Folder 5.
57   Augusta to Ellen Roddis Lempereur, May 29, 1953. RFP, WHS, Box 2, Folder 4.
58   Mary Roddis Connor to Augusta, Jan 6, 1950. RFP, WHS, Box 1, Folder 13.
59   Castillo/Lanvin suits would also have been available in the U.S. so it is not definite that this suit was purchased in Paris.
60   Castillo began his career in the 1930s in Paris. After the death of French couturier Jeanne Lanvin, he became head of the Lanvin fashion house. In 1964, he opened his own house in Paris.
61   This dress was later much altered in order to be wearable for Ellen's daughters, so it was reassembled by Edward Maeder.
62   Dior 1957 (2007), p.52.
63   These advice books became far less prevalent by the 1960s, although John Molly's 1977 title, *The Woman's Dress for Success Book*, was popular.
64   U.S. *Vogue*, Jan 1, 1941, p.21.
65   *Business North Shore*, Mar 1984, p.89.
66   *Galesburg Register-Mail*, Sep 3, 1953, p.14.

Chapter Eleven

1   The house of W.H. Roddis was sold, and burned down in 1969. Her grandparents' belongings were moved to Augusta's in 1948.
2   THF 2014.24.150. The only photograph of this suit shows Hamilton wearing it at his fiftieth wedding anniversary (see p.264).
3   The original lining of this wedding dress was replaced, the bodice expanded, and the mono-bosom* style reduced.
4   "Queen came to visit 50 years ago today", *The Sault Star*, Jul 4, 2009.
5   The timber in Sault Ste. Marie was one of the few extensive supplies of birch remaining on the North American continent.
6   This spoon, engraved "Queen Elizabeth II Visits Canada 1959", is set into a box with an enclosed card entitled "A Keepsake" with these words inside: "Presented by the Sault Windsor Hotel in commemoration of the visit of Her Majesty Queen Elizabeth II to Sault Ste. Marie, Ontario, July 8, 1959". THF 2014.24.192.
7   Recollection of Gordon P. Connor, Aug 2014. See Witter Connor 2014, p.105.
8   Recollection of Mary Connor Pierce, relayed through her sister Sara Witter Connor to Jane Bradbury in a conversation in 2011.

9   *Marshfield News – Herald*, Mar 28, 1960, p.1.

10   See obit. in *Marshfield News – Herald*, Mar 28, 1960, p.1.

11   Weyerhaeuser acquired the Roddis Plywood Corporation, Aug 1, 1960.

12   Recollection of Ann Beggs Rauff, daughter of Catherine Prindle Beggs, as shared with Jane Bradbury in Feb 2011, and again in Dec 2015.

13   Augusta to Jane Prindle Lempereur, Jan 17, 1970, p.1. RFPC.

14   Augusta to Jane Prindle Lempereur, Feb 12, 1973. RFPC.

15   H.L. Mencken, "The Mikado", *Baltimore Evening Sun*, Nov 29, 1910.

16   As confirmed by John Vollmer and Will Chandler, respected specialists in oriental dress and textiles, via email with Edward Maeder, Jan 2015.

17   As found in the Roddis house: *Smiles: A Musical Extravaganza with Home Talent*, The Adler Theater, Marshfield, Sep 2, 1929. THF 2015.10.70.

18   Refs to Richard's skill with a camera are found in many family letters.

19   Letter from Mary Newton to Catherine Prindle, Jun 24, 1900. RFP, WHS, Box 5, Folder 9.

20   Following World War I, patriotic fervor in the U.S. was reinforced by the celebration of Abraham Lincoln and George Washington's birthdays.

21   "She delighted in the magic of childhood.... Christmas, Halloween and Easter." From *Augusta Roddis: A Woman of Substance*, DAR Annual Meeting, Apr 15, 2009. RFPC.

22   Augusta Roddis to Pickie, Catherine Roddis Beggs, , Mar 14, 1963. RFPC.

23   Augusta Roddis to Jane Prindle Lempereur, Feb 12, 1973. RFPC.

24   The DAR is dedicated to patriotic, educational, and historic preservation. Augusta was a dedicated member for over 60 years.

25   Information based on a photograph from 1947. RFPA.

26   "DAR Centennial Tea", *Marshfield News – Herald*, Jun 10, 1972.

27   Catherine Roddis was a founding member of the local P.E.O. chapter.

28   Augusta to Jane Prindle Lempereur, Jan 17, 1970, p.1. RFPC.

29   Augusta to Jane Prindle Lempereur, Feb 2, 1976. RFPC.

30   Prologue of *The Confederate Pageant 1976* program. THF 2015.96.11.

31   Two programs for *The Confederate Pageant* were found in the Roddis house (1941: RFP, WHS, Box 11, Folder 1; 1976 THF 2015.96.11).

32   Ibid.

33   DAR 80th Anniversary Chris Buchanan Style Show, Oct 8, 1988. DVD courtesy of the North Wood County Historical Society, now at THF.

34   See Preface by Edward Maeder.

35   Joan Severa (1925–2015), curator at The State Historical Society of Wisconsin, 1959–90; Curator of Costumes and Textiles, 1979–90.

36   Augusta Roddis to Joan Severa, Curator of Decorative Arts, The State Historical Society of Wisconsin, Sep 12, 1972. EMC.

37   Augusta convinced fellow board members on the Hamilton Roddis Foundation to make a donation to kick-start this program.

38   Augusta Roddis to Jane Prindle Lempereur, Feb 12, 1973. RFPC.

39   Evelyn Barton Brown's niece, Cynthia Barton Kasten, to Edward Maeder, Jun 3, 2012: her aunt once told her on the phone that "I can't visit with you right now because I have Jackie Kennedy here".

40   Edward Maeder spoke to the leading designer, Cynthia Sobel, in New York City, Oct 6, 2015.

Abbreviations

DAR:	Daughters of the American Revolution
EMC:	Edward Maeder Collection
F.I.T.:	Fashion Institute of Technology
JBC:	Jane Bradbury Collection
LFC:	Lempereur Family Collection
P.E.O.:	The P.E.O. is a philanthropic women's organization dedicated to expanding the education of women. The meaning of the letters P.E.O. is a secret known only to its members.
RDC:	Roddis Dress Collection
RFP:	Roddis Family Papers, 1884–2007
RFPA:	Roddis Family Photo Archive
RFPC:	Roddis Family Private Collection
RPCR:	Roddis Plywood Corporation Records, 1897–1967
THF:	The Henry Ford
WPB:	War Production Board
WHS:	Wisconsin Historical Society Archives Division

Glossary

AUTHORS' NOTE
The exact definition of a fashion term is only valid within the context of the period in which it is used. This glossary is intended to be a general guide with basic information for ready reference.

A line
A term introduced in 1955 by couturier Christian Dior to describe apparel styled close and narrow at the shoulders and flaring gently away from the body from under the arms to the hem—resembling the letter A.

Alençon needle lace
Also known as *point d'Alençon*, this is a type of needle lace developed in Alençon, France, where Italian needle lace-making techniques (via kidnapped lace-makers from Venice) were introduced in the 1660s. This form of lace declined after the French Revolution but was revived by the Empress Eugenie during the Second Empire (1852–70), when it reached the peak of its popularity.

Alice band
A stiffened band shaped to the head to hold the wearer's hair away from the face, sometimes trimmed with matching fabric or flowers to compliment an ensemble. So-called because of its resemblance to the similar hair band worn by Alice in the illustrations of Lewis Carroll's 1865 novel *Alice in Wonderland*.

Arts and Crafts Movement
This movement (1880–1920) aimed to bring back pure design and craftsmanship, considered by some to have been overshadowed by mass production at the end of the nineteenth century. Although it began in England, the movement also gained a wide audience in America.

Art Deco
A term derived from the style made popular by *L'Exposition internationale des arts décoratifs et industriels modernes* (held in Paris in 1925) but not actually used until 1966. Characterized by rich colors, bold geometric shapes, and lavish ornamentation, Art Deco was based on, and drew inspiration from, the imagery, materials, and technology of the Machine Age.

Art Moderne
A late form of Art Deco architecture and design that emerged in the 1930s, sometimes also referred to as "Streamline Moderne". It emphasized curved shapes and long horizontal lines and was seen in all forms of industrial design, from architecture to transportation, and in interior and fashion design.

Art Nouveau
A late nineteenth-century (1880–1915) style seen in architecture and the decorative arts of the period, notable for its sinuously curving lines, rich colors, and use of exotic materials.

Ayrshire whitework
A type of embroidery made in white thread on white material, with areas of drawn thread work, used primarily for accessories, such as various forms of collars and cuffs. After 1780, it became associated with Ayrshire in Scotland, which became a center for the manufacture of muslin* (the material most often used to create this sort of embroidery).

Basque bodice
A form-fitting, boned upper garment, with or without a short skirt-like continuation. The term is from the French *Basque*, referring to the area in the western Pyrenees that spans the border between France and Spain, and the indigenous people who live there. Exotic, foreign terms were given to stylish items, quite randomly, to make them sound more interesting and desirable. In the 1890s, the term "habit basque" was also used. In the early twentieth century, this term referred primarily to a fitted bodice shape.

Bouclé
Woven or knitted fabric with a looped or knotted surface appearance, often used as fabric for sports suits. From the French for "curled" or "buckled".

Bowler
A stiff felt hat with a round crown and a narrow, curved brim. Commissioned in 1849 in England by Edward Coke, the younger brother of the second Earl of Leicester, as a hard and well-gripping form of hat that would protect the heads of his gamekeepers from overhanging branches. Bowler Brothers (Thomas and William) made the first "bowler" for James Locke & Co., a firm that originated in 1676 and has been based in London from 1765 to the present day. At first worn by working-class men, by the end of the nineteenth century the bowler was adopted by the upper-middle classes, especially businessmen. This hat is also known as a derby*, especially in North America.

Box cloth
A coarse, thick, water-resistant cloth, usually buff in color. It was often used for riding habits and other outdoor wear, including spats*.

Broderie anglaise
An all-white cotton embroidery, usually featuring a floral design, incorporating small holes, and mainly worked with buttonhole or satin stitch.

Bustle
A pad, cushion, or type of framework used to expand the fullness or support the drapery at the back of a woman's dress. It evolved from the crinoline* from 1867–72, reaching its most extreme form in the late 1880s.

Carrickmacross lace
A lace made by applying shaped pieces of sheer fabric to plain, machine-made net, with buttonhole or chain stitch, and then cutting away the material around the design. So-called after the lace school that was set up in Carrickmacross, Ireland, which enabled local women to earn a living, and thus avoid starvation, after the devastating effects of the 1846 potato famine.

Chemical lace
Also known as "burned out" lace, this was invented in Plauen, Germany in 1886 and was the most popular form of machine lace for the next century.

Chemise
Previously called a "shift", this term is French for "shirt" and was used for centuries to refer to a woman's loose-fitting, shirt-like undergarment worn next to the body. A corset and multiple petticoats were worn over it.

Chiné
A silk fabric with a subtly mottled pattern produced by warp threads that have been dyed, printed, or painted before weaving. Dictionaries claim that the term is derived from the French verb *chiner*, meaning "to make in the Chinese fashion", as derived from *Chine*, the French word for China. However, eighteenth-century French dictionaries suggest that this term is instead related to *chaîne*, the French word for "warp".

Cloche hat
A woman's close-fitting hat with a deep, bell-shaped crown and often a narrow turned brim. Derived from the French word *cloche*, meaning bell.

Cocktail dress
A semi-formal, usually short dress, worn for early evening parties. Often made from silk or other luxury fabrics.

Cravat
A man's neckcloth typically folded or tied at the front, with the ends tucked inside the shirt or coat. Derived from a style worn by the Croatians, it was adopted by the French in the late eighteenth century.

Crinoline
Derived from the French word *crin*, crinoline refers to a fabric that was made with horsehair and used as stiffening in the expanding skirt support system worn during the middle decades of the nineteenth century. The term "crinoline" was originally used to describe this stiff fabric, and first appeared in about 1830. By 1850–6, the word referred to either a stiffened petticoat or the rigid skirt-shaped structure of watch-spring steel, designed to support the skirts of a woman's dress to form the large, rounded bell shape that was popular until the mid-1860s. The crinoline silhouette was revived during the twentieth century in several forms. In the late 1940s and even the 1950s, the flounced petticoats extending the skirts became known as crinolines.

Cutaway
The cutaway is a type of man's coat in which the fabric below the waist seam is cut away from the front but leaves a pair of gradually tapered "fish-tailed" extensions at the back. Called a morning coat in England, the cutaway first appeared in the early 1840s, but was not considered "proper". According to the British magazine *The Tailor & Cutter* in 1899, the frock

coat was still the correct coat for weddings, while the morning coat was considered to be the appropriate coat for dressy, yet informal events, such as a day in town.

Decorations
Medals of honor worn by men to white tie* formal occasions, placed on the breast of their coat, with those of their native country at the top.

Derby
See entry above for Bowler. This is an American term for a bowler hat.

Dinner dress
A category of women's evening dress, usually full-length but less formal than a ball dress. It was felt that a woman's bare shoulder could be distracting for a man seated beside her at a dinner party, and therefore either short, or long, sleeved dresses were the important characteristic of a dinner dress, unless worn with a jacket. This term was used from about 1900 to the middle of the twentieth century.

Directoire
French term referring to the fashion style of, relating to, or in imitation of the one prevalent in France during the *Directoire*, the post-French Revolution period from 1795 to 1799. Originally, it was the transitional silhouette that metamorphosed into the Empire style. The Directoire style was revived in the early twentieth century, and again in the 1960s.

Drawers
These were loose, trouser-like undergarments, mid-calf length, made from cotton or linen, and usually decorated with lace, embroidery, or tucking. The term is derived from "drawing on" the garment. Drawers first appeared in France in the early nineteenth century.

Drawn-thread work
Also known as pulled thread work, this technique involves removing threads from the warp and/or the weft of a piece of even-weave fabric. The remaining threads are grouped or bundled together into a variety of patterns. Traditionally done in white thread on white fabric, it was a popular technique used to enhance shirtwaist* blouses.

Dress suit
Men's formal evening wear. Also called a dress coat and sometimes called a swallowtail coat*, a dress suit jacket is squarely cut across the front hem, unlike the cutaway* (a morning coat in Britain). Since the 1850s, the dress suit was to be worn only in the evening by men as part of the white tie* dress code, also known as evening full dress*.

Dutch Colonial Revival
A style of domestic architecture, primarily characterized by gambrel roofs, which is a subtype of the Colonial Revival style, inspired by aspects of the homes built by the early English and Dutch settlers of the eighteenth century. The Colonial Revival style arose in the United States from the late 1870s and peaked in the mid-1950s.

Flapper
The name given to any young woman of the 1920s who wore short skirts or short, sleeveless dresses and the exaggerated styles of that decade. Also associated with modern-minded women of the Roaring Twenties who lived the fast life. Originates from historic British slang for women of ill repute.

Frock coat
A low-waisted, sometimes double-breasted, man's coat with a knee-length skirt. Often worn by businessmen in the late nineteenth century.

Full dress
Evening dress suitable for formal social gatherings according to social custom. Chiefly applied to men's evening clothes, it refers to the white tie* dress code, which includes swallowtailed coats*, colloquially called "tails".

Gingham
A cotton cloth woven from threads that have been previously dyed. Most commonly woven in a pattern of squares, it was used for everyday clothing, such as aprons, and household furnishings, such as curtains.

Glove fastener
A device consisting of a loop or chain with a decorative ball, which was drawn around a pair of gloves when not in use. Also known as a "glove guard", it could be fastened to a handbag to prevent the gloves being lost.

Godet
An extra, semi-circular piece, or triangular wedge, of fabric that is set into a garment, usually a skirt, to add flare by increasing width and volume.

Gutta-percha
A type of Malaysian tree resin similar to rubber that can be easily molded to shape. This new material was introduced in England in 1843, and was heavily promoted in the Great Exhibition of 1851.

Jet
A form of lignite (precursor to black coal) that can be polished to a high luster, and was used for beads, buttons and jewelry, particularly for the various states of mourning dress into the early twentieth century. Often from Whitby, England, where it is the fossilized wood from a species of the Monkey Puzzle tree (*Araucaria araucana*). "French jet" was a term applied to the black glass imitation of the genuine material.

Juliet cap
A small openwork, crocheted or mesh cap, sometimes decorated with pearls, beads or jewels, typically worn with evening gowns or as bridal wear in the 1930s. The cap is named after the heroine of Shakespeare's *Romeo and Juliet*, set in the late fifteenth century, when this style was in fashion.

Leg-o'mutton sleeve
Also known as the "gigot" or "leg-o-lamb" sleeve for its resemblance to that cut of meat, this term was first introduced in about 1824 and evolved into various extreme shapes throughout the 1830s. It was revived in the 1890s, and variations survived into the first decade of the twentieth century.

Mono-bosom
This term refers to the voluminous bodice typical of late nineteenth- and early twentieth-century fashion, which enhanced a woman's figure, along with S-curve* corsets that thrust the bust forward and pushed the hips backward. This style of bodice is also referred to as the "pouter pigeon" shape, due to the puffed-up volume of fabric protruding over the waist.

Muslin
An open-textured cotton cloth, sometimes thin and sheer—the fineness determined by the quality of material and skills of the spinner and weaver. Used for women's dresses, and curtains. Term credited to Marco Polo (*c*.1254–1324), the Venetian merchant and traveler, who wrote that it derived from a fabric made in Mosul, now in northern Iraq. In America in the 1870s, it was used for everyday cotton fabric for shirts and bedding. The natural or unbleached variety was, and is, called "unbleached calico" in Britain.

Norfolk jacket
Named for the English Duke of Norfolk, or perhaps also after the English county of Norfolk. A Norfolk jacket is a loose, single-breasted jacket with box pleats at the front and back, and incorporates a false self-belt at the back. This style was popularized after the 1860s by the British Prince of Wales, later King Edward VII, whose country residence was Sandringham House in Norfolk. This style was revived in the 1930s, but banned during World War II due to the extra fabric required for its construction.

Paillettes
A term from the French word used to refer to small, glittering disks that can be sewn onto fabric to lie flat like fish-scales.

Passementerie
A term from the French word for trimmings, especially those featuring heavy embroideries or edgings of rich braids, beads, silks, and tinsel.

Pongee
A natural, unprocessed or raw silk fabric, light ecru in color, and originally made in China from wild silkworms. Used for adult and children's clothes, and was popular just before and after the turn of the twentieth century.

Presentation dress or gown
A dress worn to formal occasions where the wearer was expected to be "presented" to an important political person or aristocrat. Such dresses were designed for their visual impact, were often extravagant and richly decorated, and could include impressive yet cumbersome trains.

Princess-line
A form-fitting dress style featuring continuous vertical seams from shoulder to hem. This was a style of dress credited to Charles Frederick

Worth, the designer who created such a dress for Princess Metternich, the wife of the Austrian ambassador to Paris. This style, which eliminated the waist seam, was introduced in the late 1860s and went in and out of style for the next half century, including the first decade of the twentieth century.

Rayon
Rayon, also known as "artificial silk" or simply "art. silk", short for artificial silk but used frequently (and deceptively) without the period in American fashion magazines and publications of the era. Derived from the cellulose found in wood, it was less expensive than silk to produce.

Revers
A section of a garment that is turned back to show the lining or facing, such as a lapel, but it can also be used in reference to cuffs. The term "revers" comes from the French (based on Latin *reversus*, meaning returned) and refers to the opposite side from the principally viewed side of a fabric.

S-curve silhouette
The "S-curve" or "S-bend" refers to the silhouette, resembling the letter S, which was prevalent in women's fashion from the 1870s into the twentieth century, especially 1901-10, with the most extreme fashions appearing 1904-5. The straight front corsets, when laced even moderately tightly, tended to push the abdomen back, threw the breasts forward, and thus arched the back, and these corsets caused this S-curve, also contributing to what is sometimes called the "pouter pigeon" front.

Sack suit
A man's single-breasted, daytime suit, which came into common use as work and leisure wear during the mid-1880s and, by 1900, outnumbered cutaway* coat ensembles for daywear by two to one. The sack suit, with a square boxy cut similar to suit jackets today, was more likely to have coat and trousers made of the same cloth, although not always a matching waistcoat. Made with an unfitted, long jacket, with wide shoulders. The trousers tended to be cut wide in the legs.

Seersucker
A cotton fabric, the name of which originates from the Hindustani phrase *kheer aur shakkar*, meaning "milk and sugar" (probably a reference to the resemblance of the fabric's smooth and rough stripes to the smooth texture of milk and the bumpy texture of sugar). In America, the fabric, worn originally by the poor, was adopted by preppy undergraduate students in the 1920s, in the spirit of reverse snobbery. In this way, the seersucker suit transcended its roots, which originated in the South, and became synonymous with status and style in American menswear.

Shirtdress
A one-piece, tailored dress with a bodice like a shirtwaist*, often tucked, close fitted, and usually belted. Universally referred to as shirtwaist dresses in the 1950s, this style was sometimes made from rich fabrics and featured tailored collars, jeweled buttons, and plain sleeves that were often pushed up or of three-quarter length.

Shirtwaist
Commonly referred to as a "waist", this garment is a blouse made of easily laundered cotton or linen, and was almost ubiquitous by the end of the nineteenth century when the trend in women's clothing was for simpler and more practical styles. Available as ready-to-wear by 1890, some examples resembled feminine versions of a man's shirt with buttons down the front, double cuffs, and turnover collars worn with a long or bow tie.

Snood
A bag-like, netted covering for the hair, worn at the back of the head, which originated in fifteenth-century Italy, but became popular during the American Civil War. Snoods once again became fashionable after the release of the 1939 film *Gone With the Wind*, in which they were first introduced to the modern world, and also during World War II, when they were promoted as a safety measure for those women working in factories.

Soutache
Woven from a variety of materials including silk, wool, and metallic gold (and by the twentieth century, rayon), this narrow, flat, double-cord braid was applied in decorative patterns to women's dresses and suits.

Spats
Short for "spatterdashes", this shoe covering, usually made of felted woolen cloth, was popular for both men and women as outdoor wear during the first decades of the twentieth century. Not only protective and practical, they were also fashionable—until King George V appeared at the 1926 Chelsea Flower Show in London without them. They disappeared from fashion soon afterwards.

Spectator shoes or pumps
Introduced around 1925, these two-toned shoes or pumps were frequently made in contrasting colors of black, navy, red, or brown on white. Extra sewn-on toe and heel pieces of another color, sometimes with perforations and pinked edges, were also common. Originally a man's style, it was later adapted for women's shoes.

Swallowtail coats or suits
A term used to refer to the full dress coats worn by men on formal occasions. At the front, the skirt of the coat is cut away squarely at the waist so as to leave only the rear section of the skirt, known colloquially as the "tails"—two long tapering ends at the back that resemble the tails of a swallow. This is the type of dress coat still worn today as an element of the white tie* dress code.

Tailor-mades
A term used for a lady's garment or suit made from a sturdy woolen fabric such as serge. Worn with a shirtwaist* by both middle- and upper-class women, they were introduced in London in the 1880s by the Houses of Redfern and Creed. They were soon available in American stores such as Marshall Field's of Chicago.

Toiles
Toiles are exact fabric patterns cut out of unbleached cotton muslin* from which a dress could be copied. In the 1930s, they were imported duty free into America. Purchased by both designers and prestigious department stores, they made it possible for upper-middle-class women to dress in the latest styles, even accurate copies of couture gowns.

Trousseau
This term, derived from the French word *trousse*, meaning "bundle", was introduced in the mid-nineteenth century, and quickly became part of the wedding tradition. Many European countries had long traditions of wedding preparations but these were usually considered to be "folk" customs. When France, the world leader in all things fashion-related at that time, introduced the "trousseau", it was rapidly established as normal procedure in Europe and America.

Tuxedo
An American appellation for the British term "dinner jacket", the tuxedo was derived from the version worn at the Tuxedo Club, a private club dedicated to golf, located near Tuxedo Lake, about an hour north and west of Manhattan. The term originally referred only to the jacket element of the ensemble.

White tie
White tie, also called full dress*, is the most formal evening dress code in Western fashion. For men, it consists of a black swallowtail coat* worn over a white starched shirt, white waistcoat, and a white bow tie. High-waisted black trousers and shiny (often patent leather) shoes complete the ensemble. A top hat and white scarf are acceptable as accessories. Decorations* can be worn if specified on the invitation.

Widow's weeds
This term refers to the black clothes worn by a widow in mourning. It came into use in the early eighteenth century, having evolved from "mourning weeds". Weeds is an obsolete term meaning garments, as derived from the Old English word *wǣd(e)*.

Wiener Werkstätte
Term meaning "Vienna Workshops" (1903-32). Frustrated by the dominance of the florid Art Nouveau* style, Josef Hoffmann and Koloman Moser yearned for an integrated decorative idiom that was more relevant to the modern age. They founded an association of designers and craftsmen in Vienna in 1903 in order to achieve this. The cooperative lasted until 1932.

Wing Collar
A collar for a man's shirt with folded down tips. Typically worn with full dress* and formal daytime dress.

Yoke
A shaped piece in a garment that was fitted about, or below, the neck and shoulders, or about the hips from which the rest of the garment hung.

The Roddis Collection

Editorial note
The thumbnail images below have been selected to present the historical and stylistic range of the Roddis Collection, and to present full views of some garments mentioned or shown throughout the book. Arranged chronologically by category, each image includes: basic description and date; material/s each item is made from; wearer, where known (initials in square brackets – see key below; please note that Mary Isabella and Sara Frances Roddis were twins); designer or location of purchase, where known; and finally, for identification purposes, museum reference numbers for The Henry Ford (THF) or the Roddis Dress Collection (RDC), which is currently in the Jane Bradbury Collection (JBC).

[ADR] Augusta Denton Roddis
[CPR] Catherine Prindle Roddis (mother)
[CPR "P"] Catherine Prindle Roddis, "Pickie" (daughter)
[FR] Frances Roddis
[HR] Hamilton Roddis
[IAHP] Isabella Arents Hedenberg Prindle

[JPG] Jane Prindle Gammon
[MG] Martha Griffin (first cousin of CPR)
[MRC] Mary Isabella Roddis/Mary Roddis Connor
[SDR] Sara Denton Roddis
[SFR] Sara Frances Roddis
[WHR] William Henry Roddis

Crinoline dress, *c.*1856
Printed silk gauze [JPG]
THF 2014.24.54

Presentation dress, *c.*1880
Silk velvet, silk satin, "French jet" beads [JPG]
Mon. A. Angla ROBES, Paris
THF 2014.24.34

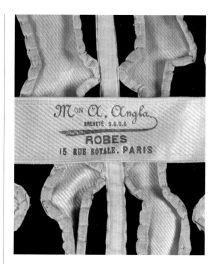

Presentation dress (label), *c.*1880
Silk velvet, silk satin, "French jet" beads [JPG]
Mon. A. Angla ROBES, Paris
THF 2014.24.34

Dress bodice, *c.*1903
Silk faille, silk chemical lace
Made by Mrs. J.A. Hunt, Detroit
THF 2014.24.11

Day dress, *c.*1906
Linen (from Philippine pre-embroidered panels) [CPR]
THF 2014.24.29

Dress, 1912
Silk pongee, linen bobbin lace inserts [CPR]
THF 2014.24.26

Evening dress, *c.*1912
Silk, glass beads [FR]
THF 2014.24.71

Evening dress, *c.*1913
Cotton, silk, glass beads [FR]
RDC 10, JBC

Coat and dress, *c.*1914
Wool twill, astrakhan fur, silk crêpe de chine,
composition buttons [SDR]
2014.24.32

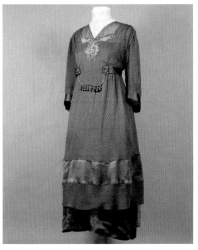

Evening dress, *c.*1917
Silk crêpe de chine, satin, glass beads [FR]
THF 2014.24.55

Day dress, *c.*1921
Silk crêpe de chine, satin [SDR/FR]
THF 2014.24.47

Evening dress, *c.*1923
Gold brocade, silk net, silk satin, black glass
beads [MG]
RDC 123, JBC

Day dress, *c.*1925
Cotton tulle, silk embroidery [CPR]
THF 2014.119.4.1

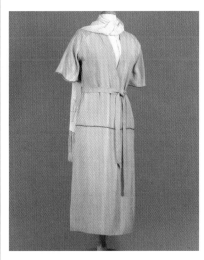

Syrian robe (made into a dress), *c.*1928
Silk, metallic gold thread [CPR]
THF 2014.24.39

Evening dress, 1932
Rayon [ADR]
THF 2014.24.72

Evening dress, *c.*1932
Silk taffeta, silk velvet, beads, rhinestones
[CPR "P"; ADR]
THF 2014.24.68

Dress, *c.*1934
Cotton/rayon, shirred beaver, metal belt
[ADR]
THF 2014.24.49

Evening dress, *c.*1938
Rayon satin-backed crêpe, rhinestone buckles
[ADR]
THF 2014.24.80

Coat, *c.*1940
Wool with mink tails [MRC]
Carson Pirie Scott, Chicago
Collection of Catherine Connor Dellin

Boudoir dress and coat, *c.*1940
Silk dress; silk gauze coat with satin appliqué
embroidery [CPR]
RDC 98, JBC

Evening dress, 1941
Rayon crêpe, silk chiffon, silk velvet ribbon
[ADR]
THF 2014.24.69

Evening dress, *c.*1950
Silk chiffon, rayon taffeta [ADR]
RDC 30, JBC

Day dress, *c.*1952
Embroidered linen [ADR]
Ruth McCulloch, Hubbard Woods
THF 2014.24.38

Day dress, *c.*1952
Cotton (fabric by Liberty of London)
Frances Brewster, Palm Beach, Florida
RDC 169, JBC

Day dress, *c*.1953
Printed silk [ADR]
Nettie Rosenstein, Blum's - North, Chicago
THF 2014.24.27

Bathing suit, *c*.1953
Embroidered cotton [ADR]
Jantzen/Made in USA
THF 2014.24.10

Day dress, *c*.1954
Linen [ADR]
THF 2014.24.41

Evening gown, 1955–8
Silk satin [ADR]
Blum's - North, Chicago
THF 2014.24.78

Evening gown, *c*.1956
Silk taffeta [ADR]
Made by CPR
RDC 5, JBC

Day dress with jacket, *c*.1957
Corded cotton, silk crêpe [ADR]
Ruth McCulloch, Hubbard Woods & Evanston
THF 2014.24.65

Day dress, *c*.1957
Cotton, cotton-rayon grosgrain ribbon
Frances Brewster, Palm Beach, Florida
RDC 47, JBC

Suit jacket, *c*.1958
Silk shantung, velvet, rhinestone closure [ADR]
Ruth McCulloch, Hubbard Woods & Evanston
RDC 64, JBC

Cocktail dress, *c*.1959
Slubbed rayon [ADR]
THF 2014.24.22

Evening dress, *c.*1960
Silk chiffon, silk satin, lace [CPR]
THF 2014.24.73

Day dress, *c.*1960
Linen [ADR]
Jay Anderson, Naples, Florida
THF 2014.24.37

Cocktail dress, *c.*1962
Pleated Irish linen [MRC]
Sybil Connolly, Dublin, Ireland
Collection of Catherine Connor Dellin

Evening dress, *c.*1965
Silk chiffon [ADR]
Bill Blass, New York
RDC 59, JBC

Dress and scarf, *c.*1972
Linen, silk scarf [ADR]
Donald Brooks, New York
THF 2014.24.61

Evening gown, *c.*1975
Printed polyester chiffon [ADR]
Graham Wren for Nettie Vogues, London
RDC 40, JBC

Evening gown, *c.*1977
Polyester ombré print [ADR]
Malcolm Starr/Elizabeth Arden, New York
THF 2014.24.76

Day dress, *c.*1977
Printed silk jersey [ADR]
Emilio Pucci, Florence, Italy, Emilio Pucci
Boutique, Saks Fifth Avenue
RDC 167, JBC

Dress with jacket, *c.*1978
Cotton [ADR]
Oscar de la Renta boutique, New York
RDC 174, JBC

Evening dress, *c.*1980
Pleated polyester chiffon [ADR]
Miss Elliette, California
RDC 83, JBC

Suit, *c.*1995
Checked bouclé rayon, cotton and silk [ADR]
Cynthia Sobel for Howard Grossman
THF 2014.119.6

Blouse with peplum, 1900–10
Linen lawn [CPR]
THF 2014.24.1

Blouse with drawn-thread work, *c.*1905
Fine linen [CPR]
THF 2014.24.4

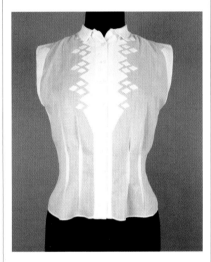

Blouse *c.*1938
White linen, shadow-work appliqué [ADR]
Label: Made in France
THF 2014.24.7

Needle lace blouse, *c.*1950
Cotton [ADR]
Venice/Burano, Italy
RDC 65, JBC

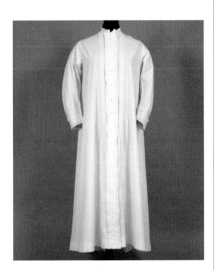

Trousseau nightgown, *c.*1874
Cotton muslin [SDR]
THF 2014.24.88

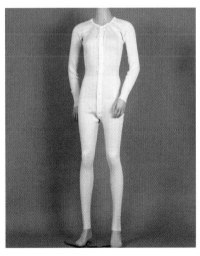

Ladies' union suit (long underwear), *c.*1890
Mercerized knitted cotton, cotton twill [SDR]
Label: Knit-to-Fit, Portage, Wisconsin
THF 2014.24.102

Chemise, *c.*1909
Cotton lawn, machine-embroidered lace
[CPR]
THF 2014.24.100

Boudoir cap, *c.*1913
Silk, couched tape lace [SDR]
THF 2014.24.128

Nightgown, *c.*1920
Silk, cotton crochet, machine embroidery
[CPR]
THF 2014.24.86

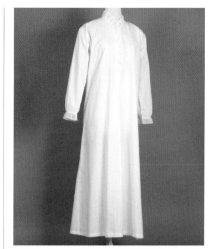

Nightgown, *c.*1930
Cotton, machine embroidery [CPR]
Marshall Field & Co. Lingerie, Chicago
THF 2014.24.87

Nightgown, *c.*1935
Red and white striped cotton [ADR]
Lord & Taylor Miss Collegiate, Chicago
THF 2014.24.84

Slip, *c.*1935
Silk satin [ADR]
THF 2014.24.99

Nightgown, *c.*1935
Silk charmeuse, cotton lace [ADR]
THF 2014.24.85

Corselet foundation, *c.*1939
Rayon, cotton, rubber [CPR]
Life/The Formfit Co./Made in U.S.A.
THF 2014.24.98

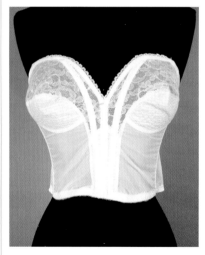

Merry Widow, *c.*1958
Cotton and feather boning [ADR]
Gay Life: Bontell/Bonwit Teller
RDC 138, JBC

Girl's hat, *c.*1900
Silk, cotton lace
THF 2014.24.172

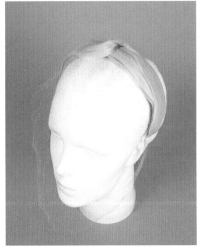

Alice band/headpiece, *c*.1948
Organza, silk veil [CPR]
Worn with Gothé dress (THF 2014.24.60)
THF 2014.24.116

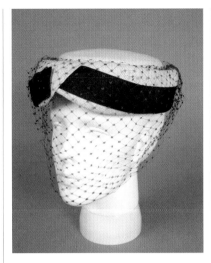

Afternoon hat, *c*.1950
Straw, silk velvet ribbon, veil
Jan Leslie, Custom Design
RDC A23, JBC

Petal hat, *c*.1951
Silk ottoman ribbon, veil
Miss Betté, The French Room, Marshall Field
& Co., Chicago
RDC A14, JBC

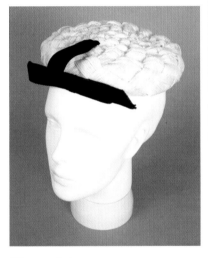

Afternoon hat, *c*.1953
Artificial straw, grosgrain ribbon [CPR]
Chapeaux Original
RDC A24, JBC

Floral hat, *c*.1953
Synthetic flowers, rayon velvet, silk veil
THF 2014.24.126

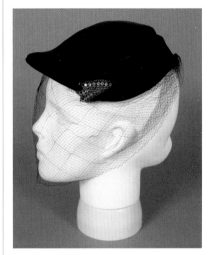

Cocktail hat, *c*.1954
Rayon velvet, rhinestones, beads, silk veil
Saks Fifth Avenue Millinery Salon, Chicago
RDC A18, JBC

Afternoon hat, *c*.1955
Fur felt, cotton velveteen, silk veil [CPR]
Saks Fifth Avenue Millinery Salon, Chicago
RDC A15, JBC

Headpiece, *c*.1955
Soutache cord, silk veil
Ruth McCulloch, Hubbard Woods & Evanston
RDC A36, JBC

Cocktail/afternoon hat, *c*.1958
Silk velvet
AMY, New York, Bonwit Teller
RDC A10, JBC

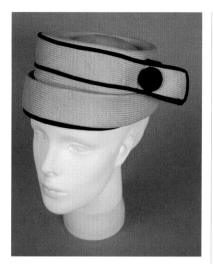

Afternoon hat, *c*.1958
Straw, grosgrain ribbon [ADR]
Chapeaux, Paris, Chicago
RDC A22, JBC

Hat, *c*.1958
Silk
RDC A17, JBC

Turban-style hat, *c*.1964
Silk dupioni
Saks Fifth Avenue Millinery Salon, Chicago
RDC A34, JBC

High button shoes, *c*.1890
Bronze leather, mother-of-pearl buttons
[SDR]
Shoecraft Shop, New York
THF 2014.24.134

Evening shoes, *c*.1930
Silk moiré, gilt leather [CPR]
Selby Arch Preserver Shoe, Cincinnati, Ohio
THF 2014.24.135

Shoes, *c*.1948
Leather, suede [ADR]
I. Miller, New York
RDC A51, JBC

Wedge shoes, 1948
Brown lizard [ADR]
I. Miller, Chicago
RDC A53, JBC

Wedge sandals, *c*.1950
Raffia, leather [CPR]
Saks Fifth Avenue, Debutante Fashions,
Chicago
THF 2014.24.132

Wedge shoes, *c*.1952
Suede, kid leather [ADR]
Wolsam Ltd/Magic Shanks by Morris Wolcock
RDC A55, JBC

Pumps, *c.*1954
Suede, kid leather [ADR]
Saks Fifth Avenue, Chicago
RDC A52, JBC

Stack-heel shoes, 1950–5
Leather [CPR]
Joseph Antell for Bally, Boston
THF 2014.24.136

Baby bonnet, *c.*1850
Fine cotton lawn, lace edging
THF 2014.24.174

Child's bonnet, *c.*1910
Silk, silk lace [SFR or MRC]
THF 2014.24.173

Infant's dress, *c.*1910
Fine linen, eyelet embroidery [SFR or MRC]
THF 2014.24.166

Infant's dress, *c.*1910
Fine cotton, machine whitework embroidery
[SFR or MRC]
THF 2014.24.167

Girl's dress, *c.*1918
Fine cotton
THF 2014.24.167

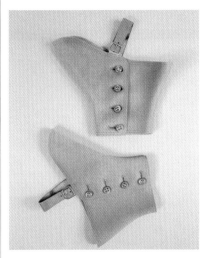

Spats, 1910–20
Wool English box cloth [HR/WHR]
Spoo & Son, Oshkosh, Wisconsin
THF 2014.24.161

Top hat, *c.*1910
Beaver, silk, leather [WHR]
Colbert, Marshall Field & Co., Chicago
THF 2014.24.157

Top hat (collapsible), *c.***1920**
Silk grosgrain (Golden Lions Rampant – logo only) [HR]
THF 2014.24.156

Waistcoat (vest), 1913
Silk [WHR]
Carver & Wilkie Carroll, McMillen Inc., Chicago
RDC 196, JBC

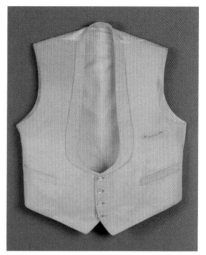

Waistcoat (vest), 1915
Ribbed silk [WHR]
Wilkie & Sellery, Tailors, Chicago
RDC 195, JBC

Shoes, *c.***1920**
Leather [WHR]
Hanan & Son, New York
THF 2014.24.158

Spectator shoes, 1930-5
Leather, rubber [HR]
Hanan & Son (Hanan's Hurdler's)
THF 2014.24.159

Man's suit (two-piece), *c.***1938**
Cotton corded weave (mock seersucker) [HR]
Lorraine Haspel, New Orleans, Marshall Field & Co.
THF 2014.24.148

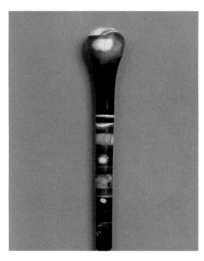

Walking stick, *c.***1913**
Stacked horn, England/Germany [WHR]
THF 2014.119.13

Ayrshire whitework embroidered cuffs, 1853
Cotton [JPG]
RDC A73, JBC

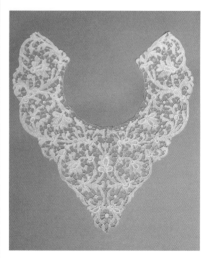

Dress collar insert, *c.***1913**
Cotton needlelace [SDR]
Venice/Burano, Italy
RDC A126, JBC

Fur muff, *c*.1910
Sable, silk [SDR]
RDC A78, JBC

Fur muff, with wrist ring, *c*.1915
Sable, silk, celluloid
THF 2014.24.107

Fur stole, 1940–50
Mink
Hansen's Empire Fur Factory, Milwaukee
THF 2014.24.106

Fan, *c*.1900
Painted silk, ebony, feathers
RDC A77, JBC

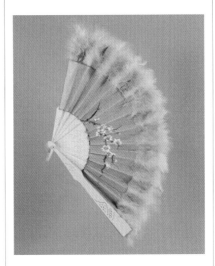

Fan, 1920–30
Painted silk, ivory, marabou feathers
RDC A76, JBC

Fan, 1920–30
Silk, gilded wood
RDC A75, JBC

Beaded neckband, 1928
Glass beads [IAHP]
France
THF 2014.24.131

Evening handbag, *c*.1940
Metallic brocade clutch purse, with
accessories
RDC A82, JBC

Handbag, *c*.1960
Metallic embroidery, glass beads [ADR]
Label: Made in India
THF 2014.24.112

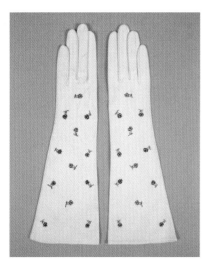

Embroidered gloves, 1948
Kid leather, silk tambour embroidery [ADR]
"le gant topaze", Paris
RDC A70, JBC

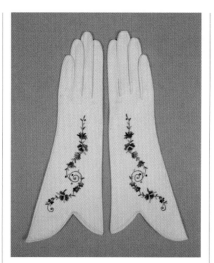

Embroidered gloves, 1948
Kid leather, silk tambour embroidery [ADR]
"le gant topaze", Paris
THF 2014.24.110

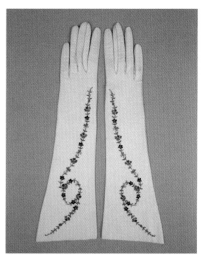

Embroidered gloves, 1948
Kid leather, silk tambour embroidery [ADR]
"le gant topaze", Paris
RDC A93, JBC

Embroidered gloves, 1948
Kid leather, silk tambour embroidery [ADR]
"le gant topaze", Paris
RDC A106, JBC

Gloves, *c.*1950
Kid leather, pearlized buttons [ADR]
Les Gants Christian Dior, Paris
THF 2014.24.111

Dance card/program, 1932
"Story Book Ball", Marshfield High School
Prom [ADR]
THF 2014.24.176

Hat box, *c.*1949
Paper, pasteboard
Saks Fifth Avenue
(travel labels: Cunard White Star)
THF 2014.24.184

Hat box, 1950–60
Paper, pasteboard
Schmidt's
(travel labels: First Class French Line)
THF 2014.24.182

Commemorative spoon, 1959
Gold plate, engraved "Queen Elizabeth II
Visits Canada 1959" [CPR/HR]
THF 2014.24.192

Bibliography

BOOKS

Aldcroft 2012
Derek H. Aldcroft, *The European Economy 1914–2000* (Routledge, 2012)

Arnold 2009
Rebecca Arnold, *The American Look: Fashion, Sportswear and the Image of Women in 1930s and 1940s New York* (I.B. Taurus, 2009)

Bartlett and Steele 1979 (2003)
Donald L. Bartlett and James B. Steele, *Howard Hughes: His Life and Madness* (André Deutsch Ltd, 1979; reprinted with revised title, 2003)

Belmont Davis 1908
Charles Belmont Davis, "The Altar of Her Beauty: A Story of a Girl who Loved Fine Clothes", *Ladies' Home Journal*, Vol. XXV, No. 7, Jun 1908

Benton 1956
Frances Benton (co-edited by the General Federation of Women's Clubs), *Complete Etiquette: The Complete Modern Guide for Day to Day Living the Correct Way* (Random House, 1956)

Bjorkman 1948
Roy H. Bjorkman, *Northwest's Most Exclusive Women's Specialty Shop: Through 25 Years, 1923–1948* (Bjorkman Company, 1948)

Blair 1988
Karen J. Blair, *The Clubwoman as Feminist: True Womanhood Redefined, 1868–1914* (1980) (Holmes & Meier Publishers, Inc., 1988)

Blanke 2002
David Blanke, *The 1910s: American Popular Culture Through History* (Greenwood, 2002)

Blum 2003
Dilys E. Blum, *Shocking! The Art and Fashion of Elsa Schiaparelli* (Yale University Press, 2003)

Boorstin 1973
Daniel J. Boorstin, *The Americans: The Democratic Experience* (Random House, 1973)

Bostock 2011
Gillian Louise Bostock, *The Roddis House: A Thread of Continuity* (Blurb, 2011)

Braden 1988
Donna Braden, *Leisure and Entertainment in America* (Henry Ford Museum, 1988)

Brinnin 2000
John Malcolm Brinnin, *The Sway of the Grand Saloon: A Social History of the North Atlantic* (Barnes & Noble, 2000)

Brooks Picken 1973
Mary Brooks Picken, *The Fashion Dictionary: Fabric, Sewing, and Dress as Expressed in the Language of Fashion* (Funk & Wagnalls, 1957)

Brown Blackwell 1874
Antoinette Brown Blackwell, "The Relation of Women's Work in the Household to the Work Outside", *Papers and Letters Presented at the First Women's Congress of the Association for the Advancement of Women* (Harper & Brothers, 1874)

Butterick 1926
Helen Goodrich Butterick, *Principles of Clothing Selection* (The MacMillan Company, 1926)

Cartier 1931
Colette Cartier, *Modern Dressmaking: The Guide to French Chic and Smartness of Dress* (The Pictorial Review Company, 1931)

Chenoune 1993
Farid Chenoune (trans. from the French by Deke Dusinberre), *A History of Men's Fashion* (Flammarion, 1993)

Click 1943
Author not named, "Slim Wartime Silhouette", *Click* magazine, Oct 1943, p.30 (available to read online at www.oldmagazinearticles.com/WW2_fashion_and_WW2-fabric_rationing_of_World_War_Two)

Clinton 1984
Catherine Clinton, *The Other Civil War: American Women in the 19th Century* (Hill and Wang, 1984)

Costantino 2007
Maria Costantino, *Fashions of the Decade: The 1930s* (Chelsea House, 2007)

Craig and Hulbert 1938–42
Sir William A. Craig and James R. Hulbert, *A Dictionary of American English on Historical Principles, Compiled at The University of Chicago*, Vols. I-IV (University of Chicago Press, 1938–42)

Creecy 1860
James R. Creecy, *Scenes in the South, and Other Miscellaneous Pieces* (T. McGill, 1860)

Cunningham 2003
Patricia A. Cunningham, *Reforming Women's Fashions 1850–1920: Politics, Health and Art* (Kent State University Press, 2003)

Davies-Strodder, Lister and Taylor 2015
Cassie Davies-Strodder, Jenny Lister and Lou Taylor, *London Society Fashion 1905-1925: The Wardrobe of Heather Firbank* (V&A Publishing, 2015)

Dawson 2007
Philip Dawson, *The Liner: Retrospective and Renaissance* (Conway, 2007)

Dior 1957 (2007)
Christian Dior (trans. from the French by Antonia Fraser), *Dior by Dior: The Autobiography of Christian Dior* (Weidenfeld & Nicolson, 1957; reprinted by V&A Publishing, 2007)

Donzel 2006
Catherine Donzel, *Luxury Liners: Life On Board* (Vendome Press, 2006)

Drowne and Huber 2004
Kathleen Drowne and Patrick Huber, *The 1920s: American Popular Culture Through History* (Greenwood, 2004)

Dworkin 1998
Susan Dworkin, *Miss America, 1945: Bess Myerson and the Year That Changed Our Lives* (Newmarket Press, 1998)

Ely 1935
Grace D. Ely, *American Fashion Designers* (RRB, University of Pittsburg, 1935)

Erenberg 1984
Lewis A. Erenberg, *Steppin' Out: New York Nightlife and the Transformation of American Culture* (University of Chicago Press, 1984)

Etulain 1999
Richard W. Etulain, *Does the Frontier Experience Make America Exceptional?* (Historians at Work) (Palgrave Macmillan, 1999)

Farneti Cera 1992
Deanna Farneti Cera (ed.), *Jewels of Fantasy: Costume Jewelry of the 20th Century* (Harry N. Abrams, Inc., 1992)

Fogg 2013
Marnie Fogg (ed.), *Fashion: The Whole Story* (Thames & Hudson, 2013)

Fukai 2006
Akiki Fukai, *Fashion History: A History from the 18th to the 20th Century*, Vol. 2 (Taschen, for the Kyoto Costume Institute, 2006)

Garfinkel and Spafford 2002
Simson Garfinkel and Gene Spafford, *Web Security, Privacy & Commerce* (O'Reilly Media, Inc., 2002)

Goddard 2011
Leslie Goddard, *Remembering Marshall Field's* (Arcadia Publishing, 2011)

Godlove Donovan 1943
Dulcie Godlove Donovan, *The Mode in Dress and Home* (Allyn and Bacon, 1943)

Golbin 2009
Pamela Golbin (ed.), *Madeleine Vionnet* (Rizzoli, 2009)

Golden 2007
Eve Golden, *Vernon and Irene Castle's Ragtime Revolution* (University Press of Kentucky, 2007)

Gordon 1990
Lynn D. Gordon, *Gender and Higher Education in the Progressive Era* (Yale University Press, 1990)

Gould Woolson 1874
Abba Gould Woolson (ed.), *Dress-Reform* (Roberts Brothers, 1874)

Green 1983 (2003)
Harvey Green, *The Light of the Home: An Intimate View of the Lives of Women in Victorian America* (Pantheon Books, 1983; reprinted by University of Arkansas Press, 2003)

Hall 1931
Helen Hall, *Correct Styles for the Individual: Pattern Making* (Sye Foundation Pattern Co., 1931)

Hawes 1938
Elizabeth Hawes, *Fashion is Spinach* (Random House, 1938)

Hawes 1943
Elizabeth Hawes, *Why Women Cry or, Wenches with Wrenches* (Reynal & Hitchcock, Inc., 1943)

Haye, Taylor and Thompson 2005
Amy de la Haye, Lou Taylor and Eleanor Thompson, *A Family of Fashion: The Messell Dress Collection, 1865-2005* (Philip Wilson Publishers, 2005)

Heatly Dulles 1890
Joseph Heatly Dulles, *Necrological Reports and Annual Proceedings of the Alumni Association of Princeton Theological Seminary*, Vol. 2 (Princeton Theological Seminary, 1890)

Hennessy 2012
Kathryn Hennessy (ed.), *Fashion: The Definitive History of Costume and Style* (Dorling Kindersley, 2012)

Herald 2006
Jacqueline Herald, *The 1920s: Fashion of a Decade* (Chelsea House Publishing, 2006)

Holt 1896
Arden Holt, *Fancy Dresses Described, or What to Wear at Fancy Dress Balls* (Debenham & Freebody and Edward Arnold, 1896)

Howell 2012
Geraldine Howell, *Wartime Fashion: From Haute Couture to Homemade, 1939-1945* (Berg, 2012)

Huston 1972
Harvey Huston, *The Roddis Line. The Roddis Lumber & Veneer Co. Railroad and the Dells & Northeastern Railway* (Harvey Huston, 1972)

Jones et al 1923
George O. Jones et al, *History of Wood County*, Wisconsin (H.C. Cooper, Jr. & Cooper, 1923)

Karamanski 1989
Theodore J. Karamanski, *The History of Logging in Northern Michigan* (Wayne State University Press, 1989)

Katz Frommer 2013
Myrna Katz Frommer, *Manhattan at Mid-Century: An Oral History* (Taylor Trade Publishing, 2013)

Kearns Goodwin 1995
Doris Kearns Goodwin, *No Ordinary Time: Franklin and Eleanor Roosevelt: The Home Front in World War II* (Touchstone Books, Simon & Schuster, 1995)

Kidwell and Christman 1974
Claudia B. Kidwell and Margaret C. Christman, *Suiting Everyone: The Democratization of Clothing in America* (Smithsonian Institution Press, 1974)

Kirkham 2001
Pat Kirkham (ed.), *Women Designers in the USA 1900-2000: Diversity and Difference* (Yale University Press for Bard Graduate Center for Studies in the Decorative Arts, 2001)

Klaffke 2003
Pamela Klaffke, *Spree: A Cultural History of Shopping* (Arsenal Pulp Press, 2003)

Kyvig 2004
David Kyvig, *Daily Life in the United States 1920-1940* (Ivan R. Dee, 2004)

Laird 1999
Helen L. Laird, "Augusta Roddis: A sketch of her life by Helen Laird", delivered at the AJ Chapter of P.E.O. meeting in Marshfield, Wisconsin, May 11, 1999 (unpublished but held at THF)

Laird 2006
Helen L. Laird, *A Mind of Her Own: Helen Connor Laird and Family, 1888-1982* (University of Wisconsin Press, 2006)

Laver 2012
James Laver, *Costume and Fashion: A Concise History* (Thames & Hudson, 5th edition, 2012)

Lewis Allen 1986
Frederick Lewis Allen, *Since Yesterday: The 1930s in America, September 3, 1929 to September 3, 1939* (Harper Perennial, 1986)

Lewis Allen 2010
Frederick Lewis Allen, *Only Yesterday: An Informal History of the 1920s* (Harper Perennial Modern Classics, 2010)

Mackenzie Stuart 2012
Amanda Mackenzie Stuart, *Empress of Fashion: A Life of Diana Vreeland* (Harper Perennial, 2012)

Maeder 1987
Edward Maeder (ed.), *Hollywood and History: Costume Design in Film* (Thames & Hudson, 1987)

Mankey Calasibetta 1988
Charlotte Mankey Calasibetta, *Fairchild's Dictionary of Fashion* (2nd edition, Fairchild Publications, 1988)

Marcus 2001
H. Stanley Marcus, *Minding the Store* (University of North Texas Press, 2001)

Matthews 2003
Jean V. Matthews, *The Rise of the New Woman: The Women's Movement in America, 1875-1930* (American Ways Series, published by Ivan R. Dee, 2003)

Mears and Bruce Boyer 2014
Patricia Mears and G. Bruce Boyer (eds), *Elegance in the Age of Crisis: Fashions of the 1930s* (Yale University Press/Fashion Institute of Technology, New York, 2014)

Miller 2006
Judith Miller, *Decorative Arts: Style and Design from Classical to Contemporary* (Dorling Kindersley, 2006)

Miller 2010 (a)
William H. Miller, *Floating Palaces: The Great Atlantic Liners* (Amberley Publishing, 2010)

Miller 2010 (b)
William H. Miller, *SS Nieuw Amsterdam: The Darling of the Dutch* (Amberley Publishing, 2010)

Miller 2011
William H. Miller, *The Last Atlantic Liners: Getting There is Half the Fun* (Amberley Publishing, 2011)

Mintz and Kellogg 1988
Steven Mintz and Susan Kellogg, *Domestic Revolutions: A Social History of American Family Life* (The Free Press, 1988)

Myers 1892
Anne E. Myers, *Home Dressmaking – a complete guide to Household Sewing* (C.H. Sergel & Company, 1892)

Myres 1982
Sandra L. Myres, *Westering Women and the Frontier Experience 1800–1915* (University of New Mexico Press, 1982)

Nesbit 1989
Robert C. Nesbit, *Wisconsin: A History*, second edition, revised and updated by William F. Thompson (University of Wisconsin Press, 1989)

Newton 1974
Stella Mary Newton, *Health, Art & Reason: Dress Reformers of the 19th Century* (John Murray, 1974)

Oliphant 1888
R.J. Oliphant, *Historical sketches relating to the first quarter century of the State normal and training school at Oswego* (S.U.C.E., 1888)

O'Neill 2014
Rosary O'Neill, *New Orleans Carnival Krewes: The History, Spirit and Secrets of Mardi Gras* (The History Press, 2014)

Palmer 2009
Alexandra Palmer, *Dior: A New Look, A New Enterprise (1947–57)* (V&A Publishing, 2009)

Post 1922
Emily Post, *Etiquette in Society, in Business, in Politics, and at Home* (Funk & Wagnalls Company, 1922)

Pridmore 2002
Jay Pridmore, *Marshall Field's: A Building Book from the Chicago Architecture Foundation* (Pomegranate, 2002)

Przybyszewski 2014
Linda Przybyszewski, *The Lost Art of Dress: The Women Who Once Made America Stylish* (Basic Books, 2014)

Queen and Berger 2006
Sally Queen and Vicki L. Berger, *Clothing and Textile Collections in the United States: A CSA Guide* (Costume Society of America Series, 2006)

Raushenbush 1942
Winifred Raushenbush, *How to Dress in Wartime* (Coward-McCann, 1942)

Ricci and Maeder 1992
Stefania Ricci and Edward Maeder, *Salvatore Ferragamo: The Art of the Shoe 1898–1960* (Rizzoli, 1992)

Roberts Compton 1980
Beulah Roberts Compton, *Introduction to Social Welfare and Social Work: Structure, Function, and Process* (Dorsey Press, 1980)

Roddis 1 (undated)
Augusta Roddis, *A Few Random Notes on the Social History of Marshfield* (an informal lecture given by Miss Roddis to her P.E.O. women's group, year unknown). An oral recording of this lecture was found in the Roddis House and transcribed by Gill Tickner with assistance from Jane Bradbury. The transcript, as well as the oral recording, is held at The Henry Ford.

Roddis 2 (undated)
Augusta Roddis, *History of the Roddis Plywood Company* (available for reference: RFP, WHS, Box 3, Folder 2)

Roddis for Bostock c.1995–6
Augusta Roddis, Grandparent Project: answers to a questionnaire about the Depression for her grandniece Gillian Bostock, for her 8th grade at Crystal Springs Uplands School of Hillsborough, CA. The document is not dated, but was written *c.*1995–6.

Rutkow 2013
Eric Rutkow, *American Canopy: Trees, Forests, and the Making of a Nation* (Scribner, 2013)

Saillard and Zazzo 2012
Olivier Saillard and Anne Zazzo (eds), *Paris Haute Couture* (Flammarion, 2012)

Schnitzler 1997
Donald H. Schnitzler (ed.), *The Marshfield Story, 1872–1997, Vol. 1: Piecing Together Our Past* (Marshfield History Project, 1997)

Schnitzler 2000
Donald H. Schnitzler (ed.), *The Marshfield Story, Vol. 2: Windows to Our Past* (Marshfield History Project, 2000)

Shields 1991
Jody Shields, *Hats: A Stylish History and Collector's Guide* (Clarkson Potter, 1991)

Siry 1988 (2012)
Joseph Siry, *Carson Pirie Scott: Louis Sullivan and the Chicago Department Store* (University of Chicago Press, 1988; reprinted 2012)

Snowden 1897
C.L. Snowden, "The Armour Institute", *New England Magazine, An Illustrated Monthly*, Vol. XVI, No. 3 (May 1897)

Soucek 2010
Gayle Soucek, *Marshall Field's: The Store That Helped Build Chicago* (The History Press, 2010)

Spanabel Emery 1999
Joy Spanabel Emery, "Dreams on Paper: A Story of the Commercial Pattern Industry", in Barbara Burman (ed.), *The Culture of Sewing: Gender, Consumption and Home Dressmaking* (Berg, 1999)

Steele 2001
Valerie Steele, *The Corset: A Cultural History* (Yale University Press, 2001)

Steele 2009
Valerie Steele, *Fifty Years of Fashion* (Yale University Press, 2009)

Steele 2010
Valerie Steele, *The Berg Companion to Fashion* (Berg, 2010)

S.U.C.E. (State University College of Education, Oswego, N.Y.) 1888
Historical Sketches relating to the First Quarter Century of the State Normal and Training School at Oswego, N. Y. (R. J. Oliphant, 1888)

S.U.C.E. (State University College of Education, Oswego, N.Y.) 1913
History of the First Half Century of the Oswego State Normal and Training School (The Radcliffe Press, 1913)

Taylor 2013
Kerry Taylor, *Vintage Fashion & Couture: From Poiret to McQueen* (Mitchell Beazley, 2013)

Taylor 1983 (2009)
Lou Taylor, *Mourning Dress, A Costume and Social History* (George Allen & Unwin 1983; 2nd edition Routledge, 2009)

Trilling and Williams Nicholas 1942
Mabel Barbara Trilling and Florence Williams Nicholas, *Art in Home and Dress* (J.B. Lippincott Company, 1942)

Ujifusa 2012
Steven Ujifusa, *A Man and His Ship: America's Greatest Naval Architect and His Quest to Build the SS. United States* (Simon & Schuster, 2012)

Vanderbilt 1952
Amy Vanderbilt, *Complete Book of Etiquette* (Doubleday & Company, 1952)

Veblen (1899) 2009
Thorstein Veblen, *The Theory of the Leisure Class: An Economic Study in the Evolution of Institutions* (Macmillan, N.Y., 1899; Oxford World's Classics, 2009)

Washington 1949
Ella Mae Washington, *Color in Dress (For Dark Skinned People)* (Langston, 1949)

Welters and Cunningham 2005
Linda Welters and Patricia A. Cunningham (eds), *Twentieth-Century American Fashion* (Bloomsbury, 2005)

Whalan 2010
Mark Whalan, *American Culture in the 1910s* (Edinburgh University Press, 2010)

Wharton 1920 (2003)
Edith Wharton, *The Age of Innocence*, ed. Candace Waid (D. Appleton and Company, 1920; reprinted by W.W. Norton & Company, 2003)

Wharton 1938
Edith Wharton, "A Little Girl's New York", *Harper's* (Aug 1938)

Whitaker 2006
Jan Whitaker, *Service and Style: How the American Department Store Fashioned the Middle Class* (St. Martin's Press, 2006)

Wilson 1941
Margery Wilson, *Margery Wilson's Pocket Book of Etiquette* (Pocket Books, Inc., 1941)

Wilson and Taylor 1989
Elizabeth Wilson and Lou Taylor, *Through the Looking Glass: A History of Dress from 1860 to the Present Day* (BBC Books, 1989)

Witter Connor 2009
Sara Witter Connor, "Wisconsin's Flying Trees: The Plywood Industry's Contribution to World War II", *Wisconsin Magazine of History*, Spring 2009.

Witter Connor 2014
Sara Witter Connor, *Wisconsin's Flying Trees in World War II: A Victory for American Forest Products and Allied Aviation* (The History Press, 2014)

Zaide 1994
Sonia M. Zaide, *The Philippines: A Unique Nation* (All-Nations Publishing Co., 1994)

DIGITAL REFERENCES (SEE DIG. REF.)

Aiello 2012
Dawn Aiello, "The Trousseau", May 23, 2012 (*Victorian Lace*): www.thehistorybox.com/ny_city/society/articles/nycity_society_weddings_article0043.htm

Bernstein
Irving Bernstein, "Americans in Depression and War" (*U.S. Department of Labor*, undated): www.dol.gov/dol/aboutdol/history/chapter5.htm

Hailey 2009
Charlie Hailey, "Sleeping Porch to Sleeping Machine: Inverting Traditions of Fresh Air in North America", *TDSR* Vol. XX, No. 11, 2009: http://iaste.berkeley.edu/pdfs/20.2d-Spr09hailey-sml.pdf

Hennell-Foley 2014
Nicholas Hennell-Foley, *The Influence of Jazz on Women's Fashion and Society in the 1920s* (*Academia.edu*, 2014): www.academia.edu/5034145/The_Influence_of_Jazz_on_Womens_Fashion_and_Society_in_the_1920s

Hoppe 1997
Michelle J. Hoppe, "The Victorian Wedding: Part One – Preparation", (*Literary Liaisons*, 1997): www.literary-liaisons.com/article003.html

Kolkman 2011
Donald Kolkman, "US Rationing during WWII Part 8: Shoes", *International Journal of Rationing 2.1* (2010): 1–4, May 5, 2011: www.rationcurrency.net/ojs/index.php/ijr/article/viewFile/43/45

Lodwick 2008
Keith Lodwick, "The film work of stage designer Oliver Messel", *V&A Online Journal*, Issue No.1, Autumn 2008, ISSN 2043-667X: www.vam.ac.uk/content/journals/research-journal/issue-01/the-film-work-of-stage-designer-oliver-messel/

Scharf 2015
Andrew Scharf, "Seersucker 'n Bourbon in New Orleans", (*RedHerring/Whitefield Consulting*), Apr 17, 2015: www.whitefieldconsulting.com/wordpress/seersucker_redddherring/

Snyder 1993
Thomas D. Snyder (ed.), *120 Years of American Education: A Statistical Portrait* (National Center for Education Statistics, 1993), p.68: http://nces.ed.gov/pubs93/93442.pdf

Stanton 2009
Shelby L. Stanton, "Limitation Order L-85: Fashion Survivability", and others in this series (*Blitzkrieg Baby*), Jul 1, 2009: www.blitzkriegbaby.de/stantonorders/july09.htm

Picture Credits

Unless otherwise stated, all images are courtesy of Jane L. Bradbury.

All photographs of the clothing and accessories, unless otherwise stated are by Gillian Bostock Ewing (gillianbostock.com), including the photographs from her book (Bostock 2011): pp.9, 19, 92, 102, 103, and 268.

All still life photographs are by Doug Mindell (dougmindellphotography.com): pp.15, 22, 42, 52, 58, 79, 84, 104, 112, 114 (fig. 95), 132, 151, 160, 186, 198, 210, 230, 262, 266, and 280.

Additional photography is by Sarah Davis (millstonephotographyservices.co.uk): pp.54 (fig. 31), 91 (figs 69 and 70), 234 (fig. 203), 243 (fig. 210), 254 (fig. 221), 261 (fig. 236), and 306 (dress collar insert). Sarah Davis also did scanning and post-production work for the photography in this publication.

The images on pp.51, 53, 113, and 306 (two waistcoats) are by Eli Dagostino.

For the family tree, all photos pp.12–13 are from RFPA, with the exception of that of Mary Roddis Connor, which is courtesy of Catherine Connor Dellin, and that of Ellen Roddis Lempereur, which is courtesy of Jane L. Bradbury.

Photographs credited to EMC, courtesy of Edward Maeder: pp.93, 144, 154 (fig. 131), 158, 159, 206 (fig. 175), and 240.

Photographs credited to RFP, Courtesy of WHS Archives Division: pp.30, 62 (fig. 37), 64, 70 (fig. 46), 75 (figs 52 and 53), 123, 189, 239, and 274. These papers are in the possession of the Wisconsin Historical Society and are held at the Nelis R. Kampenga University Archives & Area Research Center, University of Wisconsin – Stevens Point, Stevens Point, Wisconsin.

Photographs credited to RFPA, courtesy of Jane L. Bradbury: pp.9, 11, 33, 40, 44, 61, 65, 66, 67, 73 (fig. 49), 83 (fig. 61), 86 (figs 65 and 66), 96, 97, 110, 128, 129, 131 (figs 112 and 113), 139, 144 (fig. 120), 147, 162, 168 (figs 143 and 144), 175, 190, 196, 199, 200, 219, 220, 250 (fig. 216), 252, 264, 269, 271, and 272 (fig. 247). Scans made by Gillian Bostock Ewing.

Photographs credited to RFPC: pp.45, 117, 176, 178 and 267 (courtesy of Sara and Peter Bostock); 47 and 78 (fig. 56) courtesy of Grace Roddis Hoffmann; 54, 62 (fig. 38), 63, 120, 174, and 181 (courtesy JBC); 272 (fig. 246) courtesy of Douglas Lempereur.

See also, p.11 (fig. 4): Photograph by Jeff the quiet, 2010; pp.34, 35, and 237: collection of Sara Witter Connor; p.54 (fig. 30): courtesy of New York Tribune; pp.57, 70 (fig. 47), 108 (figs 87 and 88), 118 (figs 100 and 101), 136, 152 (photograph by Gillian Bostock Ewing), 192, 254 (fig. 222), and p.259 (fig. 230): From the Collections of The Henry Ford; pp.114 and 154 (fig. 132): courtesy of Commercial Pattern Archive, University of Rhode Island; p.144 (fig. 121): courtesy of the Academy of Motion Picture Arts and Sciences, Margaret Herrick Library; p.149: courtesy of New York Times Archive; p.169: courtesy of the U.S. National Archives and Records Administration; p.165: Reprinted with permission from Wisconsin's Flying Trees in World War II (Sara Witter Connor 2014), available from the publisher online at arcadiapublishing.com, or by calling +1 888-313-2665; p.188 (fig. 160): courtesy of Amberley Publishing; p.206: courtesy of U.S. Passport Service; pp.208 and 209 (fig. 181): courtesy of Elaine Greenstone; p.245: courtesy of Beverley Birks and Francesca Galloway; p.258 (fig. 227): courtesy of Betty Bjorkman; p.260 (fig. 232): courtesy of Evanston History Center, Evanston, Illinois; thumbnail images on pp.298 and 300: collection of Catherine Connor Dellin.

Index

Page numbers in *italic* refer to the illustrations and their captions

A

A line 292
Abercrombie and Fitch 227, *228*
accounts, store 233
Adair of Paris 123, *124–5*, 232
Adèle & Cie 127
Adrian 226, 238–9
advertisements 105
    Best & Co. 149, *149*
    Cadillac 208, *209*
    Chicago Sunday Tribune 152, *152*
    Cunard *188*, *198*
    De Havilland Mosquito aircraft *165*
    Justrite Corsets *93*
    Phillip-Jones 53, *54*
    Roddis Lumber & Veneer Company *57*
    Roddis Plywood Company *223*
Aesthetic Movement 36
Africa 185, 187, 204
afternoon dresses 180, *181*, 240, 249, 265, *265*
afternoon hats 215–16, *215*, 223, *223*, 265, *303*, *304*
Ahrens, Therese 223, *223*
Air Ministry (Britain) 165
aircraft *162*, 165–7, *165*, 176–7, 203
Alençon needle lace *78*, 292
Alice bands 203, 292, *303*
American Civil War 157, 279
American Lumberman 176–7
American Motherhood, Cooperstown, New York 98
American Revolution 271
AMY, New York 303
Anderson, Jay 300
Antell, Joseph 305
Anthony, Susan B. 68–9
Apfel, Iris 203
Arden, Elizabeth 300
Armour Institute, Chicago 60, 64, 67, 68, 116
Art Deco 113, 151, 189, 292
Art Moderne 151, 292
Art Nouveau 64, *70*, 75, *77*, 292
Arts and Crafts Movement 46, 92, *92*, 292
Ashburn, Mrs. 33
at-home dresses 113–14
Atlanta, Georgia 78
Atlantic City, New Jersey 71
Ayrshire whitework 292, *306*

B

baby bonnets *305*
Bachrach, Bradford *257*
Balenciaga, Cristobal 185, 242, *243*, *245*
ball dresses 190
Bally *305*
basque bodices 61, 93, 292
bathing suits 193–4, *193*, 299
Batory, M.S. 194
beadwork 120, *121*, 123, *124–5*, *307*
beards 54, *55*
Beaton, Frances, *Complete Etiquette* 239
Beautime 204, *205*
Beene, Geoffrey 250
Beggs, Catherine Roddis (Pickie) *13*
    attitude to money 234–5

childhood 97, *97*, 108
clothes 130, *130*, 143, 212, 216, *217*
    dressing up 272, *272*
    education 118–19
    theatrical productions 269
    in World War II 175
Beggs, Ellen 249, *250*
Beggs, Robert 175
Belle Jardinière 37
Benton, Frances 219
berets 242, *243*
Berlin 31
Bermuda 163
Bessi, Averado 275, *276*
Best & Co. 149, *149*, 232, 235, *236*
bias-cut dresses 137–9, 276–9, *278*
Bjorkman, Roy H. 232, 242–5, *244*, 258–9, *258–9*
black tie 219
Blackwell, Antoinette Brown 75
Blair, Karen 30
Blass, Bill 300
Blotta, Anthony 226, *226*
blouses 195
    drawn-thread work *301*
    leg-o' mutton sleeves 65, 66, *66*
    linen *301*
    needle lace *301*
    shirtwaists 65, 70–72, *70*, *72–3*, 88, 294
    shot-silk taffeta *262*
Blum's, North Chicago 174, 250, 299
Bon Ton 73
Bonwit Teller 225, 232, 302
boots 172
Bostock, Sara 21
Boston 119, 167, 232, 233, 238, 239–40
bouclé fabrics 292
    bouclé rayon suit 279, *301*
    wool bouclé suits 249, *250*, 254, *255*
boudoir cap 122, *122*, 302
boudoir dress 298
Bow, Clara 119
bowler (derby) hats 48, *49*, 52, *52*, 232, 292
box cloth 100, 292
Bradbury, Jane 10, 21, 270
braid, soutache 243, *244–5*, 294
brassieres 120, 181, *182*
Brewster, Frances 212, *213*, 222, 227, 240, 298, 299
bridesmaids 129–30, *129*, 236
Britain 56, 101, 164, 165, 194–5
brocade evening dress 297
broderie anglaise 292
Brooklyn 233
Brooks, Donald 300
Brown, Evelyn Barton 232, 275–6, *277*
Buck Rogers 151–2
buster suits 114, *116*, 266
bustles 61, 63, 292
Butterick patterns 152
buttons 254

C

Cadillac 208, *209*
Callot Soeurs 112
Camp Five Museum, Laona, Wisconsin *280*
Canada 264, 266
Canal Fulton, Ohio 23
canes 52
capes *173*, 174
card tables 136
cardigans 228
Cardin, Pierre 266

Caribbean 252
Carnegie, Hattie 212
Caronia, S.S. 198–9
carpets 92
Carrickmacross lace 216, 292
Carrington, Kay *144*, 146, *147*
Carson Pirie Scott 98, *99*, 232, *233*, 298
cartes de visite 61
Carver & Wilkie & Caroll McMillen Inc., Chicago 50, 306
Castillo, Antonio del 254, *255*
Catalina 193–4, *193*
Catholic Church 177, 222
Challacombe, Isabella *see* Hedenberg, Isabella Challacombe
Chamberlain, Neville 165
Chanel, Coco 139, 249, 279
Chantilly lace 60, *61*
Chapman, Ceil 250
charga-plates (charge cards) 233–4, *234*
chemical lace 34–5, 36, 292, *296*
chemises 25, *25*, 26, 91, 292, *301*
Chicago 48, 56, 129
    Prindle family in 62, 64, 68, 88
    shopping in 31, 232–3, 235, 240
    tailors 50, 161
Chicago Art Institute 63
Chicago Sunday Tribune 152, *152*
Chicago World's Fair (1933) 149–51, *150–51*
chiffon
    cocktail dresses 212–14, *213–14*
    evening dresses *106*, *126*, *127*, 298, 300, *301*
Child Life magazine 117, *118*
children's clothes 17, 114–16
    bonnets *305*
    buster suit 114, *116*, 266
    dresses 114, *116–17*, *305*
chiné fabrics 34, *35*, 292
christening gowns 17
Chrysler 208
church, dressing for 222–3
cloche hats 120–22, *123*, 292
clothing restrictions, World War II 168–70, *169*, 185
coatdresses 170–72, *171*
coats
    cutaway *49*, 50, 281–2, 292
    evening coats *8*, 216, *217*, 232
    frock coats 48, 293
    linings 100, *101*
    mink 239
    swallowtail 211, 294
    wool 99–100, *101*, 297, 298
    see also jackets
cocktail dresses 200, 292
    floral silk 17, 254, *256–7*
    peau de soie dress with jacket *246*, 249, *261*
    rayon taffeta 243–5, *244*
    silk chiffon and cotton lace 212–14, *213–14*
    silk taffeta 147–9, *148*
    silk with soutache braid 243–5, *245*
    slubbed rayon 299
cocktail hats 215–16, *215*, *303*
Colbert 305
collars
    detachable 100, 225, *225*
    lace 306
    men's shirts 53–4
    wing collars 294
Colonial Revival architecture 46, 97, *97*, 271, 293
Columbian Exposition, Chicago (1893) 50, 150
comic strips 151–2, 159, *159*

Condé Nast 154-6
The Confederate Pageant, Natchez 274, *274*
Connolly, Sybil 252, 300
Connor, Gordon Phelps 127-8, 131, *131*, 133, 134, 143, 188, 199
Connor, Mary Roddis 13, 97, 108, 143, 252, 280
  dance parties 137
  dressing up 272
  education 118-19
  evening coat 232
  flapper dresses 119
  in Great Depression 133
  hats 122
  shopping 238, 252-5
  travel 188, *190*, 198-9, 204
  wedding 127-9, *129*, 130-31, *131*, 234
    in World War II 167
Connor, Sara Witter 166
Connor, W.D. 48, 127, 129, 134
Connor, Mrs W.D. 30
Connor Lumber and Land Company 127
Coolseeker 202
Copeland, Jo 180, 181, 207
Copp Family Collection 17
Cornovery, Mrs. G. *271*
corsages 134
corsets 71, 93, *93*, 120, 181, *302*
cosmetics 119
cotton
  bathing suits 193-4, *193*
  day dresses 196-8, *197*, 207, 226-8, *227-9*, 240, *297-9*
  evening dresses 204, *205*, 297
  men's suits *306*
  nightgowns *301, 302*
  seersucker 162-4, 294
  sundresses *202*
  union suits *301*
cowl necks 139
cravats 54, 292
crêpe, rayon 139
  evening dresses *138*, 139, 154-6, *155*
crêpe de chine
  day dresses *297*
  dinner dresses *219*
  evening dresses *297*
crinolines 61, 201, 274, 292, 296
cuffs
  embroidered *306*
  men's shirts 54
  wartime regulations 170, 178
  whitework *79*
Cunard White Star Line 187, *188*, 196-9, *198-9*
customs duties 216
cutaway jackets *49, 50*, 281-2, 292
Czechoslovakia 123

D
dances 98, 119-20, 137, 140, 142-3, 149, 211-12, 308
Daughters of the American Revolution (DAR) 271-2, *271*, 274, 276, 280
Davidow 249, *250*
day dresses 220-23
  corded cotton *299*
  cotton print 226-8, *227-9*, 240, *298, 299*
  cotton tulle *297*
  fur-trimmed 150-51, *151, 153, 298*
  linen 246, *247, 298-300*
  printed rayon and cotton 196-8, *197*, 207
  ready-made embroidery panels 72-3, *74, 296*

silk 37, *38*
silk crêpe de chine and satin *297*
silk jersey *276*
silk pongee 99, *100*, 110-12, *111*, 296
silk print 250-51, *251, 299, 300*
silk shantung 222, 223
silk tweed 251-2, *252-3*
sports dress 173-4, *173*
checked wool 241, 242
De Havilland, Geoffrey 165-6
De Havilland Mosquito aircraft 162, 165-6, *165, 167, 177*
de la Renta, Oscar 300
decorations (medals) 293
Demorest's Monthly 37
Denton, Frances Augusta 13
Denton, Rev. Jonas 13, 23, 25
Denton, Mary Esther 13
Denton, Sara Louise *see* Roddis, Sara Denton
Denver Northwestern and Pacific Railway *70*
department stores 231-40, 245-6, 250
derby (bowler) hats 48, *49, 52, 52*, 232, 292
Dickens, Charles 134
dickey, lace *262*
Dietrich, Marlene 194
Diners Club 234
dinner dresses 187, 190, 191, *191*, 219, *219*, 293
dinner jackets 189-90
Dior, Christian 180-81, 200, 207, 212, 219, 225, 242, 251-2, *252-3*, 254-6, 308
Directoire style 73-4, *75*, 89-90, *90*, 293
doors, flush 56, 97, 108
drawers 25, *26*, 293
drawn-thread work *60*, 293, *301*
dress codes 219
Dress Doctors 156-7, 220
"dress elevators" 146
dress reform 33-4, 75-6
dress salons 240-50, *240*
dress suits 50, 293
Dressendorfer, Mrs. L. *271*, 272
dresses
  afternoon dresses 180, *181*, 240, 249, 265, *265*
  at-home dresses 113-14
  ball dresses 190
  bias-cut dresses 137-9, 276-9, *278*
  boudoir dress *298*
  bridesmaid dresses 129-30, *129*
  children's clothes 114, *116, 305*
  coatdresses 170-72, *171*
  crinoline skirts 61, 201, 274, 292, 296
  dinner dresses 187, 190, 191, *191*, 219, *219*, 293
  embroidered panels 72-3, *74*
  flapper-style 119, 120
  kimono-style *112*, 113-14, *115*, 268, *269*
  lace inserts 99, *100, 111*, 112
  mourning dresses 39, *40-41*
  presentation dress *8, 9*, 63, *64, 79*, 82-3, 231, 232, 270, 293, 296
  princess line 93, *94-5*, 261, 293
  Prom dresses 134, 137-40, *138-9*
  sheath dresses 181
  shirtdresses 173, *174*, 294
  sportswear 198
  suit dresses 246-8, *248*
  sundresses 202, 203-4
  tea gowns *130*
  wartime restrictions 168-70, *169*
  see also cocktail dresses; day dresses; evening dresses; weddings
dressing gowns *114*

ready-made embroidery panels 72-3, *74, 296*
silk 37, *38*
silk crêpe de chine and satin *297*
silk jersey *276*
silk pongee 99, *100*, 110-12, *111*, 296
silk print 250-51, *251, 299, 300*
silk shantung 222, 223
silk tweed 251-2, *252-3*
sports dress 173-4, *173*
checked wool 241, 242
De Havilland, Geoffrey 165-6
De Havilland Mosquito aircraft 162, 165-6, *165, 167, 177*
de la Renta, Oscar 300
decorations (medals) 293
Demorest's Monthly 37
Denton, Frances Augusta 13
Denton, Rev. Jonas 13, 23, 25
Denton, Mary Esther 13
Denton, Sara Louise *see* Roddis, Sara Denton
Denver Northwestern and Pacific Railway *70*
department stores 231-40, 245-6, 250
derby (bowler) hats 48, *49, 52, 52*, 232, 292
Dickens, Charles 134
dickey, lace *262*
Dietrich, Marlene 194
Diners Club 234
dinner dresses 187, 190, 191, *191*, 219, *219*, 293
dinner jackets 189-90
Dior, Christian 180-81, 200, 207, 212, 219, 225, 242, 251-2, *252-3*, 254-6, 308
Directoire style 73-4, *75*, 89-90, *90*, 293
doors, flush 56, 97, 108
drawers 25, *26*, 293
drawn-thread work *60*, 293, *301*
dress codes 219
Dress Doctors 156-7, 220
"dress elevators" 146
dress reform 33-4, 75-6
dress salons 240-50, *240*
dress suits 50, 293
Dressendorfer, Mrs. L. *271*, 272
dresses
  afternoon dresses 180, *181*, 240, 249, 265, *265*
  at-home dresses 113-14
  ball dresses 190
  bias-cut dresses 137-9, 276-9, *278*
  boudoir dress *298*
  bridesmaid dresses 129-30, *129*
  children's clothes 114, *116, 305*
  coatdresses 170-72, *171*
  crinoline skirts 61, 201, 274, 292, 296
  dinner dresses 187, 190, 191, *191*, 219, *219*, 293
  embroidered panels 72-3, *74*
  flapper style 119, 120
  kimono style *112*, 113-14, *115*, 268, *269*
  lace inserts 99, *100, 111*, 112
  mourning dresses 39, *40-41*
  presentation dress *8, 9, 63, 64, 79*, 82-3, 231, 232, 270, 293, 296
  princess line 93, *94-5*, 261, 293
  Prom dresses 134, 137-40, *138-9*
  sheath dresses 181
  shirtdresses 173, *174*, 294
  sportswear 198
  suit dresses 246-8, *248*
  sundresses 202, 203-4
  tea gowns *130*
  wartime restrictions 168-70, *169*
  see also cocktail dresses; day dresses; evening dresses; weddings

dressing up 262, 263, 268-75, 269, 271-4
dressmaking see sewing
Dumas, Alexander, *The Count of Monte Cristo* 87
DuPont Company 172
Dutch Colonial Revival architecture 46, 97, 97, 271, 293
Dutchess Royal Inc. 202

E

Egypt 113
Eisenhower, Mamie 251
Elizabeth II, Queen 261, 308
Elkhorn, Wisconsin 31, 85
Elm Grove, Bel Air, Virginia 67
embroidery
    blouses 72, 301
    Catherine Sarah Roddis's skills 67-8, 68
    cuffs 306
    gloves 252, 254, 308
    Hamburg edging 25
    handbags 223, 223, 307
    Hungarian motifs 247
    monograms 91, 91
    needlepoint 265, 266
    passementerie 172, 293
    ready-made embroideries 72-3
England see Britain
Episcopalians 46, 93
etiquette guides 109, 219, 220, 234, 239, 256
Evanston, Illinois 232, 246, 260
evening coats 8, 216, 217, 232
evening dresses
    ball dresses 190
    beadwork 123, 124-5, 297
    cotton lace 140, 141-2
    cotton organdy 204, 205
    gold brocade 297
    polyester 276, 277, 300, 301
    printed chiffon 126, 127, 300
    Prom dresses 134, 137-40, 138-9
    rayon crêpe 138, 139, 154-6, 155, 297, 298
    silk chiffon 298, 300
    silk crêpe 120, 121, 218-19, 219, 297
    silk gauze 34-6, 34-5
    silk satin 220, 220-21, 299
    silk taffeta 143-6, 144-5, 298, 299
    wartime restrictions 168
    see also dinner dresses
evening handbags 307
evening shoes 200, 304
Everson, Ann 272, 272
Everson, Tempe 272, 272
Everson, Thomas 249, 250

F

fabrics
    bouclé fabrics 292
    chiné 292
    gingham 293
    muslin 293
    piña fiber 129-30, 130
    seersucker 162-4, 294
    see also cotton; linen; polyester; rayon; silk; wool
"fancyback" jackets 163
fans 63, 86, 106, 307
Fashion Originators' Guild of America 207
felt hats 174, 175, 303
Féraud, Louis 276-9, 278
Ferguson, Miriam Amanda Wallace "Ma" 207
Ferragamo, Salvatore 172

films 109-10, 119, 146, 151, 154, 157, 163, 214, 226, 242
Firestone, Elizabeth Parke 17, 245
First Ladies Collection 17
Flanagan, Barbara 259
flappers 119-20, 293
Flash Gordon 151-2
Florida 147, 162, 163, 272
flush doors 56, 97, 108
fobs, gold 44, 52-3
The Formfit Co. 302
France 37, 101, 123-7, 242
Franklin-Ritt cars 106
Franklin Simon & Co. 88-90, 89, 232
French jet 39, 293
The French Room, Marshall Field & Company 175, 242, 303
frock coats 48, 293
full dress 293
fur 8
    coats 239
    hats 174-5, 174, 225, 235, 236
    muffs 307
    stoles 307
    trimmings 150-51, 153
furniture 92, 136

G

Gable, Clark 163
Gallagher, Louise Barnes 183, 185
Gammon, Elijah 12, 78, 79
Gammon, Jane Prindle (Aunt Jennie) 8, 60, 63, 64, 78, 78-9, 231, 270, 274
Gammon Theological Seminary 78, 79, 280
Le gant topaz, Paris 232, 252, 254
Gazette du Bon Ton 37
Germany 56, 107, 164-5, 177, 279
Gestapo 164
"Gibson Girl" hairstyle 33, 67
Gilbert and Sullivan 268
Gimbel, Adam 250
gingham 60, 88, 293
glove fasteners 252, 293
gloves 194, 206, 215, 219, 232, 250, 252, 254, 308
godets 140, 293
Godey's Lady's Book 63
Goldstein, Harriet and Vetta, *Art in Every Day Life* 156
golf 173-4, 173
Gone With The Wind 242
Gothé (David Gottlieb) 200, 201, 208, 208-9, 220
Grace Episcopal Church, Madison, Wisconsin 177-8
Grafton Hall, Fond du Lac, Wisconsin 118
Grand Rapids, Michigan 56
"Grand Tour" 56
Great Depression (1930s) 20, 133-42, 146, 150, 157, 161
Greek sculpture 139
Green, Harvey 75
Greenwich, Connecticut 199
Grossman, Herbert 279, 301
Gunther Jaeckel 224, 225, 238
gutta-percha 293

H

hairstyles 33, 65, 67, 120, 167-8, 168, 223, 294
Halloween 270
Hamburg edging 25
Hanan, John H. & Son, Inc. 54, 55, 98, 99, 162, 162-3, 306

handbags 223, 223, 307
handkerchief hems 127
handkerchiefs 91
Hansen's Empire Fur Factory 306
Harper's Bazaar 63
Haskell, Miriam 146
Haspel, Joseph 162-3
Haspel, Lorraine 162-4, 163, 232, 306
hat boxes 258, 308
hats 174-5, 194, 232, 302-4
    afternoon hats 223, 223, 265, 303, 304
    berets 242, 243
    boudoir caps 122, 122
    in church 222-3
    cloche hats 120-22, 123, 292
    cocktail hats 215-16, 215, 303
    derby (bowler) hats 48, 49, 52, 52, 232, 292
    fur felt 174-5, 174, 225, 303
    fur-trimmed 235, 236
    oversized 96, 96
    shopping for 234, 242
    silk floral hat 223, 223
    straw 303
    top hats 52, 305-6
    veils 215, 303
    velvet 303
Hatteberg Veneer Company 27, 43-6
Hawes, Elizabeth, *Fashion is Spinach* 240
Healy, George P.A. 78
Hedenberg Whitlock, Cecilia 12, 116, 117, 123
Hedenberg, Isabella Arents see Prindle, Isabella Arents Hedenberg
Hedenberg, Isabella Challacombe 12, 60, 68-9
Hedenberg, John Wesley 12, 60
hemlines 122-3, 130-31, 150, 170
The Henry Ford, Dearborn, Michigan 17, 21
Hepburn, Katharine 167, 176, 194
historic clothing 269-75
Hitler, Adolf 164
Holland-America Line 188-90
Hollywood 105, 109-10, 146, 154, 156, 157, 194, 214, 226, 239
Holy Land 112, 193
Hoover, Herbert 133
hope chests 85
housedresses 226-8, 227
Howard, Leslie 146
Hubbard Woods, Illinois 246, 260
Hughes, Howard R. Jr. 166
Hughes H4 Hercules flying boat ("Spruce Goose") 166, 177
Hugo, Victor, *Les Misérables* 265
Hunt, Mrs. J.A. 296
Huston, Harvey 48

I

Irene 226
Islamic art 123
It Happened One Night (film) 163
Italy 101, 176, 269

J

jackets
    cutaway 49, 50, 281-2, 292
    dinner jackets 189-90
    "fancyback" 163
    Norfolk jackets 163, 163, 293
    peplums 183, 185
    silk shantung 261, 299
    tuxedos 187, 189, 200, 216, 219, 219, 294
    wartime restrictions 170

winter jacket 70, *70*
    see also coats
Jamaica 163, 204
Jantzen 193-4, 299
Japan 114, *114*, 268, *269*
jazz 120
jet 39, 293
Jews, Kristallnacht 164
Jones, Henry Stewart 127, 200, *200*
Jones, Sara Roddis *13*, *280*
    childhood 97, 108
    clothes 212
    dance parties 137
    education 118-19
    hairstyle 120
    marriage 127, *128*
    travel 200, *200*
Joyce, Emmet 207
Juliet caps *144*, 146, 293
Justrite Corsets 93

K
Kaiser, Henry J. 166
Kamfes, Mrs. F. *271*
Kass, Samuel 180, *188*, 196-8, *197*, 206-7,
    206-7, 240
Kasten, Cynthia Barton 276
Kennedy, Jackie 276
Key West, Florida 162
kimonos *112*, 113-14, *115*, 268, *269*
Kirksville, Missouri 64, 93
Krasin, Gus. A. 97, *97*
Kraus, Mrs. I. Sexton *271*
Kristallnacht (1938) 164
Kungsholm, S.S. *252*, 252

L
La Crosse Tribune 149
labels 216, 231, 232
    Adair of Paris *124*
    designer labels 249-51
    Gladys Parker *159*
    Gothé *209*
    hats *243*
    Jeanne Lanvin *255*
    Phillip-Jones 53, *54*
    presentation dress *296*
    Roy H.Bjorkman *258*
    Ruth McCulloch 246, 249-50, *260*
    Samuel Kass *206*
    store labels 232, 242, 276
    tailors' labels 48
    Wilkie & Sellery 50, *51*
    Woodrow *52*
lace 140
    Alençon needle lace *78*, 292
    blouse *301*
    Carrickmacross lace 216, 292
    Chantilly lace 60, *61*
    chemical lace *34-5*, 36, 292, *296*
    cocktail dresses 212-14, *213-14*
    collars *306*
    dickey *262*
    evening dresses *124-5*, 140, *141-2*
    inserts 99, *100*, *111*, 112
    overdresses 200-203, *201*
Ladies' Home Journal 71, 75, 156
Ladies' Literary Society, Milwaukee 30
Ladies' Shakespeare Club, Marshfield 30
Ladies' Travel Class, Marshfield 29-31, *30*, 185
Laird, Helen L. 27, 48, 182-3

Laird, Melvin R. 128, 131, *131*, 143
Lake, Veronica 159
Lake Placid, New York State 212
lampshades *112*
Lanvin, Jeanne 254, *255*
leather, wartime rationing 172
Leddell, Frances *13*, 23
leg-o' mutton sleeves *65*, 66, *66*, 293
Leigh, Vivien 242
Lempereur, Douglas 220
Lempereur, Ellen Roddis *13*, 143, *250*
    attitude to money 235
    childhood 108, 116-17, *117*, 128, 131, *131*
    coat 168
    cocktail dress 17, 231, 254, *256-7*
    hairstyle 167-8, *168*
    learns to fly 20, 177
    letters 238, 239, *239*
    marriage 177-8, *178*, 254
    shopping 233
    travel 191, 203
    in World War II 167
Lempereur, Glen 177-8, *178*, 254
Lend-Lease agreement 166
LePere, Mrs. H.A. *271*
Leslie, Jan 303
Leviathan, S.S. 107-8, *107*, 162
Liberty of London 227, 298
Lieberberg and Kaplin 259
LIFE magazine 168, 174
Lincoln, Mary Todd 60
linen
    blouses 72, *301*
    cocktail dresses *300*
    day dresses 246, *247*, *296*, *298-300*
linings
    coats 100, *101*
    revers *294*
London 48, 105, 165, 185, 194-5
Long Island 175-6
LOOK magazine *158*
Lord & Taylor *178*, 302
Los Angeles 56
Lusitania, R.M.S. 101

M
McCall's Magazine 152-4, *154*, 266
McCall's patterns *139*, 152-6
McCardell, Claire 181
McCulloch, Bruce 260
McCulloch, Ruth 245-9, *247-9*, 260, *260-61*,
    265, *276*, *280*, 298, 299, 303
Madison, Wisconsin 119, 129, 177, 232
Maeder, Edward 9, 10-11, 275
magazines 109, 170
maids of honor 236
mail order 109, 232-3
make-up 119
Maklary Ladies Tailors 99-100, *101*
Maltitz, Baron von 164
Manhattan, S.S. *199*
Marcus, H. Stanley 169-70
Marshall Field & Company *52*, 52, *92*, 162, 175,
    232, 233, 240, 242, 302, 303, 305
Marshfield, Wisconsin *16*, 23
    Central Avenue *28*, *101*, *106*
    education in 185
    in Great Depression 135
    in the 1920s 106-7
    Roddis family home in 8, *9*, 10, *11*, 14-16,
    27-30, 36-7

Roddis Lumber & Veneer Company 18, 43,
    45-8, *45*, 56-7, 86
    social life 28-31, 271-2, *271*
    W.H. Roddis as mayor of 55
    in World War I 103
Marshfield Centennial 270-71, *272*
Marshfield Daily 37
Marshfield High School 308
Marshfield News Herald 216
Marshfield School Board 185, 246
Marshfield Times 30, 45, 137
Marshfield Women's Club 29
Martha Weathered, Minneapolis 198, 240, 259
Maxwell, Vera 181
Mayflower Hotel, Washington, D.C. 275-6
medals of honor 293
Mendham, New Jersey 23
men's accessories 52-3, *306*
men's clothing 16-17, 48-54, 170, 232
    see also shirts, suits *etc*
"Merry Widow" brassiere 181, *182*, 302
The Merry Widow (operetta) 164, 182
Metropolitan Museum of Art, New York 185
Metropolitan Opera, New York 242
Miami 204
Middle East 112-13
The Mikado (operetta) 268
Miller, Annie Jenness 33
Miller, Bess 212
Miller, I. 304
Milwaukee, Wisconsin 24-5, 27, 31, 43, 45, 48,
    71, 129, 232, 268
Milwaukee Academy 43
mink coats 239
Minneapolis 56, 232, 233, 242, 259
Miss America Pageant 207
Miss Elliette *301*
Mississippi River 163
Mr. John 242, *243*
La Mode 37
Modern Dressmaking 156
Mon A. Angla *83*, 232, *296*
Mondovi, Wisconsin 31
money, shopping 233-4, *234*
"money-back guarantees" 233
mono-bosom 73, 293
monograms 91, *91*
Motion Picture 144
mourning clothes 39, *40-41*, 67, 116
movies *see* films
muffs *307*
muslin 293, *301*
Myerson, Bess 207

N
napkins 91, *91*
Natchez, Mississippi 274
National Recovery Administration 134
National Suit Company 73-4
neck band, beaded 123, *307*
neckties 54
needlepoint 265, *266*
negligées *114*
Neiman Marcus 169-70, 251
Nettie Vogues *300*
New Look 180-81, 207, 225
New Orleans 59, 119, 123, 156, 162, 275
"New Woman" 69, 71
New York 25, 31, 48, 56, 98, 105, 149, 161, 199,
    232, 235, 240
New York Couture Group 208

New York Stock Market 133
New York Times 149, 182
New York World's Fair (1939) 172
New York World's Fair (1964) 208
New Yorker 165
newspapers 109
Newsweek 222, 223
Newton, Mary Prindle 12, 68, 269
Nieuw Amsterdam, S.S. 188–92, *188–90*, 194, 200, 219
nightgowns 17, 26, *301, 302*
Norell, Norman 101
Norfolk jackets 163, *163*, 293
Northbrook Court shopping center, Illinois 246, 260
Northwestern University 63, 64, 68, 69, 85, 143, 146, 150, 275
Nyack, New York State 24
nylon
  blouses 195
  stockings 172

O

ocean liners 187, 188–92, *188–9*, 196–203, *196, 198–9*
O'Hagan, Helen 242
O'Hara, Dorothy 214
Oklahoma City 56
Onondaga Silk Company *197*, 198, 207
organdy evening dress 204, *205*
Oswego Normal and Training School, New York State 24, 157
Oxford shoes 162, *162–3*, 238

P

pageants 274, *274*
paillettes 293
paisley shawls 79
Palestine 112, *113*, 262
Palm Beach, Florida 212, 232, 240
Palmer-Ward Family Collection 17
Panic of 1893 44–5
paper patterns 139, 152–6, *154*, 172, 208, *266*, 275
parasols *112*, 114, *114*
Paris 105, 165
  hats 194, 242
  influence of Parisian fashion 110, 112, 139, 152, 156, 185
  New Look 180–81
  shopping in 123, 127, 194, 215, 232, 252–4
Paris Exposition (1878) 79
The Paris News 180
Park Falls, Wisconsin 47, 55, *162*
Parker, Gladys 146–9, *148, 158–9, 159*
parties 137, 140–43, 211–16
passementerie 172, 293
Patou, Jean 152, *152*
patterns, paper 139, 152–6, *154*, 172, 208, *266*, 275
Pearl Harbor 166
peau de soie cocktail dresses 249, *261*
Peck, Gregory 163
P.E.O. Sisterhood 272
peplums 183, *185, 301*
perfume 198, *206*
permanent waves 120
petticoats 180, *181*
Philadelphia 233
Philippines 72, *74*, 130, 176
Phillips-Jones 53, *54*
Pictorial Review 114
piña fiber 129–30, *130*

playing cards *261*
plays 268–9, *269*
plywood, aircraft production 165–7, 176–7
Poiret, Paul 110, *110*, 113
Poland 183
Polaroid sunglasses *188*, 194
polyester evening dresses 276, *277, 300, 301*
pongee silk 99, *100*, 110–12, *111*, 293, 296
Portia Club, New Orleans 107
Portland, Oregon 233
Post, Emily 190
  Etiquette in Society, in Business, in Politics, and at Home 109
Post, Marjorie Merriweather 17
"pouter pigeon" shape 72, 293
Praia Botafogo 223
presentation dress 8, *9*, 63, 64, *79, 82–3*, 231, 232, 270, 293, *296*
princess-line 93, *94–5, 261*, 293
Prindle, Arents Legore 12, 65
Prindle, Edith Isabella 8, *9*, 12, 64, 67, *67, 79, 83*, 88, 90–91, 93, 270
Prindle, Isabella Arents Hedenberg 12, 60–67, *61, 64, 67, 69, 74–5, 87*, 88, 116, *123*, 272
Prindle, Jane Catherine 12
Prindle, Jason Richards 12, 61–3, 67
Prindle, Lucy Adelaide 12, 65, 67, 69
Prindle, Mary Maria *see* Newton, Mary Prindle
Prindle, Miriam Elisabeth 12, 67
  education 143
  hats 122, *123*
  ink sketches *62–3*, 63–4, *70, 71, 75*
  letters 60, 70, 71, 238
  suit 20, 73–4, *75*
  winter jacket *70, 70*
Prindle, Richard Hedenberg 12, 65, 67, 269
Prindle family 59–76, *60, 65*
Prohibition 106–7, 280
Prom dresses 134, 137–40, *138–9*
Prsybyszewski, Linda 156
Pucci, Emilio 275, *276, 300*
pumps *see* shoes
Purdy, Mrs. F. Cole *271*

Q

Queen Elizabeth, R.M.S. 196, 200, *200*
Queen Mary, R.M.S. *188*, 196, 240
Quirt, Barbara 216
Quirt, Howard 216, *219*

R

railroads 47
"rape drapes" 214
rationing, World War II 167, 172, 195
Rauff, Ann 212, 216
rayon 139, 294
  bouclé rayon suit 279, *301*
  cocktail dresses 243, *244, 299*
  day dresses 150–51, *151, 153*, 173–4, *173*, 196–8, *197*, 207
  evening dresses *138*, 139, 154–6, *155, 297, 298*
  shirtwaists *181*
"Red Top", Marshfield, Wisconsin 24, 27–8, 36, 46, 47
Reichman, Florence 174, 175
Renaissance 33, 36
revers 294
Richardson, Janice 220
Rio de Janeiro *188–9*, 219, 223
Roddis, Augusta Denton 11, *13*, 23, *144, 147*
  afternoon dresses 240

attitude to money 235
brassieres 181, *182*
childhood 98, 108, *110*, 114, 116–18, *116–17*
cocktail dresses 146–9, *148*, 212–15, *213–14*
collection of clothes 8, *9*, 10–11, 14–15, 17–18, 21, *267*, 274–5, 279, 281
day dresses 150, *151*, 204, 223, 227–8, *228, 241*, 246, *247*, 250–52, *252–3*
death 279
dinner dresses 219
dressing up 262, *263*, 270–75, *271, 272*
early life 103
education 118, 134, 136–7, *143*
evening dresses 143–6, *144–5*, 154–6, *155*, 190, *190–91*, 220, *221*
gloves 215, 219, 252
golf 173–4
on her grandmother 40
in Great Depression 134–5, 157, 161
hairstyle 168, *168*
hats 174–5, 194, 215, 242
last years 266–7
letters 134–5, 137
on Marshfield 28–30
mohair sweater 146, *147*
parties 137, 140–43
political views 183
postwar life 183–5
Prom dress *134*, 137–40, *138–9*
shopping 231, 232, 234, 235–40, 242, 246, 252
social gatherings 212
suit dresses 246–8, *248*
suits 204, *224, 225*, 235, *237, 238–9*, 249, *250*
sundress 202, 203–4
swimsuits 194
theatrical productions 268–9
travel 157, 164–5, 187–8, *188*, 190, 192–8, *192, 199*, 203–4
in World War II 172, 175–6, 182–3
Roddis, Catherine Prindle 12, 14, 59–60, 78, *86*
  afternoon dress 180–1, *181*
  at-home dress 113–14, *115*
  attitude to money 234–5
  blouses 66, 72
  children 97, 98, 108, *110*
  children's clothes 114–16
  coat 99–100, *101*
  coatdress 170–72, *171*
  day dresses 110–12, 227–8
  death 266
  dressing up 269
  dressmaking 17, 65, 152–6, 173, *266*
  early life 64, *64, 66–7*
  education 66–7, 143
  embroidery 60, 67–8, *68, 265*, 266
  evening coat 216, *217*
  evening dresses *126*, 127, 140, *141–2*, 200–203, *201*, 219–20, *219, 220*
  fiftieth wedding anniversary 263, *264*, 279
  French clothes 123–7
  golf 173–4
  in Great Depression 133–4, 157, 161
  hats *174*, 175, *265*
  home 97–8, *97, 102–3*
  last years 263–6
  letters 11, *19*, 194
  marriage 18, 31, 56, 85–96, *86, 94–6*, 129, 140, 279
  Middle Eastern dress 112–13
  in the 1920s 106, 107
  shoes 98, *99*

shopping 232, 233, 234, 238, 242–3
suits 185, 225–6
teaching career 85
travel 112–13, 157, 164, 188, *188*, *190*, 191–2, 193, 199–200, *200*, 203
waist cincher *73*
in World War I 101–2
Roddis, Catherine Prindle (Pickie) *see* Beggs, Catherine Roddis
Roddis, Ellen Cecilia *see* Lempereur, Ellen Roddis
Roddis, Frances Mary *13*, 14, 31, 48–50, 59, 129, 156
and Catherine's marriage 88, *90*
clothes 110–12
early life 26, 28–9
inheritance 39, 57
letters 33, 71
in the 1920s 107
teaching career 85
theatrical productions 269
in World War II 167
Roddis, Hamilton *13*, 14, 17, 26, 48, *86*
attitude to money 234–5
cars 106
children 97, 98, 102–3, 108, 118–19, 127
collars 54, 100
death 266
dinner jackets 189–90, *219*
education 28, 31
and Ellen's elopement 178
family life 102
fiftieth wedding anniversary 263, *264*
in Great Depression 20, 133–6, 143, 161
home 97–8, *97*, *102–3*
last years 263–5
marriage 36, 59, 85–96, *86*, *96*, 140
in the 1920s 106, *107*
postwar life 185
and the Roddis Lumber & Veneer Company 18, 39, 55–6, 57, 86–7, 107–8, 157, 267
shoes 54, 162
spats 100–1, *162*
suits 162–4, *162*, 232, 281–2
theatrical productions 269
travel 112, 157, 164, 187, 188, *188*, 189–90, 193, 199–200, *199*, *200*, 203
in World War II 161, 164–6, *176*, 178
Roddis, Mary Augusta *13*, 106–7
Roddis, Mary Isabella *see* Connor, Mary Roddis
Roddis, Sara Denton *13*, *24*, *33*, *99*, 107
chemises *25*, *25*, 26, 91
dresses 31–6, *32–5*, 37, 140, 231, 270, 272
early life 23–5, 157
life in Marshfield 27–31, 36–7, 45, 62
marriage 25–7
mourning clothes 39–40, *40–41*
and the Roddis Lumber & Veneer Company 26–7, 37–9
Roddis, Sara Frances *see* Jones, Sara Roddis
Roddis, Thomas Richard *13*
Roddis, William Henry *13*, 17, 40, 43–57, *44*, 106, 211
clothes 31, 48–54, 161–2, 232, 281–2
death 37–9, 57
derby hat 232
early life 43
life in Marshfield 27–9, 107
marriage 18, 25, 26–7
Roddis Lumber & Veneer Company 18, 20, 27, 43–7, 55–6

Roddis, William Henry II (Bill) *13*, 164
buster suit 114, *116*, 266
early life 98, 110, *110*, 116, *117*, 135, 136
dressing up 262, 269
in World War II 161, 166, *175*, 176
Roddis Bulletin 176, 178
Roddis (Hamilton) Foundation 21
Roddis Lumber & Veneer Company 45, 157, 222
catalogs 57, *108*, 162
flush doors 56, 97, 108
in Great Depression 134–6
growth of 43–7, 55–7, 265
and S.S. *Leviathan* 107–8, *107*
and Roddis family home 97
wall panels 135, *136*
W.H. Roddis's death 37–9
in World War II 161, 164–7, 176–7, *176*, 178
Roddis Plywood Corporation 185, 223, 263, 266
Roddiscraft 175
Romeo and Juliet (film) 144, 146
Roosevelt, Eleanor 172, 200, 208, *209*
Roosevelt, Franklin D. 166
Rosenstein, Nettie 180, 207, 250–51, *251*, 299
Rotary Club 188
Rubin, Ruth 207
Russeks 232, 235, 237
Russia 97, 183

S

S-curve silhouette 294
sack suits 50, 294
St. Alban's Episcopal Church, Marshfield, Wisconsin 46, 223
Saint Laurent, Yves 251–2
St. Lawrence Seaway 264
Saint Mary's School, New York State 118, 134, 136
Saks Fifth Avenue 225, *225*, 235, 238, 241, 242, 250, 303, 304, 305, 308
San Francisco 98, 105
sandals *304*
satin 37
evening dresses 220, *220–21*, 299
slips *302*
wedding dress *94–5*
waist cincher 72, *73*
Saturday Evening Post 209
Saulte Ste. Marie 264
Schiaparelli, Elsa 198
Schmidt's 308
science-fiction 151
scrapbooks 68–9
Sears & Roebuck 233
seersucker 162–4, 294
Selby Arch Preserver Shoe 304
Seminole tribes 272
separates 181–2
Seventeen Magazine 206
Severa, Joan 10, 275
sewing 60, 62–3, 65, 67–8, *68*, 69–70, 75, 152–6, 172–3
sewing machines 48, 87, 266
Sexton, Ellen 118, 135, 142, 232, 236, 270
Shakespeare, William 30, 46, 164
shawls 79, *83*, 204
Shearer, Norma *144*, 146
sheath dresses 181
Sheldon, Edward 24
ships, transatlantic 187, 188–92, *188–9*, 196–203, *196*, *198–9*
shirtdresses *173*, 174, 294

shirt studs *162*
shirts 48, 53, *54*, 100, 281
shirtwaists 65, 70–72, *70*, *72–3*, 88, *181*, 294
Shoecraft Shop, New York 304
shoes 17, 304–5
beaded leather pumps 98, *99*
evening shoes 200, *304*
high button shoes 262, *304*
men's *54*, *55*, 161, 162, *162–3*, *306*
in the 1920s 127, *128*
Oxford shoes 162, *162–3*, 238
peau de soie pumps 98, *99*, *106*
silk *83*
spats 100–101, *162*, 294, *305*
spectator shoes 238, *239*, 294, *306*
stack heel shoes *305*
wartime restrictions 172
wedge shoes *304*
shopping 231–57, 282
shorts 194
Siempelkamp 164, 177
silk
afternoon dresses 265, *265*
cocktail dresses *245*, 254, *256–7*
day dresses 37, *38*, 173–4, *173*, 222, 250–52, *251–3*, 299, *300*
dinner dresses 219, *219*
evening dresses 34–6, *34–5*, 120, *121*, 123–7, *124–5*, *297–9*
hats *303*, *304*
mourning dresses 39, *40–41*
nightgowns *302*
shantung jackets *261*
silk chiffon dress 32–3, *33*
silk gauze dress *80–81*, *296–7*
silk jersey dress *276*
silk pongee dresses *99*, 100, 110–12, *111*, 293, *296*
silk shantung jackets *299*
two-piece ensemble *75*, *76–7*
waistcoats *306*
wartime restrictions 172
see also satin; taffeta; velvet
Simplicity patterns 208
Simpson, Adele 207, 249
skirts
bustles 61, 63, 292
crinoline 61, *201*, 274, 292, 296
hemlines 122–3, 130–31, 150, 170
New Look 180–81
slacks 194
sleeves
"bishop" *75*
leg-o' mutton 65, 66, *66*, 293
slips *302*
Smithsonian National Museum of American History, Washington, D.C. 17
smocking 68
smoking 119
snoods 294
Sobel, Cynthia 279, 301
soutache braid 243, *244–5*, 294
South Africa 193
South America 185, 188–9
spats 100–101, *162*, 294, *305*
specialty dress salons 240–50, *240*
spectator shoes 238, *239*, 294, *306*
Spoo & Son 305
spoon, commemorative *308*
sports dresses 173–4, *173*, 198
SPOT magazine 159

"Spruce Goose" (Hughes H4 Hercules flying boat) 166, 177
stack heel shoes 305
Stanton, Elizabeth Cady 75
Stanwyck, Barbara 159
Starr, Malcolm 300
stockings 172
stoles, fur 307
stores 231–40, 245–6, 250
Stout, Mary S. 13
Stratford-upon-Avon 164
straw hats 303
studs, shirt 162
Stuttgart 164
suffrage, women's 68–9, 107
suit dresses 235, 237, 246–8, 248
suits, men's 48, 50–51, 184, 185, 216, 232, 306
    cutaway suits 49, 50, 281–2, 292
    dress suits 50, 293
    sack suits 50, 294
    seersucker suits 162–4
    swallowtail 211, 294
    three-piece suits 50
suits, women's 225–7, 249
    bouclé rayon 279, 301
    Directoire style 73–4, 75, 89
    hounds-tooth pattern suits 224–5, 225
    walking suits 88–90, 89–90, 232
    wartime restrictions 170
    wool bouclé 249, 250, 254, 255
    wool gabardine 178, 179, 183, 185, 226, 226
sundresses 202, 203–4
sunglasses 188, 194
swallowtail coats 211, 294
swimsuits 193–4, 193, 299
Switzerland 165
Syria 112–13
Syrian robe 297

taffeta
    afternoon dresses 180, 181
    cocktail dresses 147–9, 148, 243, 244
    dress ensemble 272, 272–3
    evening dresses 143–6, 144–5, 298, 299
tailor-mades 50, 74, 294
tailors, men's clothing 50–51
Taylor, Lou 20
tea gowns 130
Texas 135, 180
theatrical productions 176, 268–9, 269
Tiffany, Louis Comfort 36
The Tiger 140
tiles 139
TIME magazine 156, 250
To Kill a Mockingbird (film) 163
toiles 294
top hats 52, 305–6
transatlantic ships 187, 188–92, 188–9, 196–203, 196, 198–9
Trigère, Pauline 207, 249–50
trousers 170, 172, 194
trousseaux 25–6, 85, 88, 91, 128–9, 234, 294
Troy, New York State 43
Truman, Harry S. 185
Tuck, Desmond 196
The Tulsa Tribune 159
Tutankhamen, King 113
tuxedos 187, 189, 200, 216, 219, 219, 294
tweed day dresses 251–2, 252–3
28 Shop, Marshall Field & Company 240, 242

underwear
    brassieres 120, 181, 182
    chemises 25, 25, 26, 91, 292, 301
    corsets 71, 93, 93, 120, 181, 302
    drawers 25, 26, 293
    slips 302
    union suits 301
union suits 301
United States Bicentennial (1976) 275
University of Wisconsin 28, 31, 48, 86, 177
Upham, W.H. 27
US Congress 166
US Navy 176

valets 199
Vanderbilt, Amy, Complete Book of Etiquette 234
Veblen, Thorstein, The Theory of the Leisure Class 39
Vedder, Virginia 137
veils 67, 215, 303
velvet
    evening coats 216, 217
    hats 303
    presentation dress 8, 9, 63, 64, 79, 82–3, 231, 232, 270, 293, 296
Venetian lace 33, 301, 306
Vertes, Marcel 198
Victoria Falls, Zambia 204
"Victory Suits" 170
Vigée Le Brun, Louise Élisabeth 267
Vionnet, Madeleine 137–9
Vogelman, Philip A. 207
Vogue 37, 109, 119, 120, 127, 140, 159, 180, 203, 225, 232, 235
Vogue patterns 154–6, 208

waist cinchers 72, 73
waistcoats 50–51, 51, 306
walking sticks 52, 53, 306
walking suits 88–90, 89–90, 232
Wall Street Crash (1929) 118, 131, 133
War Production Board (WPB) 169–72, 169, 182
Warner's 181, 182
Washington, D.C. 232, 276
Washington, George and Martha 262, 269
watches 53
Weatherill, Bernard 184, 185
weddings 219–20
    Barbara Quirt 216–19, 219, 220
    bridesmaids 129–30, 129, 236
    Catherine Sarah Prindle 86, 93–6, 94–5, 263, 264, 279
    Mary Isabella Roddis 127–31, 129, 131
    Sara Frances Roddis 127, 128
    trousseaux 25–6, 85, 88, 91, 128–9, 234, 294
wedge shoes 304
Wellesley College, Boston 167, 177
West Indies 187
Western Union 233
Weyerhaeuser 266
Weyerhaeuser, Frederick 44
Wharton, Edith, The Age of Innocence 239–40
Whitaker, Jan 233
white tie 219, 293, 294
whitework 79, 292, 306
widow's weeds 294
Wiener Werkstätte 100, 101, 294
Wilkie & Sellery 49, 50, 51, 306

Williams, Mrs. R. 271
wing collars 294
Wisconsin 14, 16, 44, 47, 106
Wisconsin Central Railroad 27, 47
Wisconsin Historical Society (WHS) 10–11, 21, 275
The Wizard of Oz 150, 239
Wolsam Ltd 304
women
    dress reform 33–4, 75–6
    education 69
    suffrage 68–9, 107
Women Airforce Service Pilots (WASP) 177
Woodrow 52
wool
    berets 242, 243
    bias-cut dress 276–9, 278
    coatdresses 170–72, 171
    coats 99–100, 101, 297, 298
    day dresses 239, 241, 242
    jacquard shawl 83
    men's clothing 50
    suit dresses 246–8, 248
    suits 178, 179, 183, 185, 224–5, 226, 226, 235, 237
Woolson, Abba Gould 75
Work Projects Administration 172–3
World War I 98, 100, 101–3, 105, 107–8, 165–6
World War II 18, 20, 56, 164–80, 182–3, 194
Wren, Graham 300

Yalta Conference (1945) 182–3
yoke 294

Zambia 204
Zerner, Irene 208

Acknowledgements

The writing of this book would not have been possible without the knowledge, advice, and encouragement of family and friends, and from the many people we met during the course of our research. We are ever thankful to the Roddis family members, in particular: to Sara Bostock for saving the clothes, letters, and ephemera from the Roddis house, and to Douglas and Janice Lempereur, as well as the Roddis cousins, who assisted her; to Gillian Bostock Ewing, for her sensitive photography of the Roddis Collection and the Roddis house and for creating the family photo archive; and to Peter Bostock, who continued to assist even years later, when additional documents and photographs needed to be sorted and scanned. We also thank the many other Roddis relatives who shared memories and information with us, especially Grace Roddis Hoffmann, Ruth Roddis, Jackie Brownell, Ann Rauff, Ellen Everson, David Jones, Roddis Jones, Jarl Jones, Catherine Connor Dellin, Gordon and Sigrid Connor, Jennifer Connor, and Sara Witter Connor, who also shared her own research. We are particularly grateful to the Hamilton Roddis Foundation, whose support made possible our initial documentation and research.

For the expert assistance with preparing the clothes for photography, we thank our dear friend June Gaeke. Elias Dry Cleaners of Walton Street, London, performed miracles, and we also appreciate the assistance of the Elias tailor, Shirley Lee Laws. We are grateful to those who shared important expertise and information with us: Karen Augusta, Cynthia Barton Kasten, Beverley Birks, Betty Bjorkman, Brad Casselberry, Francesca Galloway, Elaine Greenstone, Anita Hayes, Paula Madden, Janet Messmer, Debbie Miller, Shirley Mook, Jan Norris, Nancy Pick, Nancy Rexford, Elizabeth Semmelhack, Matt Severson, Cynthia Sobel, Ralph Steiner, Philip Sykas, Kerry Taylor, Steven Ujifusa, and Ruth Wachter-Nelson. Our thanks go to Gill Tickner for her audio transcription. We are also indebted to our readers: Zara Anvari, Jeanine Head Miller, Helen Laird, Shirley Mook, Kiki Smith, Sonnet Stanfill, Haydn Williams, Marilyn Zoidis, and especially Lou Taylor, all of whom read and commented on the original manuscript, and offered expert advice. Any errors that remain are our own.

Administrators and curators from The Henry Ford recognized the potential of the Roddis Collection. These include Christian Overland, Spencer Medford, Marilyn Zoidis, Marc Greuther, and especially curator Jeanine Head Miller, who gave us helpful feedback in the early stages, and worked tirelessly to bring about the acquisition and subsequent exhibition of the Roddis Collection. Additional assistance from The Henry Ford was provided by Charles Sable, Frances Faile, Jan Hiatt, and Christine Jeryan.

We are particularly grateful to Valerie Steele for her support, and for her foreword. We cannot praise enough the professionalism of our editor, Rebeka Cohen, whose support and editorial assistance were invaluable. We also thank Doug Mindell for his still life photographs. Additional thanks go to photographers Eli Dagostino and especially Sarah Davis, who performed the massive task of organizing and processing hundreds of photographs for this book. We are indebted to Myfanwy Vernon-Hunt for designing the book so beautifully. We also thank Tom Windross, and his team at V&A Publishing, for bringing this book to fruition.

Co-authoring a book requires patience and mutual respect, and we were lucky enough to enjoy both. Our deepest thanks go to our closest family members and friends, who put up with our book obsession for years yet cheered us on regardless. Edward thanks Iskander. Jane acknowledges that she could never have co-written this book without the patience and support of her husband, Ivan, and her sons, George and David. A special thank you is extended to the late Joan Severa, who connected Edward Maeder to Augusta Roddis in the first instance. Finally, we both thank Augusta Roddis for saving nearly everything in her house.

First published by V&A Publishing, 2016
Victoria and Albert Museum
South Kensington
London SW7 2RL
www.vandapublishing.com

Distributed in North America by Abrams, an imprint of ABRAMS

© Jane Bradbury and Edward Maeder

The moral right of the authors has been asserted.

This book is published to accompany the exhibition "American Style and Spirit: 130 Years of Fashions and Lives of an Entrepreneurial Family", to be held at Henry Ford Museum, Dearborn, MI, U.S.A., from Nov 5, 2016 to Apr 2, 2017.

Hardback edition
ISBN 978 1 85177 889 8

Library of Congress Control Number 2016930364

10 9 8 7 6 5 4 3 2 1
2020 2019 2018 2017 2016

Front jacket illustration: Day dress with metal belt, c.1934. THF 2014.24.49 (p.153).

Back jacket illustrations: "Cocktail" evening dress by Gladys Parker, 1934. THF 2014.24.36 (p.148); formal portrait of Augusta Roddis by Kay Carrington, 1937. THF 2015.10.62 (p. 147); kid leather gloves, c.1950. THF 2014.24.111 (p.308).

Half title: Circular rhinestone buckle (detail) of evening dress, c.1938. THF 2014.24.80 (p.155).

Frontispiece: Rear view of day dress (detail) by Samuel Kass, 1945. THF 2014.24.59 (pp.197 and 207).

Page 295: Evening dress (detail), 1928. THF 2014.24.48 (p.126).

Project Editor: Rebeka Cohen
Designer: Myfanwy Vernon-Hunt | this-side.co.uk
Proofreader: Jenny Wilson
Indexer: Hilary Bird

Collection photography by Gillian Bostock Ewing | gillianbostock.com
Still life photography by Doug Mindell | dougmindellphotography.com

Printed in China.

V&A Publishing

Supporting the world's leading museum of art and design, the Victoria and Albert Museum, London